THIS IS A VOLUME IN THE

Minnesota Library on Student Personnel Work

EDITED BY E. G. WILLIAMSON

AFTER HIGH SCHOOL – *what?*

by RALPH F. BERDIE

with chapters by
WILBER L. LAYTON *and* BEN WILLERMAN

The University of Minnesota Press, Minneapolis

✒ Preface

DR. BERDIE's report extends the series begun by J. B. Johnston in 1914, when he became dean of the College of Science, Literature, and the Arts at the University of Minnesota. Dean Johnston was concerned with the wasted efforts of many students who were not capable of profiting from their educational opportunities. Johnston's habit of thinking gained in his own research in neurology led him to search for ways of identifying insufficient aptitude before enrollment in college. In this connection, he initiated studies which sought an answer to the basic policy question: "Who should go to college?" This question was, and continues to be, a major query confronting educators.

Johnston believed deeply in the responsibility of a state university to serve the state through conservation of human talent. This conservation was to be achieved by the fullest possible educational development of each individual according to his capabilities. But the university was not an institution open to enrollment of all students who desired to come or who could financially afford to enroll. Rather it was to be reserved for those whose intellectual powers were such that they could master university-level materials.

Identification of a few high points in the University of Minnesota's long search will serve to establish firmly the significance of the present study. Professor Van Waggenen, a pioneer in group psychological testing, was the first one at the university to use the Army Alpha intelligence test, made available to him in 1919 through the efforts of Professor Yerkes following his Army psychology experiences in classifying men according to their capabilities. It was hoped that much could be transferred of Army methodology and technique to the problem of classifying students before instruction. Professor Paterson was brought to the university in 1922 to develop specialized tests for college students, since earlier tests for the general population were not differentiating at this high level of aptitude. And Professor Paterson proposed to administer the tests, not in college after the student was enrolled, but rather in the senior year of high school so that the student and his advisers could base counseling upon objective appraisals of college aptitude. And our state-wide testing program of high school students has continued uninterrupted to the present day.

But there was a second and in many ways equally fundamental development stemming from Johnston's search. The mere identification, objective though it is, of latent talent does not automatically lead to the most intelligent planning by students. The appraisal of aptitude is itself a technical process and one concerning which parents and students need assistance. Therefore, these educational pioneers initiated the development of a personal counseling program, using faculty advisers in helping students base their plans upon objective appraisal of capabilities. It was the hope that comparable counseling programs would be organized in the high schools, and the university would provide objective test data for the underpinning of high school counseling programs.

Dr. Berdie's study is a new step in advance of this early development. It is a further refinement of our knowledge of why many students with adequate and even promising aptitude do not go to college and thus train their latent capacities to the maximum. The study also suggests that the mere availability of scholarship money does not widely serve as an effective inducement to college attendance for many promising students. And there appear to be many personal and familial blockings in the fullest possible use of aptitudes, blockings that may require individualized counseling as a substitute for the present mass appeals used by so many professional societies who seek to recruit students en masse.

One may confidently anticipate that the last possible answer is not yet known with respect to Dean Johnston's early question and many more studies, similar to the present one, will be required.

E. G. WILLIAMSON

DEAN OF STUDENTS AND PROFESSOR
OF PSYCHOLOGY

University of Minnesota
February 24, 1954

◪ Acknowledgments

THIS volume results from the cooperative efforts of many persons. First, the 25,000 students who provided us with information about their plans, their interests, and their backgrounds, should be given appreciative recognition. Next, Dr. Wilbur Layton, Dr. Ben Willerman, and Dr. Theda Hagenah of the Student Counseling Bureau of the University of Minnesota cooperated in planning and conducting the study. Dr. Edward Swanson of the Student Counseling Bureau assumed responsibility for collecting and analyzing the follow-up information. Most of the basic tabulations were performed by Edward Mehsikomer. Mrs. Jane Wold Headley conducted the interviews that provided a source for many important hypotheses.

Financial support was provided by the University of Minnesota's Graduate School and the Office of the Dean of Students, the Commission on Human Resources and Advanced Training, and the Commission on Financing Higher Education.

The author also wishes to acknowledge the fine spirit of cooperation which relates the high schools and the colleges in Minnesota, cooperation which owes much to the generous and consistent support given by the Association of Minnesota Colleges to the Minnesota State-Wide Testing Program. The project reported in this volume can in a way be viewed as a research extension of this program.

Finally, the author wishes to express a deep debt of personal and professional gratitude to Dean E. G. Williamson of the University of Minnesota whose careful planning and organization over a period of many years has made such projects possible and whose broad experience brought into closer focus many of the problems with which this study is concerned.

R. F. B.

University of Minnesota
February 15, 1954

vii

Contents

Tables

Part One · Who Chooses College

1

Manpower and Education

Manpower is a term increasingly used during recent years. It implies that the potential of our civilization rests in the men for whom that civilization exists. It suggests that the driving force of that civilization is found in those men, that the action upon which our society rests is the action of those men.

The connotations of the term *manpower* are dynamic in character. Manpower means action, energy, drive, performance, achievement, construction, development, social progress. As social organization becomes more complex, an increasing number of problems demands more manpower and better manpower. More men must work and the work they do will be more and more exacting.

"It seems . . . evident that our society is rapidly developing more specialized activities, vocations, and professions, each one presupposing that a supply of personnel will be available of very high innate ability and with special training. The aggregate of these demands, when seen over against the character of the population, seems to make it clear that we do not possess the requisite number of highly competent personnel to satisfy these demands. We are paralleling in the field of human resources the phenomenon which is becoming more and more characteristic of America, that our demands for material resources rapidly outstrip our supply." [1]

Thus manpower is this country's most valuable natural resource. Classifying men as a resource to be used has unpleasant connotations for some people, but such a concept is not necessarily degrading since manpower, along with timber, or metallic ores, or animal products, is used for man's own betterment.

Just as other natural resources have to be processed and subjected

3

to various degrees of refinement, so does manpower. Raw petroleum, as it comes from the ground, has a limited number of uses. So does manpower, unselected and untrained. Petroleum refined to various degrees can be used for running tractors and diesel engines, for running automobiles, for running high-speed airplanes, and for making complex dyes and necessary chemicals. The degree of the refinement of petroleum depends upon the purposes for which the final product is to be used. Manpower also must be refined progressively as more exacting demands are placed upon the final product.

For men the refinement process consists of education and training. Men, as raw materials, pass through a process which is not outside of themselves, but which is essentially a part of themselves, and as they progress through this process, they acquire new knowledge and develop new skills and become increasingly competent social and moral beings.

What determines the height to which any given person progresses on this educational and training ladder? In a democratic society with a population homogeneous in terms of abilities and with opportunities unlimited, each individual should have an opportunity to decide for himself his educational and occupational future in light of his own interests and in light of his information about society's needs.

"A democratic society has obligations to provide *opportunities* for individuals to develop and use their talents, and the interests of society require that such opportunities be made attractive, but no one in a democracy can be *compelled* to use the opportunities available to him. The role of education in this connection is to equip the individual to use the opportunities that will best utilize his abilities and to guide him in making decisions that will serve both his own interests and those of society."[2]

In such a hypothetical society with a homogeneous population, the free choice of the individual would be almost unlimited. Our democratic society today, however, is not a society where people are homogeneous in terms of abilities nor do we have unlimited opportunities. Thus, educational and vocational choices of individuals are limited both by the individual's inherent characteristics and by the opportunities available. But, working within these limitations and frequently attempting to modify them, we endeavor to maximize the freedom of choice for each individual and to provide to each person a set of alternatives from which he can choose; our hope is that one alternative will be more attractive and more promising than all others and that the final choice can be made on the basis, not of chance, but of reasoned decision.

To utilize this maximized freedom of choice, the individual must be aware of his own potentialities and capacities, his own basic interests and personality characteristics, his own abilities and aptitudes, and he must also have full and complete information about the opportunities that await him and the nature of the world that surrounds him. These types of information, however, are not in and of themselves sufficient to allow him to utilize a freedom of choice.

The individual also must have skills that will allow him to use this information in a rational and an emotionally acceptable manner. He must have developed problem-solving techniques that can be applied to important practical problems touching upon his own personal development. He must know how to obtain information, how to evaluate information, how to consider alternatives, how to arrive at decisions, and how to base actions upon decisions once his final goals are selected. Having the state, the school, or the family maximize freedom of personal choice does little good unless the individual himself is prepared to make use of such freedom.

The freedom and wisdom of choice and factors determining the direction of the choice are of concern to all of society.

"The United States, now more than ever before in our history, needs to have its ablest citizens either in positions of large immediate social influence (such as public administration, business and labor leadership, journalism, teaching) or in work of great potential future benefit (such as research in the natural and social sciences, philosophy, and criticism, and the creative arts). Men and women of superior talents are needed for such positions, but talent alone is not enough. They must also have special training that will develop their talents along lines required by the complexities and specializations of contemporary life. And they must have a sense of social responsibility and other qualities of character that will direct the use of their talents toward socially beneficial ends." [3]

That this matter is not of importance exclusively to the individual is attested by the interest shown in manpower problems by many groups, particularly during the past decade. Among the groups vitally interested in manpower problems at the present time are these: Office of Scientific Personnel of the National Research Council; Commission on Financing Higher Education; Commission on Human Resources and Advanced

Training; Conservation of Human Resources Project; Working Group on Human Behaviour of the Department of Defense; Personnel Division of the Armed Services; Selective Service System; National Security Resources Board; Office of Defense Mobilization; Department of Labor; Manpower Planning Division of the Adjutant General's Office; and National Manpower Council. These groups are making, for the first time in American history, extensive attempts to inventory the potentialities of the American population and to study carefully the manpower problems faced by our complex society.

The answer to the question Who should be educated for what? can be determined only upon resolution of several different philosophical points of view. It is an answer dependent upon values, and the question must be approached in terms of what is wanted for individuals and for society. The question of *how* people should be selected and educated, although still dependent upon values, is one that can be approached more directly and empirically. Once we have some point of agreement regarding who should be educated for what, then it will be easier for us to approach the second question systematically.

There are essentially two divergent educational philosophies that find expression in this country today. Exponents of both philosophies appear to be in full agreement with J. B. Johnston, long-time dean at the University of Minnesota, when he said: "It seems to me that an intelligent, successful and enduring society will provide educational facilities to enable each individual to secure training for some occupation suited to his native abilities or endowments, so that he may perform his share of the world's work in a field which he can work at best." [4]

But beyond this there is considerable disagreement. The one educational philosophy, briefly summarized, assumes that the number of persons capable of benefiting from higher education is relatively small and that higher education is for a limited number of intellectually selected individuals. This is the European theory of educating only the intellectual elite. The other philosophy assumes that a large share of our population can benefit from higher education. As stated in the report of the President's Commission on Higher Education, "It must always be remembered that at least as many young people who have the same or greater intellectual ability than those now in college do not enroll because of low family income." [5] The first philosophy would steer into higher education small numbers of carefully selected individuals who would then be given rigorous and thorough education probably along somewhat traditional lines. The second philosophy, however, assumes that an increasing number of individuals will be brought into institutions of higher learning and that the programs of these institutions should be varied to meet the varying demands of this vast number of persons.

These two philosophies are perhaps directly related to two different points of view regarding the needs of society for trained manpower. One point of view is presented in a book by Seymour Harris, *The Market for College Graduates*.[6] Harris fears that American institutions of higher learning will produce too many college graduates. He assumes a relatively limited and fixed demand for college graduates, particularly in terms of vocational requirements, and apparently feels that the demand is now being met, if not exceeded. He fears that college graduates, unsuccessful in finding work in jobs they have anticipated, will become frustrated intelligentsia and that they will provide raw material for an American fascistic movement. His assumptions are based upon both a static society and a static system of higher education.

The years since World War II have demonstrated that ours is far from a static society, and educators have expressed the fervent hope that higher education is not rigidly fixed in traditional patterns but that a dynamic pattern is emerging in our colleges and universities in response to the accelerating changes in our society. These changes have led to competition for college-trained young people instead of the oversupply Harris prophesied. As the Commission on Human Resources and Advanced Training reports:

"The growing interest in these problems comes partly from a fear that our increasingly technological civilization requires so many experts in so many different fields that our needs may soon outrun our supply of young men and women with the intelligence, the interest, and the motivation necessary to become scientists, engineers, doctors, or qualified specialists in other fields. One evidence of this fear is the growing number of efforts to persuade bright students to enter particular fields. Examples are the Fellowships of the Atomic Energy Commission, the Scholarship and Fellowship provisions of the National Science Foundation, and the Fellowships and special inducements offered by the Veterans Administration and the Public Health Service to students interested in careers in the mental health fields. The Holloway Plan was enacted by Congress in order to secure a larger number of college-trained Navy officers. If Congress approves the prospective extension of the Holloway Plan to the Army and Air Force, the competition for the ablest of our college graduates will be further increased." [7]

If the need of society is for more, not fewer, college graduates, if the philosophy that many can and should benefit from higher education is to dominate, then it is important (1) to determine at what points young people must decide on their future course; (2) to find out how many go to work and how many continue in school; and (3) to discover what the factors of heredity and environment are that influence their decision.

CHOICE POINTS FOR YOUTH

In a relatively free society such as we have, the actions of young people follow upon decisions made in response to certain pressures but under conditions providing a maximum freedom of choice. These choice points occur at irregular intervals and for different persons there are varying numbers of such choice points. One point of choice occurs when a child leaves elementary school. At that time the child must decide whether to continue general schooling, to obtain practical and vocational training, or to leave school entirely and embark upon his work career, providing the law allows him to do so. A second choice point occurs at the beginning of or during the high school career of the individual, when he must decide whether he should emphasize the high school curriculum leading to college, to immediate vocational opportunities, or to terminal general education.

Another important choice point occurs at the conclusion of high school. Then the student must decide whether he is to continue in school, find a job, marry, or undertake some other course of activity. It is this third choice point, occurring immediately after high school, that is the main concern of this volume.

Obviously, these choice points are not independent of each other. A student may in the eighth grade decide he is going to become a lawyer. To reach that goal he will require a certain amount of college training. No further choice points may occur because his decision has been made and his path is laid out before him. His choice will be reviewed periodically and his decision will be reconsidered but an actual choice will not again be made. On the other hand, a person may postpone a choice until much later in his life, he may make a choice and then change his mind and make another choice, or he may expand his choice or choose more specifically.

The types of alternatives facing high school graduates are relatively few in number. A senior graduating from high school can enter college, find employment (either with members of his family or with other persons), enter some noncollegiate school such as a business or trade school, continue in a post-high-school course, begin nurses' training, or enter military service.

Within each of these types of alternatives, however, the possible choices are many. Approximately 2000 colleges and universities are available to high school seniors. Job opportunities are found in 20,000 to 40,000 different kinds of occupations. Hundreds of hospitals and schools of nursing provide training for nurses. Schools of vocational agriculture, schools for electricians and radio repairmen, schools for beauticians, and similar noncollegiate schools are widely distributed through the entire country. Even the military provides a choice so far as it encourages selective enlistment and placement.

WHO CHOOSES WHAT

No general figures are available reporting what high school graduates in the United States do after graduation. Figures are available over the past several years for certain samples of high school graduates, however, and these provide a general picture, although not a complete one.

Goetsch found that in a group of 1023 high-ability Milwaukee high school children in school between 1937 and 1940, 35 per cent of the high school graduates attended college.[8]

Anderson and Berning, studying 22,306 graduates of Minnesota high schools in 1938, found that one year after graduation, according to the reports of high school principals, 35 per cent were employed full time, 7 per cent were employed part time, 12 per cent were unemployed, 23 per cent were in colleges or universities, 12 per cent were in other schools, and 11 per cent were unidentified.[9]

A follow-up study nine years later of a sample of these students from Minnesota high schools indicated that 13 per cent of the entire sample earned college degrees.[10] Nearly 80 per cent of the scholastically more able high school graduates received some college training and slightly more than one third of these capable students earned a degree. The results of this study also indicated that capable high school students entering college immediately after high school had a far greater chance of obtaining degrees than did capable students who delayed entrance to college until a year or more after graduation from high school.

A somewhat similar study of Minnesota high school graduates was made on the class of 1945 one year after graduation.[11] The figures for that year are badly distorted because of the war (two thirds of the men who graduated in 1945 were in the armed forces one year later), but if corrections are made to exclude the students who were in military service, approximately 50 per cent of these high school graduates were at work, fewer than 2 per cent were unemployed, approximately 25 per cent were in a college or university, approximately 6 per cent were in other schools, and 17 per cent were in other pursuits.

The figures obtained in 1938 and in 1945 indicated that one year after high school graduation, approximately one quarter of male high school graduates in Minnesota and approximately one fifth of female high school graduates were in college.

A study of 1949 high school graduates in Arkansas, based on information obtained from high school superintendents, indicated that 39 per cent of these students were employed one year after graduation and 35 per cent were attending some school: 31½ per cent were in college, 2½ per cent were in technical or trade schools, and 1 per cent were in business schools.[12] The remainder were neither employed nor in school; many of them presumably were in the armed forces.

Other studies begin with younger students. McGrath reported that although 90 per cent of all fifth-graders have the ability needed to complete high school, only 40 per cent do so.[13] He estimated also that although 32 per cent of all fifth-graders have the ability to complete college, only 7 per cent graduate. McGrath's figures indicated that 17 per cent of high school graduates complete college. Each year, according to McGrath, we fail to train 55 per cent of those who could finish high school and 76 per cent of those who could finish college. McGrath is concerned with the specter in our academic halls: "Another entire student body for every college and university just as able as those normally enrolled."

Hollinshead, in a report prepared for the Commission on Financing Higher Education, estimated that of children of the age of eighth-graders, 20 per cent have left school by the time they finish the eighth grade and 40 per cent have left school by the time they finish the tenth grade.[14] He estimated that 45 per cent of the age group of high school graduates actually graduate from high school and that by the thirteenth year in school, 83 per cent of the age group have dropped out of school, leaving only 17 per cent of this group in college. According to his figures, approximately 8 per cent of the total age group of college seniors actually graduate from college.

In general, one obtains the impression that slightly fewer than half of our American young men and young women graduate from high school and that of these graduates somewhat more than 25 per cent attend college with between one third and one half obtaining employment directly after high school graduation. Smaller proportions of students are married, enter business schools or other noncollegiate schools, enter the armed forces, or are unemployed.

DETERMINANTS OF AFTER-HIGH-SCHOOL PLANS

The question of *why* — why do some high school students go on to college while others, equally qualified, drop out? — is of course much more complex than determining how many of a given group go to college and how many get a job.

Some of the factors that are commonly considered to affect the high school student's decision are these: age of student at high school graduation, sex of student, marriage plan of student, vocational interest of student, interest student has in school, financial resources of student, ethnic background of student, size of family, order of birth, age of parents, occupation of parents, education of parents, job markets, availability of college scholarships, and proximity of training institutions.

Because of the complex patterning of these conditions, the relationships existing between any one of them and the plans made by high school graduates remain poorly defined. Here we have a problem that nicely exemplifies Carter Good's statement, "It should be made emphatic that the inferring of causes is an extremely difficult and precarious matter, especially in social fields where relationships are so complex that it is nearly impossible to determine definite causes." [15]

Despite the difficulties involved, many writers have attempted to list and study the factors influencing the high school student's decision. Reeves, for example, gives these reasons why youth do not go to college:

Restricted curriculums and educational facilities
Limited financial resources of youth
Geographical barriers
Differences of different racial or ethnic groups in desire for education

Discriminatory techniques of admissions offices
Sex and admission
Race barriers
Religious barriers
National origin as barrier
Type of college control and admission policy [16]

The National Child Labor Committee reported that "The major reasons for school leaving as disclosed by the national survey, are, in the order of importance: increased employment opportunities, expectation of the draft, economic need, lack of interest in academic work, and restlessness, insecurity, or social maladjustment." [17] Although the National Child Labor Committee was concerned primarily with the drop-outs before the twelfth grade, the same reasons may well apply to drop-outs occurring between the twelfth and thirteenth grades inasmuch as failure to continue on to college after high school graduation constitutes one type of school drop-out.

The Minnesota Commission on Higher Education found another important factor:

"The hurdle between high school and college cannot be described solely in terms of financial burden or lack of college facilities, though these factors are highly important. In spite of improved economic circumstances, the proportion of graduates who attended college increased but slightly between 1938 and 1945. Beyond a relatively short commuting range, greater distances from college facilities did not seem to be related to college attendance, probably because young people who attend college from these areas may require a high degree of motivation or they are unlikely to make the extra effort. Steps need to be taken, of course, to ease the financial strain and reduce the distance factor by a system of scholarships or some other means whereby the most able graduates who ought to go to college from all communities are encouraged and assisted in so doing. But many excellent college risks, and many parents, evidently are not convinced that college education is worth while. They do not see that one, two, or four years of post-high-school education will better equip young men and women for the immediate tasks of earning a living, establishing a home, and carrying out the responsibilities of citizenship." [18]

Hollinshead, in *Who Should Go to College in America*, presented reasons for attending college in this paragraph:

"But this one-third who went to college is by no means a random group who just happened to go. We can identify the group in several ways. Those of high ability and good academic record were more apt to go than their less able classmates. Those whose parents had high incomes or were in the professional classes were more apt to go than those who had lower incomes or lower social status. Girls went less frequently than boys, even though their abilities were as high or higher. Negroes do not go in the same proportion as whites. High school graduates in certain regions of the country do not go in the same proportions as those in other regions. Urban young people were more apt to go than rural young people. Those who were near a college were more apt to go than those farther away. And those with a strong drive for a vocation which required college training were more apt to go than those of equal status and no strong vocational interest." [19]

These generalizations are fairly obvious and many studies provide substantial evidence warranting them. But none of the studies reported cover a broad sample of high school students and none analyze a sufficiently large range of variables. Some evidence is available, however, on almost every one of the variables relating to after-high-school activity that have been mentioned here. In the following sections which summarize this evidence the emphasis is on factors directly related to college attendance. This does not imply that these are the only or even the most important problems. But it cannot be denied that college attendance is extremely important, both from the standpoint of society and from the standpoint of many millions of individual students. Nevertheless college attendance should not be considered without also taking into account other alternatives, and therefore comparisons will always have to be made between the students who plan to attend college, those who plan to work, and those who have other plans.

Ability. Almost every investigator approaching problems of higher education has taken into consideration the influence of intellectual ability upon college attendance. Intellectual ability of high order is limited and the importance of identifying and developing this ability is too obvious to need expansion.

"Since only about one per cent of the population has the type of intelligence required for the solutions of complicated scientific problems and only 300 persons out of every million can be said to fall within the brilliant class, the importance of developing and utilizing the capacities of these well-endowed individuals as fully as possible is a matter of the greatest national importance."[20]

Anderson and Berning reported in the study of Minnesota high school graduates of 1938 that of those in the upper 30 per cent of the group in ability, two thirds were not in college. An unpublished study of Minneapolis public high school graduates of 1946 found that of the graduates in the upper 10 per cent of their class on the basis of college aptitude test scores, 52 per cent were in college one year after graduation and 21 per cent were at work. Of the students in the second 10 per cent, 53 per cent were in college and 17 per cent at work. Of the students in the third upper 10 per cent, 31 per cent were in college and 28 per cent were at work, and of the students in the ninth 10 per cent, 16 per cent were in college and 43 per cent were at work.

Morehead, in his study of Arkansas high school graduates of 1949, found that 54 per cent of the students who were in the upper one quarter of their high school classes on the basis of college aptitude test scores were in college, 57 per cent of the upper one tenth were in college, and 14 per cent of the lower one quarter were in college. Benson followed up a group of people who were given intelligence tests in grade six and found that these test scores bore a significant relationship to college attendance.[21] Phearman, in a study done in 1946 in Iowa, found that of the students who were in the top 2 per cent on the Iowa tests, 92 per cent entered college.[22] Somewhat similarly, Terman found that of his gifted children, taken from the upper 1 to 2 per cent of the population in intelligence, 88 per cent entered college.[23] Hollinshead has estimated that 40 to 45 per cent of students in the upper one fifth of the population on the basis of intelligence tests go to college.

The evidence leaves little doubt that there is a strong tendency for our college students to come from the more intellectually capable of our high school graduates and that a much larger proportion of brilliant high school graduates than of the more mediocre students attend college. There is a substantial relationship between intellectual ability, as shown by scores on college aptitude tests, and college attendance.

The very size of the relationship between general aptitude and college attendance suggests that many types of ability are not being utilized effectively: "When people are selected from many fields of specialization on the basis of measures of general ability, the total potential supply for all of these fields is restricted to those persons who possess satisfactorily high general ability. It seems reasonable to assume, however, that work in different fields of specialization calls for somewhat different types of ability. Since the specialized abilities are not perfectly correlated with each other, the total potential supply could be increased by selecting people for each specialty in terms of the particular abilities required for that specialty. Relatively little effort has been devoted to isolating special abilities required by different types of work. But some attempts have been made and further work of this type should be initiated both because it might increase the total potential from which specialists could be drawn and also because the results might lead to better selection of people for the individual fields of specialization." [24]

High school achievement. High school achievement, as shown by grades in high school, is significantly related to college aptitude. Correlations between high school grades and college aptitude test scores are in the range of about .50. As one would expect, grades in high school bear a strong relationship to college attendance; in fact, a survey of the available data indicates that high school grades are perhaps more closely related to college attendance than are college aptitude test scores.

The American Council on Education (A.C.E.) publication *On Getting into College* reported that high school achievement is the second most important factor in determining college attendance (family background having been found to be the most important factor).[25] Of high school graduates in the upper quintile of their class, 59 per cent applied for admission to college, whereas of the students in the lowest quintile, only 17 per cent applied for admission.

Keller, in his study of Minnesota high school graduates of 1945, found that of students in the upper 10 per cent of their high school class, 52 per cent were in college, of students in the upper 30 per cent of their high school class, 41 per cent were in college, and of students in the lower 70 per cent, 16 per cent were in college. The study of Minneapolis high school graduates of 1945 indicated similar trends.

Anderson and Berning, in their study of Minnesota high school graduates of 1938, found that of Minnesota high school students in the upper one tenth of their high school class, 64 per cent continued schooling after leaving high school (no more than 50 per cent in college, however), of students in the fifth decile, 33 per cent continued schooling, and of students in the lowest decile, only 17 per cent continued schooling.

In general it is quite evident that the student who is a good student in high school is much more likely to attend college than is the student who has not achieved well in high school.

Age. There is evidence suggesting that age is somewhat related to college attendance. In her study of high-ability students in Milwaukee followed up in 1940 after high school graduation, Goetsch found that there was a tendency for children who were young at the time of graduation from high school to attend college to a greater extent than older children. Of superior students under seventeen years of age at the time of high school graduation, 50 per cent attended college, whereas of the superior students who were over twenty years of age at the time of graduation from high school, fewer than one tenth attended college.

Sex. Goetsch also found a greater tendency for boys to attend college than for girls. In the A.C.E. study, the sex of the student was found to be the third most influential factor in determining whether or not the student attended college. The *Fortune* Survey, reported in 1950, indicated that parental attitudes differed according to the sex of the child and that there was a strong feeling on the part of the parents that college would be more beneficial for boys than for girls.[26] This sex difference is of particular interest in the light of the lack of a corresponding sex difference in college aptitude. In fact, on the basis of high school grades, the average girl is superior in academic performance to the average high school boy. A large share of the waste of high ability, then, is undoubtedly due to the sending of too few women on to higher education.

Financial resources. Lack of money has been regarded by many people as the primary reason for young people of high ability failing to attend college.

President Truman in his message to Congress in 1950 said: "Primarily because of low family income and of the high cost involved, more than half of our young people who would benefit from a college education are now unable to attend."

Commissioner of Education McGrath in 1950 wrote: "Since low parental income is the principal deterrent to college attendance, the key to the matter, as far as potential students are concerned, is some plan of providing financial assistance adequate to remove this handicap."[27]

College attendance is a costly behavior in our society today. Even in our least expensive colleges, having a minimum of tuition, a bachelor's degree costs between $3000 and $4000, not including the money that a student would be making if he were working rather than attending college. Assuming that the average high school student can make at least $2000 a year immediately after high school graduation, four years in college, including the cost of college and the money unearned, looms to the grand figure of $11,000. The studies that have been reported indicate that students with money more frequently attend college than students without money. Many students without financial resources enter college, but most college students tend to come from economically relatively stable homes.

Gallagher estimated in 1950 that probably one half of youths with ability and ambition for college are blocked because of low parental income and inadequate existing money aids to students.[28] Goetsch found that of the high-ability students she studied who were not in college, 64 per cent said they were not in college because of lack of money. She found that of the students coming from families in the top financial brackets, 100 per cent were in college, whereas of the students coming from the lowest financial brackets, only 20 per cent were in college.

Barber, in a study of high-ability high school graduates in Pennsylvania in 1949, found that 34 per cent of the 111 not in college gave as the reason lack of money.[29] Baker reported that of 910 high school students from Pennsylvania with I.Q.'s of 110 or above, 93 per cent of the students coming from the high economic groups graduated from high school and 57 per cent attended college, whereas only 72 per cent of the students coming from lower economic groups graduated from high school and only 13 per cent went to college.[30] Keller, in his study of Minnesota high school graduates of 1945, reported: "In spite of the improved economic conditions of 1945, lack of family finances was the reason given most often for the failure of these high-ability students to go to college — accounting for almost three tenths of this group." [31] The Educational Policies Commission reported that lack of financial resources is the main but not the only reason for this waste of talent.

A more sophisticated approach to this particular problem was shown by Hollinshead, who said: "More careful study of the financial problem has indicated that it is difficult to isolate and is apt to be one of a complex of factors discouraging an individual from college attendance." [32] Along this same vein, the Educational Policies Commission stated: "The economic barrier to advanced education and professional careers rarely represents itself suddenly at a critical moment of decision. Generally, the circumstances of poverty or near-poverty operate over a period of years to condition the whole pattern of hopes and plans which shape the life of an individual." [33]

Thus ample evidence exists that many students fail to go to college because they lack funds, but additional evidence suggests that lack of funds in and of itself is not a sufficient reason for not going to college and that the relationship between financial resources and college attendance is not a direct one.

Paternal occupation. In a society where there is less than complete occupational mobility, one would expect a relationship between the occupations of fathers and the educational and occupational plans of sons. This is the case as shown by reported investigations.

Anderson and Berning, in their study of 1938 Minnesota high school graduates, said: "Children of fathers in the first three groups listed on the Anderson-Goodenough Occupational Classification Scale attended college in higher proportions than children of fathers in the other five groups. This is true for graduates of comparable ability. The probability that a farmer's child with high scholastic ability will attend college was quite low in comparison with the probability for able graduates in other occupational groups. The farmer's child in the upper 30 per cent of his class had one chance in four of attending college; the chances were only one in three for those in the highest tenth." [34]

Keller, in his study of 1945 Minnesota high school graduates, found: "Almost two women in every three whose fathers were professional men had enrolled in a college or university upon graduation from high school. At the lower end of the occupational scale, on the other hand, for every daughter of an unskilled laborer who was in college during 1945–46, fifteen had not enrolled." [35]

The A.C.E. study, *On Getting into College*, found that 73 per cent of the children of professional men and executives applied for admission to college, 48 per cent of the children of small business proprietors applied for admission, and 21 per cent of the children of factory workers applied for admission.

In the study of Minneapolis public school high school graduates of 1946, 50 per cent of the children of professional men were in college a year after graduation and 22 per cent were at work. Of the children of semiprofessional men, 37 per cent were in college and 29 per cent at work. Of the children of clerical workers, 20 per cent were in college, and 38 per cent were at work, and of the children of semiskilled laborers, 9 per cent were in college and 43 per cent were at work.

Thus, there is a marked tendency for children of fathers high on the occupational ladder to attend college to a far greater extent than do the children of fathers in other occupations. Inasmuch as there are many more children coming from nonprofessional homes, it is safe to assume, however, that a large proportion of our college students do not come from professional homes in spite of the fact that most of the children from professional homes do go to college.

Family background. Financial resources and paternal occupation are not the only factors in the family background that have been shown to be related to college attendance. Attitudes of parents are very important in determining whether or not children attend college. The *Fortune* Survey revealed that 83 per cent of the parents interviewed wanted their sons to attend college while 10 per cent were opposed; 69 per cent of the parents wanted their daughters to attend college while 21 per cent were opposed. Of the parents of the boys, 66 per cent thought college would benefit their sons from an occupational point of view, 19 per cent felt it would help their sons lead a fuller life, 15 per cent felt that college would provide necessary knowledge and education, and 10 per cent thought it would increase social poise, provide social contacts, and enhance prestige. Of the parents of the girls, 48 per cent felt that college would help their daughters occupationally, 20 per cent felt that college would help their daughters lead a more complete life, 16 per cent felt that college would provide necessary knowledge and education, and 18 per cent felt that their daughters would benefit socially by attending college.

The A.C.E. study found that of the children of fathers who had attended college 65 per cent applied for admission to college, whereas of the children of fathers who had only grade school education only 21 per cent had applied for college admission. Hollinshead has stated: "A rough estimate is that half the present student body of the average college is in that particular college because of the influence of relatives or friends of its clientele."[36] If this kind of influence is so effective in determining which colleges students attend, certainly it is powerful in determining whether or not students attend college.

Goetsch's data suggested that the age of the parent, the size of the family, and the child's place in the family are influential in determining whether or not children attend college.

Hollinshead summarizes the possible influences of these family factors in this way: "But the rewards of such economic mobility or movements up the ladder as education provides now seem to go in largest proportions to the groups the sociologists classify as lower- or middle-class. The upper-class does not rely particularly on education to maintain its position, and the so-called lower-class lacks stimulation for education which is in part caused by lack of ability but in larger part is caused by lack of motivation in the home or surrounding environment. This lack of motivation stems from lack of cultural materials such as books, periodicals, and neighborhood cultural influences. The children of ministers and schoolteachers, however, reach the top rungs of the educational ladder out of all proportion to their numbers. Allowing many exceptions, those who gain most in social status and economic improvement from education seem to come from secure, modest homes with loaded bookshelves. One of the crucial determiners of college-going is family attitude. If there is a family tradition of college-going, if there is a family respect for learning, then the youngster will go even at considerable sacrifice. (Sometimes family tradition leads the student to go or try to go to the wrong college for him.) If there is no such tradition or respect, the youngster is not apt to go, even though there may be plenty of money to send him." [37]

Nationality origin and religion. Goetsch found that nationality background was related to college attendance. A greater proportion of the high school graduates she studied went to college if they came from Scandinavian, Yugoslavian, Rumanian, Bulgarian, or British homes than if they came from French, Italian, or Greek homes. The A.C.E. study found that 68 per cent of high school graduates coming from Jewish homes, 36 per cent of those coming from Protestant homes, and 25 per cent of those coming from Catholic homes applied for admission to college. Stetter, as reported by Havighurst, found that of high school graduates studied in Connecticut, 57 per cent of the Catholics applied for admission to college, 63 per cent of the Protestants applied, and 87 per cent of the Jews applied. [38] There can be little question that a relationship exists between ethnic and religious background and college attendance.

Geography. Students in various parts of the country attend colleges at differential rates, and within a given section of the country proximity to a college influences the extent to which high school graduates attend college.

Anderson and Berning in 1938 found: "A significantly higher percentage . . . of graduates who lived within a radius of ten miles from a college were in school and fewer were at work. It seemed to make a difference whether a college was located in a graduate's backyard, but otherwise the location of a college was of little significance in affecting college attendance." [39] Keller reported: "Better than one graduate in four (27 per cent) who resided within ten miles of a college was attending college a year after graduation, as contrasted with approximately one in six of those who lived beyond this distance." [40]

Basing his index on the total population between 5 and 17 years of age, Hollinshead reported that the index of the number of students in college in California was twelve, in Minnesota ten, in West Virginia five, and in Mississippi four. Thus there are large differences among the states regarding the relative number of people in college in this age group. Russell, in a survey made of school officials, found that in most states educational facilities in colleges and universities were sufficient to care for veterans but in Georgia, Massachusetts, New Jersey, North Carolina, and South Carolina, veterans had difficulty in getting into college.[41] This perhaps reflects some geographical differences in accessibility to higher education.

The A.C.E. study revealed that in cities with a population of more than one million, 44 per cent of high school seniors applied for admission to college; in small towns, 26 per cent applied for admission; and of the children of farmers, 21 per cent applied for admission to college.

There can be little question that where a student lives has an influence upon his attending college.

Extracurricular activities. The A.C.E. study suggested that students who participate in extracurricular activities tend to go to college more frequently than do nonparticipants. Of the boys studied, 53 per cent of the officers in student activities applied for admission to college, 52 per cent of those with high participation applied for admission, and only 29 per cent of those with low participation applied for admission. Havighurst, in *Elmtown's Youth*, provided ample evidence of the relationships among participation in extracurricular activities, family background, and academic ability.[42]

Attitudes of students. Several variables related to college attendance can be classified under this rubric. Satisfaction or dissatisfaction with school undeniably plays an important part in determining whether or not students remain in school. Segel has said: "In the study on which I am working, which is mostly documentary, it appears that this frustration, this dissatisfaction of secondary school pupils, probably really develops during the elementary period. As far as that is concerned, it may develop even before that. Studies made of parents suggest that children who have been brought up in a democratic home do much better socially in school." [43]

Keller, in his study of 1946 Minnesota graduates, found that lack of interest in school was given as a reason by one out of sixteen high-ability students who were not in college. The Educational Policies Commission explains some of this: "Inflexibility of curriculum and teaching method constitutes a formidable barrier to the development of the gifts of exceptional children." [44]

On the basis of studies in several midwestern communities, Havighurst generalized about barriers to higher education as follows: "Motivational barrier is at least as important as the economic barrier." Barber reported that of 111 high-ability high school pupils not in college (students in Pennsylvania), 20 per cent were not in college because they lacked academic interest, 12 per cent were not in college because they lacked a serious purpose, and 13 per cent were not in college because they preferred to go to work. The *Fortune* Survey revealed that 10 per cent of able high school graduates would not go to college under any circumstances, even though money were available.

McGuire suggested that these factors are important in considering the motivation of high school pupils for college: aspiration level, personal attributes, social techniques, value attitudes, status anxiety, emotional approach to problems, and compensatory behavior.[45]

Goetsch found that plans for marriage and related attitudes interfered with college to a slight extent, preventing 1 per cent of the boys and 5 per cent of the girls from seriously considering college.

THE IMPORTANCE OF FURTHER STUDY

This review of the available information on why high school graduates do or do not attend college reveals that many useful facts have been uncovered. As we have indicated, however, not one of the investigations reported has been based on adequate and comprehensive samples of young persons and many important hypotheses have not been examined carefully. Some investigations involving large samples of students have been concerned with only a small number of variables. Other investigations, evaluating the effects of many determinants, have been based upon small or limited samples.

The findings of many of these investigations have suggested the ultimate importance of both economic conditions and cultural conditions in determining whether or not high school graduates attend college. In no case, however, has an attempt been made to compare the differential effects of these two types of variables and few facts have been presented to show that cultural variables other than those most directly related to economic variables, such as occupational level of father, really influence what a high school graduate does. Little acceptable evidence is available to support the frequently stated hypothesis that the cultural level of the home plays an important part in determining whether or not children attend college.

In light of this lacuna in our existing information — and in light of the important manpower problems facing us during these mid-century decades — the present study was undertaken in 1950 by the staff of the Student Counseling Bureau in the Office of the Dean of Students at the University of Minnesota.

There were special opportunities in Minnesota for such research resulting, first, from the Minnesota State-Wide Testing Program and, second, from the spirit of cooperation existing between Minnesota high schools and colleges. Each year extensive information is collected by the Minnesota colleges from all high school seniors in the state and this information is utilized effectively in counseling and instructing students, both by the high schools and by the colleges. This information is collected by means of a comprehensive inventory of college aptitude and high school achievement made each winter in Minnesota high schools. Since little additional effort would be required to extend this inventory to cover students' plans and their socio-economic backgrounds, all needed information on many variables affecting college attendance could be easily obtained from a large sample of high school students. Thus, the study was begun under unusually favorable conditions.

The specific purpose of the present study was to investigate the factors determining college attendance with particular attention to a comparison of determinants related to economic status and those related to cultural or educational status. We will present in detail the statistical results of the study, but first the next three chapters will discuss the students behind the statistics, the plan of the study and the general trends in the data, and the implications of the findings.

NOTES

[1] From the Report of the Conference on Human Resources and the Fields of Higher Learning, quoted in the Educational Testing Service *Annual Report*, 1949–50 (Princeton, N.J.: Educational Testing Service, 1950).

[2] Educational Policies Commission, *Education of the Gifted* (Washington, D.C.: National Education Association, 1950), p. 3.

[3] *Ibid.*, p. 2.

[4] John B. Johnston, *Scholarship and Democracy* (New York: D. Appleton-Century, 1937), p. 1.

[5] President's Commission on Higher Education, *Higher Education for American Democracy* (New York: Harper, 1948), p. 1.

[6] Seymour E. Harris, *The Market for College Graduates and Related Aspects of Education and Income* (Cambridge, Mass.: Harvard University Press, 1949).

[7] Commission on Human Resources and Advanced Training, *Plans for Studies of America's Trained Talent*, Report No. 2, Washington, D.C., March 9, 1951.

[8] Helen G. Goetsch, *Parental Income and College Opportunities* (New York: Bureau of Publications, Teachers College, Columbia University, 1940).

[9] G. L. Anderson and T. J. Berning, "What Happens to Minnesota High School Graduates?" *Studies in Higher Education*, University of Minnesota Committee on Educational Research, Biennial Report, 1938–40 (Minneapolis: University of Minnesota, 1941), pp. 15–40.

[10] G. Lester Anderson, "What Happens to Minnesota's High School Graduates," in Minnesota Commission on Higher Education, *Higher Education in Minnesota* (Minneapolis: University of Minnesota Press, 1950), pp. 102–15.

[11] Robert J. Keller, "The Minnesota Public High School Graduates of 1945 — One Year Later," in *Higher Education in Minnesota*, pp. 81–101.

[12] Charles Morehead, "What's Happening to Our High School Seniors," *Journal of Arkansas Education*, 23:12–13 (April 1950).

[13] Earl J. McGrath, "On the Outside — Looking In," *School Life*, 32:56–59 (January 1950).

[14] Byron S. Hollinshead, *Who Should Go to College in America* (New York: The Commission on Financing Higher Education, Columbia University Press, 1951), p. 25. (Later published as *Who Should Go to College*, Columbia University Press, 1952.)

[15] Carter V. Good, A. S. Barr, and Douglas E. Scates, *The Methodology of Educational Research* (New York: D. Appleton-Century, 1941), p. 545.

[16] Floyd W. Reeves, "Barriers to Higher Education," *Phi Delta Kappa*, 31:214–24 (January 1950).

[17] *New York Times*, Sunday, April 1, 1951, p. E 9.

[18] *Higher Education in Minnesota*, pp. 99–100.

[19] Hollinshead, p. 25.

[20] Conservation of Human Resources, Eli Ginzberg, director, *Progress Report, June 1951* (New York: Graduate School of Business, Columbia University, 1951).

[21] Viola E. Benson, "The Intelligence and Later Scholastic Success of Sixth-Grade Pupils," *School and Society*, 55:163–67 (Fall 1942).

[22] L. T. Phearman, "Comparisons of High School Graduates Who Go to College

with Those Who Do Not Go to College" (Dissertation, Education Department of Graduate College of the State University of Iowa, Iowa City, June, 1948).

[23] Lewis Terman and Melita Oden, *The Gifted Child Grows Up* (Stanford, Calif.: Stanford University Press, 1947).

[24] Commission on Human Resources and Advanced Training, *Plans for Studies of America's Trained Talent.*

[25] *On Getting into College* (Washington, D.C.: American Council on Education, 1949).

[26] *Fortune,* Supplement, September 1949, pp. 1–16.

[27] McGrath, p. 57.

[28] Buell G. Gallagher, "Necessity for Federal Aid to Students in Higher Education," *Educational Record,* 31:26–29 (January 1950).

[29] Leroy E. Barber, "Why Some Able High-School Graduates Do Not Go to College," *School Review,* 59:93–96 (February 1941).

[30] Frank E. Baker, "Education for All Youth at Social Expense," *Progressive Education,* 23:180–82 (March 1946).

[31] Keller, p. 96.

[32] Hollinshead, p. 60.

[33] Educational Policies Commission, p. 24.

[34] Anderson and Berning, p. 38.

[35] Keller, p. 87.

[36] Hollinshead, p. 31.

[37] *Ibid.*

[38] Invitational Testing Conference, Educational Testing Service, *Proceedings of Invitational Conference on Testing Problems* (Princeton, N.J.: Educational Testing Service, 1951), p. 28.

[39] Anderson and Berning, p. 33.

[40] Keller, p. 88.

[41] John D. Russell, "Could They Get into College," *Higher Education,* 3:1–5 (February 15, 1947).

[42] August Havighurst, *Elmtown's Youth* (New York: Wiley, 1949).

[43] David Segel, *Why Do Boys and Girls Drop Out of School and What Can We Do About It?* U.S. Office of Education, Circular No. 269, 1950, p. 34.

[44] Educational Policies Commission, p. 29.

[45] Carson McGuire, *Social Status, Peer Status, and Social Mobility.* University of Chicago, Committee on Human Development, January 1949.

2

The Cast of Characters

IN 1949, before we actually began the work of designing this study, a series of open-ended interviews were held with high school students in order to help us formulate hypotheses and develop appropriate methods. Jane Wold, a University of Minnesota counselor, conducted the interviews with 139 graduating seniors from four Minneapolis schools. These 56 boys and 83 girls constituted a sample of students having either a high school percentile rank or a percentile score on the American Council on Education Psychological Examination, based on norms for college freshmen, of 80 or above. Of the boys, 44 were planning to enter college and 12 had other plans. Of the girls, 37 were planning to enter college and 46 had other plans.

These students were selected by the interviewer from lists containing the names and the test scores of all students in the schools. After the students to be interviewed were identified, arrangements were made with the high school principals and high school counselors to have the students brought to an interviewing room in the school building and the interviewer spent approximately one-half hour conducting an unstructured interview that had as its primary purpose the identification of factors influencing the student in making his plans for after high school. The interviewer took careful notes while the interviews were in progress and later prepared a complete report containing both factual information and her impressions. These notes were studied carefully during the designing of the study and the preparation of questionnaires and of the interview schedule.

These interviews resulted not only in important hypotheses but also in a series of case histories that provide a reference for the results of the study.

Translating statistics into flesh and blood people is difficult. Even though one has had much experience working with people similar to those in the group upon which the statistics are based, means, medians, correlation coefficients, and standard deviations are removed so far from the actual people in whom we are mainly interested that accurate perceptions of human problems are often nearly impossible.

Analysis of the information presented in this report revealed that for the group of approximately 25,000 high school seniors studied, the probability that any one student would attend college was diminished if that student came from a home where the parents were divorced. This in and of itself is an interesting and meaningful generalization. It becomes much more meaningful if we see some of the dynamics underlying Grace Nelson's decision not to attend college, for Grace was a girl from a broken home.

The statistical results, therefore, are being introduced with this series of brief case histories. These case histories are stories of people who are the main characters in the report that follows. The histories emphasize strongly that no two persons are alike, that the factors determining decisions regarding college and post-high-school careers are identical for no two persons, but also that many common factors run through the lives of all and that the influences playing upon many persons are similar. No two persons react alike because they come from broken homes but the fact that a person does come from a broken home tends to increase the probability that a certain course of action will occur. These histories illustrate that although people are different from one another they tend to respond in a somewhat similar fashion to equivalent conditions.

The interviewer's notes provide the basis for the case histories as presented here.

GRACE NELSON

Grace is an only child and her parents are divorced. Her father, a college graduate, is a newspaper reporter living in a western city and her mother, a high school graduate, is a housewife.

Grace's high school percentile rank is 75 and her percentile score on the A.C.E. Psychological Examination is 83. She has good academic aptitude and has been a better than average student in high school.

After graduation from high school, Grace plans to work in an office. When interviewed, she was working part time doing general office work but she knew of a possibility of a job in another company. I asked why she decided to work in business and she said that she took typing in school and it seemed as though this were the only thing she could do. Since the tenth grade she has been taking the commercial course. She decided on that course in order to be able to take typing since that was the only way she could take typing in her school. Before the tenth grade she had been thinking about becoming a commercial artist but she changed her mind in the tenth grade when she did not get along well with her art teacher. She said she enjoyed art very much in junior high school.

"When I graduate from high school," Grace said, "I want to get out and save money, especially because I plan to get married within a year or so. College doesn't make sense." Grace then went on to say that she has always disliked school. "So I guess I decided against college way back. I would rather be at home than at school." She said she likes to cook and work at other household activities.

All of Grace's friends are going to work except one. "If I went to college, it would be to learn something. I would like to take Spanish and English." I tried to discover the source of Grace's attitude toward school. She told me she absolutely hates to be told what to do, especially when she intends to do it anyway. She said she also dislikes the large group associations that go along with high school and she dislikes clubs and prefers to be with just a couple of people. I would infer that Grace is not very popular in school.

Her father wants her to go to college and she thinks he favors further training because he went to college and liked it himself and because he had always enjoyed studying. "He thinks I should too." He has always been anxious for Grace to obtain good grades. Last summer he brought up the subject of college, and she thinks that she might be able to obtain financial help from him for further schooling but that she would not want it. Her mother feels that the decision regarding college is entirely up to the daughter.

I checked the cumulative record card and noticed that Grace has always obtained high achievement test scores with relatively low I.Q.'s reported on the Otis, I.Q.'s in the range of 96 and 104. I also noted that there had been a history of migraine headaches. In the interview, Grace appeared to be somewhat suspicious and supersensitive. Her decision not to attend college is apparently based in part upon her attitudes coming from her family situation and some unpleasant experiences she has had in high school and perhaps in part upon a more deep-seated emotional problem.

MARY BLACK

Mary's father is a railroad baggage man who entered high school, but Mary does not know whether or not he graduated. Her mother completed the eighth grade and is a housewife. Mary is the oldest of four siblings.

In her high school class Mary has a percentile rank of 88, indicating that her grades on the average are superior to the grades of 88 per cent of the students in her graduating class. On the A.C.E. Psychological Examination her percentile score is 92, if we use norms for college freshmen. Undoubtedly, she has sufficient academic ability and educational skills to do satisfactory work in college.

In response to a question during the interview concerning her post-high-school plans, Mary said, "I've got a job. I'll be working for three attorneys as their secretary. One of my neighbors who is a lawyer told me about the job."

Mary expects to enjoy her job very much. She has wanted to be a stenographer since she was ten years of age. She thinks she originally obtained the idea from the movies. In the ninth grade, she had to prepare a written report on an occupation and she chose stenography, read books on that occupation, and really made her decision at that time. Throughout high school she has been pleased with the commercial course she has been taking. I asked how she felt about college and she said she thought it would be fun to go but she could not since she did not have enough academic credits. Actually, with her academic record, it would be possible for her to enter any college in the state regardless of the number of academic credits she has, but students, parents, and counselors frequently are not aware that colleges do not rigidly adhere to the statements they so blithely publish in their bulletins. Mary said she also lacks funds for college.

She told me that she would rather earn some money to buy clothes and to enjoy herself than go to college, although she did say she thought it would be fun to go to a small school.

All her friends are going to work, none are entering college. "If I were to be something else, like a nurse, I'd go." But because she has always wanted to be a stenographer, she sees no point in taking college training. The idea of college activities appeals to her, however.

I asked about her parents' attitudes and she said that her father has not said much. "But mother says a girl wastes time in college, and then just gets married. Dad tends to agree with her. My mother points out girls in the neighborhood who went to college and didn't make anything of it." Her parents are happy about her job and Mary is quite certain that they prefer she follow through on her chosen occupation.

Mary impressed me as being a rather reserved young lady but pleasant and cooperative. She will probably be an unusually good secretary and the opportunity with the attorneys seems to be an excellent one for a girl coming out of high school without any experience. The job should challenge her superior ability.

WALTER WILSON

Walter is the son of a minister and the oldest of three siblings. His father completed college and had some seminary training and his mother graduated from high school and completed nurses' training. At the time of the interview she was a housewife.

Walter's high school percentile rank is 94 and his percentile score on the A.C.E. Psychological Examination, with college freshmen norms, is 70. Obviously he has sufficient academic ability to complete college work satisfactorily.

Walter wants to attend college but he does not have enough money to attend immediately after graduation from high school, so he is planning on working for a year and then entering college a year after he graduates. He hopes to save enough money while working to pay most of his college expenses during the first year. He plans to enter a small denominational college in Minneapolis.

Walter has not decided upon a major in college although he has seriously considered a general business course. I asked why he wants to go to college and he said that he wants the superior preparation that you can obtain from college. He thinks that college will be helpful "for facing life, and you're better off in school. It keeps you from working for a couple of years. I got the idea of going to college because everybody else goes. Then too, my folks expect me to go, and most of my boy friends are going." In discussing further his reasons for going to college, he said, "Half of the reason is just to go and be with the kids. Then too, people look up to college grads, and college students seem to mature faster. Then too, you can work yourself up a notch higher socially."

Walter wanted to be a doctor when he was in elementary school but later he considered this was more or less a dream. He has usually liked school. His outside interests include sports and some reading, although he used to do much more reading when he was younger.

Walter's parents have more or less taken for granted that he will be going to college. Recently his father asked him whether he was going to start school in the fall or wait a year. Walter said his mother also favors college but does not say much. Walter might be able to obtain slight financial assistance from his family but he does not want to take any money from them and wants to be able to handle all his own college finances.

ALICE FOLEY

Alice's father is a machinist who completed the sixth grade and her mother, a high school graduate, is a housewife. Alice has one older sister, who completed high school and works in a local office, and a younger sister.

On the A.C.E. Psychological Examination, Alice earned a percentile score of 85, with norms for college freshmen, and her high school percentile rank is 55. She told me that she is going to try to get some kind of office job. She has taken the commercial course in high school and has been satisfied with it. I asked why she had taken the commercial course and she told me that her older sister had taken typing and liked it and that this sister, who had had the academic course in high school, had encouraged Alice to take the commercial course. She also thought that this sequence of subjects sounded interesting.

As a child, Alice said, she thought she would like to be an airline stewardess but changed her mind because she did not want to take nurses' training, which was required at the time. I asked her how she feels about college and she told me that she has never wanted to attend college. "I don't think it can do me much good. I would like to work and get my own money. I think I've learned about plain subjects, and I would like rather to get some office work." If she ever were to attend college, she thinks that she would like to take a science course. However, she feels that college would involve a long time and that it would be expensive. She expressed her feeling that it would be fun to go to college for a while but certainly not for the full four years. She stressed the fact that she would like to be able to bring home a salary.

Alice said her father likes her plan to find an office job and that he has never mentioned college. In talking about her mother, she said, "She doesn't urge college either. I don't think she thinks I'd learn much either." She told me that her parents have never cared much about her grades one way or the other.

In regard to her high school achievement, she said that she has never worked hard in school. Outside activities, including reading and just loafing on the beach, have taken a great deal of her time.

She is a pert, cute, and on the whole quite an unacademic-looking young lady, who was rather embarrassed and shy in the interview.

JOAN CARLSON

Joan's father died when she was eleven months old and she does not know how far he had gone in school. Her mother completed the ninth grade and at the time of the interview was working as a waitress. Joan has one younger brother who is in school.

Her high school percentile rank is 91 and her percentile score on the A.C.E. Psychological Examination is 53. She probably has sufficient ability to do successful college work.

She hopes to obtain a job after graduating from high school so that she will be able to save money and enter the university in the fall. She wants to take a medical technology course and she decided on the university because she would thus be able to live at home and "because it has the best medical center." In her twelfth-grade modern problems class she studied medical technology and felt then that she would be interested in it. She thinks she has much information about medical technology, and she knows a medical technologist who has discussed this profession with her in some detail. She described medical technology as a "challenge," saying that it is a new field and that it is not over-crowded. She added that she likes chemistry.

"When I was little, I didn't want to go to college. It sounded like an awful lot of work. Then in ninth grade I knew I didn't want to take the commercial course so I decided on college." She feels that a high school diploma is not enough and that she really would like to get someplace and that a college degree is necessary in order to do that. Then too, she thinks that she will like college. "Maybe it's the glamour of it." Most of her friends are going to college.

Joan emphasized that she has always liked school and when I asked her what she liked about school, she said she has been especially enthusiastic about activities. She has played in the school band, plays the piano, and enjoys summer sports. She seemed to emphasize these things in school rather than academic work. She mentioned too that in regard to medical technology she had visited a hospital and also attended a job conference on this occupation.

Joan's mother wants her to attend college. She herself wanted to be a nurse but could not obtain the necessary training and consequently, she has to work as a waitress.

FRITZ JOHNSON

Fritz's father completed the tenth grade and then obtained training in a vocational school. His mother also completed the tenth grade and is a housewife. His older brother left school after the eleventh grade and then joined the army and one younger brother is still in school.

When I asked Fritz about his plans he said, "My folks want me to go to college, but I'm not so sure. I've had enough school for a while. I may feel differently in the fall. I'm seriously considering service."

Fritz has been working part time for the streetcar company and is considering continuing with that company full time during the summer. "Right now I feel that I'm sort of young for college and I don't know exactly what I'm going to take." He said that he has given some thought to high school social science teaching.

Apparently his brother has influenced him considerably. "He has influenced me quite a lot. He didn't like school. When he comes home, he is always talking about the good times he has, and I have a desire to travel. If I didn't start at the U. this fall, I'd go into the Army for sure. Then I'd enter the U. after my release. I've more or less wanted to go to college. My mother and relatives have always wanted me to go."

Fritz said that he has always liked school, partly because of the social life involved. He likes being with a large group of people. His brother has always had a different set of principles. "He hangs around with a different kind of crowd, and my brother was influenced by the fellows he goes around with. I've always felt that the more education you get, the better."

He reported that to him the students at the university look so old that they make him feel immature. He thinks he would grow up a little in the service and perhaps fit into college better after being released from service. He seems particularly worried about the social relationships involved in college. He expressed no doubt about his ability to meet the academic competition in college in spite of the fact that his A.C.E. Psychological Examination percentile score is only 40. His high school percentile rank, however, is 95 and he undoubtedly has perceived himself in the past as a satisfactory or far better than average student.

Both of Fritz's parents want him to go to college and they would help him with his college expenses. I had the impression that he would attend college the following fall.

DOROTHY BROWN

Dorothy's father graduated from high school and then went to business school. He is an advertising salesman. Her mother, a housewife, completed four years of college. Dorothy has one older brother, who is an engineer, and a younger sister. Her high school percentile rank is 90, and her percentile score on the A.C.E. Psychological Examination is 83, with norms based on college freshmen. She has enough ability and sufficient educational skills to do better than average work in college.

Dorothy is planning on working in a civil service position doing general office work. Early in school she considered becoming a nurse. Until the beginning of this year she had planned on college and had taken the academic course but she had changed her mind definitely about college "because I'm going to get married. I'm engaged." Her parents want her to attend college. "They've always wanted me to." She said that they had been urging it for years but finally gave up. Her father stressed the security given by a college education and a degree. She was a little defensive in the interview and I suspected she has been having a continual battle with her parents at home. She thought I was just another person she had to convince regarding the advisability of her marrying rather than going to college and she brought up factors such as "having your children when you are young" and "working together to build up your life."

None of Dorothy's friends are going to school. She thinks she can obtain an education by other routes than formal training. She likes music and enjoys reading and she intends to keep up her interests and proficiency in French by reading French books and magazines.

She impressed me as being somewhat older than the average graduating senior although her chronological age is average. Apparently much of her time recently has been spent building up a good solid case for marrying directly after she graduates from high school.

JAMES BENSON

James's father, who completed the eighth grade, died when James was a small boy. His mother is a high school graduate who works as a waitress. He has an older brother, twelve years his senior, who graduated from high school, went to business school, and was then married.

James hopes to become a radio announcer. He wants to enter college next fall and has chosen the university because he thinks that the facilities there are better than those at other schools. He attended a job conference at one of the radio stations and the man who talked to him there discouraged him from attending any small local radio school. He reported that he had studied radio announcing in his modern problems class and became quite interested in the field as a result of reading about it. James said he has always planned on attending college. "You have to have a college education to get any kind of a job." He has always liked school and most of his friends are going on to college.

He has considered taking accounting in college because figures are easy for him to work with. He said too, "I think it's good to get as much education as you can." His brother has told him that he wishes he had completed college.

He reported that he has talked his mother into his going to college and that she now favors it. He will have a little help from home but will have to work part time and rely on his savings.

SHIRLEY COLE

Shirley's father graduated from high school and, after one year of college, started to work for a department store, finally becoming a department manager. Her mother, also a high school graduate, works as a saleslady in another department store. Shirley has one younger brother and a younger sister.

Although Shirley has a high score on the A.C.E. Psychological Examination, a percentile score of 90 with norms based on college freshmen, her high school percentile rank is 11. She has good academic aptitude but in high school has never performed effectively.

Shirley said that she would like to go to art school if she could because she would like to do work in advertising, possibly fashion drawing. She has always enjoyed the art courses she has taken in high school. When she was in elementary school she wanted to be a nurse but in junior high school she began to consider art more seriously and planned her high school program with art in mind. Her parents have always favored art as a vocational goal since they feel she has the talent required, and she has received encouragement in this direction from a junior high school teacher. Her father wants her to go to art school and will help pay for her training there and her mother also favors the art school program. Shirley said she has always wanted to attend college but has never known what she would take. Until high school, her parents had planned on sending her to college but they then decided they just could not afford that. Shirley considers art a good second choice. She thinks that she has enough ability to get through college but she does not think she would like to take art in college, primarily because she does not want to teach art.

I questioned her regarding her good aptitude test scores and low grades in high school. She said that she has always wanted just to get by. She reported that she received superior grades in junior high school and in elementary school but then there were not so many things competing for her time. She said she later concentrated on having a good time. She belongs to a girls' club and she has found that social relationships mean more to her than "just getting good grades." Her friends are not very ambitious and none of them are in the honor society. In trying to figure out why she has done so poorly in high school, she said, "I think I was kind of meek in junior high and in grade school. I used to work harder and seemed to get more satisfaction out of grades." She said that her parents have never put any pressure on her or demanded that she do better in school than she was doing. Her parents would like her to have a cultural background but as far as I could tell, she meant by the word "cultural" things involving manners and poise. I asked about the magazines read at her home and she said *Harper's Bazaar, Cosmopolitan, Life,* and *Seventeen.* I did have the feeling that Shirley does not know much about college.

In our interview, Shirley was relaxed and poised. I checked the cumulative record form but there was nothing there that would help to explain her marked academic underachievement. Neither did I note any negative feelings coming to the surface when she spoke of her parents. If her underachievement is not due to her relationships with her parents,

I would hypothesize that the most potent factor here is the standards set by Shirley's companions. She seems to have accepted their values in regard to the significance of high school grades and further education.

Sam's father graduated from high school and business school and is employed as an auditor. His mother, a high school graduate, is a housewife. One older brother graduated from college and is in business and a younger sister is still in high school.

Sam is a superior student who has a percentile score on the A.C.E. Psychological Examination of 100, with norms for college freshmen, and who ranks at the top of his high school graduating class with a high school percentile rank of 100.

He plans to enter college next fall and major in engineering. He selected his college on the basis of his brother's recommendation and feels that he will obtain the best training for engineering there. He has also considered medicine and a number of other alternatives but he thinks that engineering offers relatively broad training and that the scientific work there can be utilized in a number of other fields. During the summer following graduation from high school he plans to work full time. Most of his friends are going to school.

Sam's parents insist that he attend college. "Mostly around our house, it's just logical that you should go. My folks say they don't care too much about what kind of occupation I get out of it, just so I get there. It's just five years and then you have your whole life to use it in." Sam also expressed the feeling that his parents seem to have the opinion that a degree will automatically make him better. They are quite aware of the prestige value of a degree, he said. His father has many contacts with lawyers and other college graduates and emphasizes the social "smoothness" offered by college; he also feels that a degree looks good on application forms. I asked Sam what he thought about the cultural advantages of college and Sam replied that although he would like to take some courses in music and art, his parents are not much interested in the cultural aspects of college. "You don't want to waste your time taking music and art."

Sam said that his spare-time activities include reading, wood carving, and photography. He regularly reads several periodicals about photography.

ROGER BELL

Roger's father is a truck driver, his mother a housewife, and he said that he does not know how much education his parents had. I began by asking him what his vocational and educational plans are. He said that his brother-in-law is a carpenter who will be able to get him an apprenticeship. He plans to start as a carpenter's helper after graduating from high school. He seems to be fairly certain in this decision. He said that carpentry pays good money and he appeared quite pleased with the prospect of working in this area. I asked him about other alternatives and he said that in the ninth grade he had thought of architecture but had lost interest in this field when he had to draw some plans for a house in a high school technical drawing course. If the carpentry apprenticeship does not materialize, he plans on getting some other kind of job.

Roger said he has absolutely no ambition to attend college and that college just does not appeal to him. He knows students who are attending and has heard stories about the amount of studying they need to do. He said that he could just see himself in a predicament since he nearly always procrastinates. Actually, he has never really considered going to college. "Nobody else I have ever known well has ever gone." His closest friends either are in the army, have quit school, or are attending a vocational school.

Roger has extremely good college aptitude as shown by his percentile score of 98 on the A.C.E. Psychological Examination, which compares him with college freshmen. He has been an above average student in high school as shown by his high school percentile rank of 69. He said that he has never pictured himself as "a straight A student," nor can he see himself as a doctor or "anything like that." He would not, he said, like the hours that a doctor has to work. "I like to go out in the evenings." Roger seems to have no conception of any intrinsic satisfaction that a man might get out of his job. He seems interested only in material, external rewards. In talking about carpentry, he said that he will get a starting wage of $1.65 an hour and that he will be able to buy himself a car. When I said that some students decide to go to college for other than practical reasons, for example, for social contacts and prestige, he laughed and said that he has plenty of social contacts on his present job in a service station. Roger said that anything he decides will be agreeable to his parents. His mother once mentioned casually that she would like him to go to college but his father has never said anything about this. His older sister left school before graduating from high school.

I asked Roger if he has done much reading and he said in junior high school he read many books in order to earn a certificate given to people who had read a certain number. He claimed that during the last two years he has not taken a single book out of the library and that he just has no desire to study. He spoke much of sports and activities of a non-academic nature.

It was my impression that financial reasons were not the basic factor in this boy's decision to terminate his education. He has practically no information regarding the kinds of training that would be available in college and several times he repeated, "Carpentry will earn me a living," as if this is all he cares about and sees no reason for working further.

LYMAN SLATER

Lyman is another high-ability student as shown by his A.C.E. Psychological Examination percentile score of 96, with college freshmen norms. He has been an outstanding student in high school as shown by his high school percentile rank of 94. His parents own and operate a corner store. His father had approximately four years of formal education in Poland and his mother, who is a housewife, completed the fifth grade. Lyman has two brothers and a sister; the sister is a high school graduate, the older brother an electrical engineer, and the younger brother a university student.

Lyman said, "I'm pretty sure I'm going to college but would like to have a little fun first." He is planning to work full time during the summer following high school graduation. His parents will help him with some of his college expenses but he is toying with the idea of entering military service for a while. He dislikes having to buckle down to school again so soon after graduating from high school. He feels that in the service he might obtain some practical training. In regard to his parents' attitudes, he said that his parents have always encouraged college. "It runs in the family. First one started and then all the rest followed." He frequently expressed the feeling that he is not ready for college. If he could only settle down, he feels, he would have no qualms about entering college in the fall. As it is, he is always running around. He has a motorcycle and likes the lighthearted life he leads.

His reason for going to college is mainly practical. "It seems to me that nowadays you almost have to go on to college." He feels that high school has been almost too easy and that he has been spoiled there. He intends to save some money during the summer and will probably work part time if he decides to start school in the fall. He said he needs more information about college before actually beginning school.

With his ability I imagine he has been able to progress through high school at an easy rate without much trouble or effort, and from his brother's experience, he probably realizes that he will need to work much harder if he is to do well in the science courses he wants to take if he goes to college. He knows that eventually he will need to come to grips with this problem but wants to postpone it as long as possible. He appears to be quite immature and might do better work in college if he postpones entering for at least a year. Apparently he cannot perceive himself in the role of a hard-working student.

MICHAEL BAILEY

Michael's father, a foreman in a manufacturing plant, completed the eighth grade. Michael's mother, a high school graduate, is a housewife. Michael has one older, married sister who completed the eleventh grade.

During his senior year in high school, Michael has been working in a store part time and he prefers the type of work he is doing to working in a factory, an alternative he has considered. He has already been accepted for a job in a hardware store as soon as he graduates from high school and he hopes to move up into sales work in the store. "My dad told me that you have to start at the bottom to get any place." He is contemplating taking a sales course at the vocational high school during the summer, since his job at the hardware store during the summer will be only part time.

Michael's percentile score on the A.C.E. Psychological Examination is 63 and his high school rank is 88. He has always been a good student in high school and has sufficient ability to do satisfactory work in college. He has considered attending college and taking a major in political science, but he has decided that is too broad a course to be practical. He added that he really has not taken the right kind of courses in high school, since he has not taken the difficult academic subjects. He also mentioned that he does not have enough money to attend college. He reported that the dean of men in his high school told him that with a major in political science it would not be hard to get a government job.

"So long as I have the chance for a good job, I thought I might as well take it. If I went to college, I'd just go to get a diploma so I could get a good job. I feel I don't need college now that I have a good job."

In junior high school, Michael said, he had wanted to leave school because he felt that it was too monotonous, but throughout high school he has enjoyed his work. He had a chance to apply for a scholarship but neglected to submit his application because he did not want to write the autobiography that the application involved. His principal offered to apply for a scholarship for him but Michael decided against this. In high school, modern problems and history have been his favorite subjects.

Michael's father has shown little enthusiasm for college. "He doesn't think college would be much good. He doesn't understand about it and thinks it is a waste of time or something." Michael said that his mother does not know much about college either and consequently does not want him to go. If he were to go, he would have to pay all his own expenses.

Michael impressed me as being a straightforward, interesting young fellow. I could not figure out why he is not interested enough in college to compete for scholarships. He feels, apparently, that he can do quite well in the world by working up rather than trying college. It appears that personality and emotional and family background are a lot more important here as determinants of this boy's plans than is his lack of financial resources.

BILLY BEAR

Billy Bear is a high-ability student who has been an excellent achiever in high school. His percentile score on the A.C.E. Psychological Examination is 99 and his high school percentile rank is 100. Billy's father is a cattle dealer who completed the eighth grade and his mother is a housewife who graduated from high school. There is one younger brother in the third grade and an older brother who worked his way through college and graduated last year. The older brother at the time of the interview was doing graduate study, working for a Ph.D. in technology.

Billy plans to enter the university to take the pre-law sequence. He thinks that his aptitudes suit him for law and he eventually would like to do some work in the foreign service or become a diplomat. Recently he has been considering entering military service for a year or two because he thinks this might "help me grow up a little." He would prefer to go to a college where he would live away from home, but this is not feasible financially. He thinks that there might be a possibility of his going away at some later date, after completing three years of college or after earning a bachelor's degree.

He considers his reasons for wanting a college education to be of a practical nature. He is aware of his own immaturity and believes that college might help him solve some problems of a personal nature. Billy said that he has always taken college for granted. "Way back in junior high school, when people asked me what I was going to be, I and my parents always said I would go to college." He thinks that part of the reason for this is that his brother obtained excellent grades and that school is very easy for Billy. It has just seemed "sort of natural" to the family.

Billy is a good-looking, large boy, who in the interview appeared to be self-conscious and ill at ease. As the interview progressed, he relaxed. I noted that his fingernails were well bitten, his speech was filled with slang, and frequently he would say, "this here" and "ain't." Another student I talked to told me that Billy tries very hard to fit in with the group, and even though he is very bright, he tries to act like the other students. But they tend to realize that this is not really natural for him. Billy seems to be aware of some personal or emotional problem. He thinks that the solution to this problem involves his moving away from home, but because of the financial factor, he will be unable to do this during the next year or two, and consequently is seriously thinking of entering the military service as an alternative to college.

JULIA WILSON

Julia's father, a high school graduate, is a refund clerk in a department store. Her mother, a housewife, is also a high school graduate. One younger brother and one younger sister are still in school.

Julia plans on entering college next fall to major in home economics or dietetics. She became interested in the field as a result of discussions with her aunt who is a home economist. She also obtained information recently during a job conference at a local college.

In high school she has been an excellent student as shown by her high school percentile rank of 91, but her college aptitude is questionable as indicated by a percentile score of 13 on the A.C.E. Psychological

Examination. She has been seriously considering college during the past few years in high school. Previously, she planned on going to business school. When she started to take bookkeeping and other commercial courses in high school, however, she found that she disliked them and changed her mind regarding business training.

I asked why she wanted to go to college and she said that she thinks home economics is a good field and that she could use in her home the training that she would receive. Then she mentioned that she would like to have "a higher social life." Nearly all of Julia's friends are going to college. She will work during the summer and she intends to continue working part time while going to school.

Julia told me that her parents are not enthusiastic about her going to college, particularly from the financial point of view. "I think I have them talked into it. My dad's old-fashioned. He says that I would just get married anyhow. The teachers here at school have talked with him but he thinks that I should just get into civil service in the business field."

Julia thinks that her mother would like to see her go to college but that the family will not be able to give her financial help. She did say, however, that she will be able to live at home and not have to pay any of her living expenses. Julia said that her father would like her younger brother to go to college "even though he isn't very intelligent."

HELEN JAMES

Helen's father completed the eighth grade, worked as a streetcar conductor, and then retired. Her mother, a housewife, also completed the eighth grade and was a domestic servant before her marriage. Helen has three older brothers and sisters. One of her brothers completed the eighth grade and at the time of the interview was in the air force, the other graduated from a vocational high school and is an electrician. Her older sister completed the eleventh grade and is a salesgirl in a department store.

Helen has been a good student in high school, her high school rank being 74. Her percentile score on the A.C.E. Psychological Examination is 90 and all the evidence indicates that she could do better than satisfactory work in college. In response to my question regarding post-high-school plans, Helen said, "I'll have to work for a few years. I do hope that I will be able to save enough money for college."

While in high school she has been working part time in a variety store where she intends to continue full time because she likes her job. Throughout high school she has taken a commercial course. In the ninth grade when she had to select a course the commercial course sounded best but later she decided she would be more interested in working with children than she would be in doing shorthand and typing. In the ninth grade, she said, "They told us commercial subjects would be the best for girls. It interested me then." Her parents also felt that commercial work would make the best career for her. They did not force her to take the commercial course but told her that she ought to take the course which interested her. However, as far as I could tell, her family did influence her in the direction of the commercial course and at the time, she herself thought it would be satisfying.

I asked when she first had the idea of going to college to train for child welfare work and she said she thought of this just recently and it might stem in part from her Sunday School teaching. When I questioned her further about practical plans for college, she said, "I haven't really inquired about tuition and so on, but I thought it would take a few years to save enough." If she had sufficient funds, she said, she would just love to go to college. She is considering more than the monetary advantages of college training. Her parents would not be able to give her any help at all for college.

Helen is quiet, serious, and sweet appearing. She is active in church work and reads a great deal, particularly the magazines her family subscribes to, including the *Saturday Evening Post*, the *Ladies' Home Journal*, and the *Reader's Digest*.

TED LORY

Ted is a high-ability boy and an excellent student. His percentile score on the A.C.E. Psychological Examination is 90, if we use norms for college freshmen. His father completed the eighth grade and is a salesman and his mother, a housewife, also completed the eighth grade. One older sister, a high school graduate, works as an office clerk and an older brother is a sophomore in college.

Ted plans to enter the university in the fall following his graduation from high school. He hopes to work at a full-time job during the summer. When I asked him why he decided to go to college, he said, "It will be easier later on if I have an education. There will be more of a chance for having security and cash." He said that these were the most important reasons. In high school he has been most interested in science. "I really don't know what I want at the university. I considered taking tests to help me find out." He intends to try chemistry courses during his freshman year and possibly major in that subject. I asked him just where and when he got the idea of going to college and he told me that "it just seemed to be the thing to do. As far as that goes, my folks want me to go." He said that he has always taken college for granted. His teachers have encouraged him also. He expresses little interest in college from the point of learning. He himself is afraid that he might tire of almost any major. But, he said, "I don't mind school; I kind of like it. It beats work; you get something out of it that you can keep. If you can get through, you might as well go." On the whole, Ted feels that the fastest road to success leads through college.

I questioned him about his feelings concerning the social and cultural opportunities at college. He replied, "As far as I have heard, the university doesn't have any social life. As far as culture goes, you can't get it if you don't already have it. Maybe after years and years you might get to like it, like olives." He told me that he has tried listening to symphony records, but just cannot get himself to like such "highbrow stuff." Some of his friends are going to college and some are going to a vocational school.

LORRAINE COOK

Lorraine's father owns a garage and is an auto body man. He completed the tenth grade and her mother, a housewife, completed the ninth grade. She has an older sister in college. Lorraine has been a superior student in high school as indicated by her high school percentile rank of 90. Although she has considered high school pretty much as a big joke and claims she has done practically no work, she has still maintained a superior grade average. Her percentile score of 57 on the A.C.E. Psychological Examination indicates that she has about as much college aptitude as the average college freshman.

She is planning to attend a private liberal arts college, saying that she has always wanted to go to this school because she can learn more about her religion there. She intends to work part time and hopes to major in library science. She realizes that the university would cost less money but feels that she is too young for the university. She became interested in library work through working part time for the last fifteen months in a library. She said she is "just crazy about library work."

Her parents have always planned on her attending college and took out an insurance endowment when she was born. Another reason Lorraine gives for planning to attend college is that she has always liked school. Her mother has often said that she wishes she had completed high school and definitely wants her daughter to complete college. Lorraine was one of the few students interviewed in her school who mentioned other than pecuniary or social reasons for going to college. She said that she would like to have a "general all-around education and also would just like to know a little bit more."

EDWARD MARK

Edward's father is a high school graduate who is a foreman in a manufacturing plant. His mother, a housewife, is also a high school graduate. He has one brother who graduated from high school and is working and a sister who is in college.

Edward is a top-ranking student in his graduating class, with a high school percentile rank of 100. On his college aptitude test score he received a percentile score of 100, with norms based on college freshmen. Undoubtedly he will be an extremely capable student in college.

He is planning to enter the university and major in chemistry and is considering taking advanced degrees if that is possible. He has been planning on this since he was in the seventh grade when he first received a chemistry set as a Christmas present. Since that time he has maintained a chemical laboratory in his basement. Even before deciding on chemistry he had always thought of attending college. He thinks that the main reason for his interest in college is that he has always earned exceptionally good marks. "You can't get very far with only a high school education." He repeatedly said that he wants to learn as much as he possibly can about chemistry.

He has already received a scholarship that will pay the expenses of his first year in college. He also has some savings and there does not seem to be a financial problem here.

Edward's parents definitely want him to attend college. They feel that he will be able to advance much faster with a degree and generally consider that "college pays." I imagine that this boy also has had a lot of encouragement to continue in school from his teachers. In talking about his feeling toward college, Edward said, "With me it is a practical means to an end."

As the reader peruses the results presented in the next chapters and examines the statistics that follow, it may be well worth his while to refer back occasionally to these case histories to remind himself that the statistics really represent people and that all generalizations to be made in these studies are based on individuals. The mass of data summarized in this volume was obtained from motivated persons — boys and girls who liked or disliked school, who were or were not vocationally and educationally ambitious, who were reacting to a complex pattern of family and school situations. The data are meaningful only insofar as the reader looks beyond the statistics to the people they represent.

3

An Overview

THE hypotheses explored by the Minnesota study of 1950 grew naturally out of the series of interviews with high school students reported in the last chapter. One can find easily, even in a quick reading of these case histories, recurring themes and patterns. Keeping these in mind, we framed four hypotheses.

The information collected in this study allowed us to test these hypotheses. Rigorous tests of the hypotheses, of course, will be impossible until more exact methods of quantification are developed. Actually, one might well decide not to call these statements hypotheses but rather to call them impressions, and perhaps we are not accepting or rejecting hypotheses but rather verifying impressions.

The primary hypothesis approached here was that an inordinate waste of talent characterizes our educational system. Many young persons with superior abilities, although interested in obtaining advanced training, fail to do so. Many other superior young persons even fail to show an interest in such training. Much of the intellectual talent in this country, as well as much of the other varieties of talent, is never developed and fails to contribute to the happiness of the individual or the welfare of society. How great is this waste?

A second hypothesis was that ecological factors are related to this waste of talent. To what extent are our metropolitan youths, our farm youths, and our small-town youths able to take advantage of educational opportunities?

A third hypothesis was that psychological factors are related to this waste of talent. What part do an individual's interests and motivations play in his educational decisions? A part of this hypothesis is that sex differences mark the extent to which our youths are able to utilize their

48

talents. To what extent are men more likely to use their talents than are women?

The most important and the most interesting hypothesis was perhaps the most complex. We know that the extent to which young people are able to utilize their abilities is determined in part by the economic level of the home. Also, the extent to which they actually utilize these talents is dependent upon the cultural level of the home. Now the economic and the cultural levels of the home are closely interrelated but have a far from perfect relationship. For instance, currently the cultural level of the secondary school teacher's home is somewhat higher than the cultural level of the home of a construction worker. At the same time, the economic level of the construction worker's home is considerably higher than the economic level of the teacher's home. What is the probability that a child of high ability who comes from a steel worker's home with an annual income of $9000, and an average parental education of tenth grade, will go to college? What is the probability that a high-ability child who comes from a teacher's home with an annual income of $5000, and an average parental education of sixteenth grade, will attend college? What are the relative roles of economic and cultural levels in determining the extent to which students utilize their talents? Our fourth hypothesis was that both economic level and cultural level of the home are closely related to a child's plan for education after high school.

Once we had the hypotheses to be tested clearly in mind, the experimental design of the study could be planned and methods devised for collecting information.

A basic questionnaire, later entitled "After High School — What?" was prepared by a committee consisting of Dr. Wilbur Layton, Dr. Ben Willerman, Dr. Theda Hagenah, and the writer. An early draft of the questionnaire was given to a class of high school seniors from a metropolitan school and the questionnaire was then revised and printed. A reproduction of the questionnaire is presented on pages 51–54.

The basic data for the study were obtained between January 15 and February 15, 1950, when copies of the questionnaire were sent to each of the public and private high schools in Minnesota, along with the American Council on Education Psychological Examination and the Cooperative English Test used in the Minnesota State-Wide Testing Program. Completed questionnaires were obtained from approximately 93 per cent of all high school seniors. Complete coverage of all high school seniors in the state was not obtained because some students were ill or absent the day the questionnaires were distributed, a half-dozen schools did not participate in the State-Wide Testing Program, and in a few of the participating schools the request to distribute the questionnaire was denied. Because of the high proportion of returns, however, no attempt was made to determine whether or not those from whom data were not available were typical of those who completed the questionnaire.

When the questionnaires were returned, some of the responses required coding before the data could be punched on IBM cards. The code pertaining to "occupation of father" was devised particularly for this study and was based upon the classification system used in the United States census and upon other systems used in the past at the University of Minnesota. This same code was used in categorizing the occupational choices of the students as they were written on the questionnaire. A parallel code was developed for classifying the occupation of the mother. After all the information on the questionnaires was coded and after the questionnaires were checked for complete coding, the data were punched on IBM cards which were then available for tabulation and analysis.

Before the questionnaire data were analyzed, the total group was divided, first according to sex and then according to rural-urban differences. Three "living area" groups were used. First, all students who indicated they lived on a farm were included in the "farm group." Next, all students coming from Minneapolis, St. Paul, Duluth, and suburban schools were included in the "metropolitan group." All other students, coming from smaller cities and towns, were included in the "nonfarm group." (For convenience, the farm and nonfarm students are sometimes grouped together as "nonmetropolitan.") Then each of these groups was again divided on the basis of expressed plans for after high school. Thus, there were a variety of groups for study, such as a group of boys from farms planning to attend college, a group of girls from cities planning to work, a group of boys from small towns planning to enter military service.

During the time when the questionnaire data were being collected, plans were being made to interview the parents of all the students in one town in order, first, to confirm some of the information collected in the questionnaire and, second, to gather types of data, particularly those relating to parental attitude, that could not efficiently be collected through the questionnaires. The decision was made to interview the

H.S._____1-3

Iden. No._____4-6

After High School—What?

For High School Seniors

In order to provide information about what high school seniors are planning for the next year and to show the reasons for these plans, you are being asked to answer the questions below.

Write in the answer or place a check mark (√) after the appropriate word or phrase.

7-31. Name (Print)_____
       Last   First   Middle

32. Male_____(0) Female_____(1)   33-34. Age last birthday_____years

35. Your marital status: Single_____(0) Engaged to be married_____(1) Married_____(2)

36. Father living: 37. Mother living: 38. If both parents are alive, are they separated or divorced:
     Yes_____(0)   Yes_____(0)   Yes_____(0)
     No_____(1)   No_____(1)   No_____(1)

39. Occupation of father: (Check after the item which applies)

   Profession (lawyer, banker, doctor, teacher, minister, dentist, etc.) ....(0)
   Owns or manages business (store, gas station or garage, photography or barber shop, insurance
       agency, hotel or cafe, repair shop, newspaper, etc.) ....(1)
   Office work (bookkeeper, cashier, postal clerk, etc.) ....(2)
   Sales (insurance, real estate, retail store, etc.) ....(3)
   Owns or manages farm ....(4)
   Skilled tradesman (carpenter, electrician, machinist) ....(5)
   Factory worker (laborer, farm laborer, janitor, mine laborer) ....(6)
   Other occupations: (Be specific) _____(   )
                                          (Write in name of occupation)

40. Occupation of mother before marriage: 41. Occupation of mother now:

   _____(   )   Housewife ....(0)
        (Write in name of occupation)
                                                    Other_____(   )
   Don't know ....(0)   (Write in name of occupation)

42. Education of father: (Check highest level attained)   43. Education of mother: (Check highest level attained)

   Did not attend school ....(0)   Did not attend school ....(0)
   Some grade school ....(1)   Some grade school ....(1)
   Completed eighth grade ....(2)   Completed eighth grade ....(2)
   Some high school ....(3)   Some high school ....(3)
   Graduated from high school ....(4)   Graduated from high school ....(4)
   Business or trade school ....(5)   Business or trade school ....(5)
   Some college work (including teacher   Some college work (including teacher
       training) ....(6)   training) ....(6)
   Graduated from college ....(7)   Graduated from college ....(7)
   Holds more than one college degree ......(8)   Holds more than one college degree ......(8)

51

44. Of your **older brothers,** how far in school did that **one** go who went farthest? (If you have no older brother check opposite number 0; otherwise place a check mark after the phrase which tells how far he went)

Have no older brothers ....(0)

Left school before entering high school........(1)

Left school before graduating from high school ....(2)

Left school after graduating from high school ....(3)

Attended college but left before graduation ....(4)

Graduated from college ....(5)

Now attending college ....(6)

45. Of your **older sisters,** how far in school did that **one** go who went farthest? (If you have no older sister check opposite number 0; otherwise place a check mark after the phrase which tells how far she went)

Have no older sisters ....(0)

Left school before entering high school........(1)

Left school before graduating from high school ....(2)

Left school after graduating from high school ....(3)

Attended college but left before graduation ....(4)

Graduated from college ....(5)

Now attending college ....(6)

46. What language other than English is spoken in your home? (Place a check mark after the item which applies)

None ....(0)

French ....(1)

German ....(2)

Italian ....(3)

Jewish ....(4)

Scandinavian (Danish, Finnish, Norwegian, Swedish) ....(5)

Slovakian ....(6)

Other_____(   )
        (Write in)

47. Which of the following ways best describes how your family gets its income? (Check after the **one** phrase which **best** applies)

Professional fees or business profits (Including profits from farms) ....(0)

Fixed salary (Paid on a monthly or yearly basis) ....(1)

Wages (Paid on an hourly or daily basis and depending on number of hours worked) ....(2)

Income from investments (Stocks, bonds, real estate, insurance) ....(3)

Pensions (Government or other) ....(4)

48. Check after the **phrase** which best describes your family's income:

Frequently have difficulty making ends meet ....(0)

Sometimes have difficulty in getting the necessities ....(1)

Have all the necessities but not many luxuries ....(2)

Comfortable but not well-to-do ....(3)

Well-to-do ....(4)

Wealthy ....(5)

49. Course or curriculum taken in high school: (Check after the **one** which **best** describes your course)

Commercial_____(0) Agriculture_____(1) Shop or Technical_____(2) College Preparatory_____(3)

General_____(4) Other_____(   )

50-65. Check the most important reason or reasons why you originally selected the course you checked in item 49:

50. Only one offered in school ...._____

51. Teacher's advice ...._____

52. Counselor's advice ...._____

53. Parent's advice ...._____

54. Required to by school ...._____

55. Brothers or sisters took it ...._____

56. Seemed easiest ...._____

57. Required to by parents ...._____

58. Was best in this work ...._____

59. Fitted vocational plans best ...._____

60. Course seemed most interesting ...._____

61. Friends took it ...._____

62. Brother's or sister's advice ...._____

63. "Everyone else" took it ...._____

64. Don't know ...._____

65. Other_____(   )
        (Write in)

66. **What are your plans for next year (1950-51)? (Check the one plan you are now most seriously considering)**

1. Get a job _____(0)   If yes, what kind of work? _____ 67-68
2. Work for parents _____(1)   If yes, what kind of work? _____
3. Go to college _____(2)   If yes, which college? _____ 69-70
4. Go to trade school _____(3)   If yes, which school? _____
5. Go to business school _____(4)   If yes, which school? _____ 71-72
6. Go to other school _____(5)   If yes, which school? _____
7. Do postgraduate work in high
    school _____(6)
8. Enter the Military Service _____(7)
9. Other _____(   )

73-80. Check the reasons for making the plans you indicated above: Iden. No._____(1-6)
7-14.

73. To prepare for a vocation _____
74. To be with old school friends _____
75. To get a liberal education _____
76. To start making money quickly _____
77. To please parents or friends _____
78. To be independent _____
79. To make friends and helpful connections _____
80. (1)

7. It is "the thing to do" _____
8. Foregone conclusion, never questioned why _____
9. Will enable me to make more money _____
10. "Everyone here" does this _____
11. Tired of studying, have had enough education _____
12. Only thing I can afford to do _____
13. Like school _____
14. Other _____(   )

15. Are you planning to be married within the next year?   Yes_____(0)   No_____(1)

16. If you are going to college next year (1950-51), to what extent will your family help you pay expenses?

Pay all my expenses _____(0)   Pay some of my expenses _____(2)
Pay most of my expenses _____(1)   Pay none of my expenses _____(3)

17. If you are not going to college, would you change your plans and attend college if you had more money?

Yes_____(0)   No_____(1)

18. If you checked "Yes" to the last item, how much more money would you need to attend college?

Enough to pay all   Enough to pay about   Enough to pay less than
my expenses _____(0)   half my expenses _____(1)   half my expenses _____(2)

19. If you are not going to college, could you afford to go if you wished to go?

Could afford it easily _____(0)
Could barely afford it _____(1)
Could afford it but it would involve many sacrifices _____(2)
Could not afford it _____(3)

20. How does your family feel about your going to college?

Insists that I go _____(0)
Wants me to go _____(1)
Is indifferent _____(2)
Doesn't want me to go _____(3)
Won't allow me to go _____(4)

21-22. In what occupation do you think you will most probably be working ten years from now? Naturally you won't know for sure but make the best guess you can

_____(   )

23-24. What vocation do your parents wish you to follow? _____(   )

25. Do you have a furnace or central heating in your home? .... Yes_____(1)   No_____(0)

26. Do you have running water in your home? .... Yes_____(1)   No_____(0)

27. Do you have both hot and cold running water? .... Yes_____(1)   No_____(0)

28. Do you have an electric or gas refrigerator? .... Yes_____(1)   No_____(0)

29. Do you have a telephone in your home? .... Yes_____(1)   No_____(0)

30. Does your family own or rent a deep freeze unit or a locker? .... Yes_____(1)   No_____(0)

31. Do you have electric lights in your home? .... Yes_____(1)   No_____(0)

32. Do you have a television set in your home? .... Yes_____(1)   No_____(0)

33. Does your family own your home? .... Yes_____(1)   No_____(0)

34. Do you live on a farm? .... Yes_____(1)   No_____(0)

35. How many people live in your home? .... _____(   )

36. How many rooms are there in your home excluding the bathroom? .... _____(   )

37. How many people excluding yourself sleep in your room? .... _____(   )

38. How many passenger cars does your family own? (Check) 0_____, 1_____, 2 or more_____

39. What is the year and make of your family's newest car? Year_____ Make_____(   ) (   )

40. Approximately how many books does your family have in your home?
    (Check appropriate category)

    0- 9_____(0)   25-49_____(2)   100-up_____(4)
    10-24_____(1)   50-99_____(3)

41-55. Which of these magazines does your family subscribe to or regularly buy?

    _____41 Saturday Evening Post   _____50 Fortune
    _____42 Reader's Digest   _____51 Time
    _____43 Liberty   _____52 Life
    _____44 Holiday   _____53 Look
    _____45 American   _____54 Better Homes and Gardens
    _____46 New Yorker   _____55 Atlantic Monthly (0)
    _____47 Newsweek   _____55 Foreign Affairs Quarterly (1)
    _____48 Collier's   55 Others_____
    _____49 Harper's   _____

56-80. To which of these organizations does your father or mother or both belong?

    _____56 P.T.A. or Mothers' Club   _____71 Kiwanis
    _____57 American Legion or V.F.W.   _____72 Shrine
    _____58 Rotary   _____73 Ladies' Aid
    _____59 Knights of Columbus   _____74 League of Women Voters
    _____60 Elks   _____75 Neighborhood or other social card
    _____61 Masons   playing group
    _____62 Eastern Star   _____76 Study or literary club
    _____63 Odd Fellows   _____77 American Automobile Association
    _____64 Rebeccas   (AAA)
    _____65 Lions   _____78 The Sportsman Club
    _____66 Moose   _____79 American Ass'n of University
    _____67 Labor Union   Women (0)
    _____68 Farm Bureau   79 Others_____
    _____69 Grange   _____
    _____70 Chamber of Commerce or Community   _____
             Business Club   _____

80 (2)

54

parents of all the students in one town rather than to attempt to interview a sample representative of the state as a whole because of the difficulties involved in drawing a satisfactory sample.

A town in southern Minnesota, 70 miles from Minneapolis, with a population of 10,645, was selected. Primarily a farming town, it contained a few diversified industries and was fairly typical of Minnesota towns as far as available economic indices revealed. It was far enough from a metropolitan area so that it could not be considered a suburban or commuting town.

An interview schedule was then developed. The preliminary form was tried on a sample of parents of students who had participated in the development of the questionnaire, and after a few revisions in the wording of the questions, a final form was adopted. The interviewers, selected from a group of university staff members who regularly conducted interviews, were given a two-hour training session on the use of the prepared schedule. The interviews were made in April 1950 just before the students' graduation from high school. A list was prepared of the names of all graduating seniors who were residents of the town and then the group was divided into two random halves. For one half, all the mothers were interviewed, and for the second half, all the fathers. The interviews required between 20 and 30 minutes, and all but 3 in the sample of 93 parents were located and cooperated by providing information. The interview schedules were completed by the interviewers during the interview and the information contained on these schedules was then coded and tabulated for analysis.

Because the basic questionnaire data were collected before the seniors had actually graduated from high school, the analysis had to be in terms of what these seniors *planned* to do after high school rather than in terms of what they actually *did* after graduation. Although such plans are indicators of important attitudes and therefore are of interest in themselves, the hypotheses to be tested here could be verified only if expressed plans held a close relationship to what the students really did. A follow-up study was therefore planned for the summer of 1951, one year after these seniors graduated from high school. This follow-up study had as its purpose not only the determination of the validity of after-high-school plans but also the identification of factors influencing the extent to which students expressing an interest in entering college actually applied for admission to college. What determines the extent to which students who have certain plans follow those plans?

From the approximately 25,000 questionnaires returned by graduating seniors in 1950, a 10 per cent sample was selected and studied intensively. All of the questionnaires were sorted according to high schools and then divided into two groups, metropolitan high schools and nonmetropolitan high schools. From the metropolitan questionnaires, 650 boys' and 650 girls' questionnaires were selected. The number selected from each metropolitan school depended on the relation of the total number of students in that school to the total number in the metropolitan sample. The ratio of selection from each school by sex equaled 650 divided by the number of metropolitan seniors of that sex, this figure multiplied by one-half the number of seniors in that high school. If we call that ratio x, every xth male student from each high school and every xth female student were selected. The same procedure was used to select 650 boys and 650 girls from the nonmetropolitan schools.

Then a follow-up questionnaire and an accompanying letter were prepared and sent to the selected sample during June 1951. A follow-up card was sent approximately two weeks later and a second follow-up questionnaire was sent approximately two weeks after that to those who had not replied. Then an interviewer proceeded by telephone to call systematically each student in the sample from the Minneapolis–St. Paul area who had not yet responded. Data from the follow-up questionnaires were then coded and punched on IBM cards for tabulation and analysis. The percentage of students in the follow-up study who responded was 77.

For practically all high school seniors, scores on the 1947 college edition of the American Council on Education Psychological Examination and on the Cooperative English Test, Mechanics and Effectiveness of Expression, Form Y, and high school percentile ranks were available. The report contained in this volume does not include results based upon the English tests.

The information obtained not only allowed the hypotheses in question to be tested, but also provided sociological and psychological descriptions of this broad segment of Minnesota youth. It was possible to appraise the hypotheses in light of the obtained information and at the same time to perceive this group of Minnesota youths in relation to their social, educational, economic, and family backgrounds.

SUMMARY OF FINDINGS

The information obtained from the questionnaires and the interviews provided answers to the questions we asked originally. Much talent is being wasted in Minnesota. Ecological and geographical factors related significantly to this waste of talent. Psychological factors are also related to this waste. Finally the results left little question that whether or not a qualified student attended college was in large part dependent upon both the cultural and the economic status of his family. To maximize the probability that an able student will go to college, have him born into the right home.

These results can be summarized best in terms of the hypotheses implicit in the investigation.

Waste of talent. Of the Minnesota youth studied, approximately 35 per cent of all high school seniors planned to attend college, and the follow-up study revealed that the number of students who actually attended college was almost exactly equal to the number who, before graduation from high school, planned to attend college. This figure is close to the estimate arrived at by Hollinshead: "The entering college group we had estimated is approximately one-third of all high school graduates in 1950." Almost two-thirds of Minnesota high school graduates did not enter institutions of higher learning. The proportion of Minnesota high school graduates attending college in 1950 was, however, more than 50 per cent greater than in 1939, when Anderson and Berning found that 23 per cent of Minnesota high school seniors enrolled in college.

The report of the President's Commission on Higher Education estimated that one half of all our young people should attend college for at least two years. Since fewer than one half of the appropriate age group graduate from high school, this would imply that a group as large as our total group of high school graduates could benefit from college training. Hollinshead, on the other hand, estimated that 35 per cent rather than 50 per cent of our young people could benefit from at least two years of college. If we accept this more conservative figure, the implication is that a group approximately 75 per cent as large as our group of high school graduates should attend college, as compared with the 35 per cent who actually attend.

Of the Minnesota students who had superior ability for college work, as shown by a score of 120 or above on the A.C.E. Psychological Examination, more than two thirds were planning to attend college, or approximately twice as many of these capable students were planning to attend college as was true for the entire group of students. Of the 3939 students who had A.C.E. scores of 120 or above, however, 32 per cent were not planning to attend college. Thus, for every two exceptionally well-qualified students who were planning to attend Minnesota colleges there was one high school graduate equally qualified who was not planning to attend college.

These figures cannot be compared exactly to the figures presented by Anderson and Berning inasmuch as different score definitions of "high ability" were used, but the authors of the earlier study found that if one considered the upper 10 per cent of the high school graduating class, for every student in that group who attended college there was one student in that same group who did not attend college. For every graduate ranking in the upper 30 per cent of his class and entering college, two graduates also ranking in the upper 30 per cent were not entering college. The figures from the 1950 group suggest that there has been much improvement during the intervening years and our waste of high-ability talent, in terms of nonattendance at college, is not as great now as it was at the time of the earlier studies. The waste is still considerable, however.

Ecological factors. Where a person lives has been found to bear a direct relationship to his chances for attending college. In the Minnesota study, students coming from metropolitan areas were most likely and students coming from farms were least likely to attend college. The students coming from metropolitan, farm, and nonfarm areas differed very slightly in terms of college aptitude and the proportions of persons in each of these three areas who had sufficient ability to do college work were nearly the same. The extent to which these three groups planned on college, however, varied greatly.

Earlier studies in Minnesota and elsewhere have demonstrated that a high school student is more likely to attend college if a college is within his immediate vicinity. All students living in metropolitan areas in Minnesota have easy access to colleges, whereas the colleges located outside of the metropolitan areas provide easy access only for a few students who live within the immediate area of the college. A large proportion of the students who live outside of the metropolitan areas in Minnesota do not live within commuting distance of a college and this factor of geography explains in part why some students qualified to do college work do not attend college.

Sex differences. Of the high-ability boys, 25 per cent were not planning to attend college; of the high-ability girls, 38 per cent were planning for activities other than college. Thus, the waste of talent among girls is approximately 50 per cent greater than the waste among boys.

No practically significant differences in college aptitude were found between the boys and girls studied here but the differences between the sexes in the number planning to attend college were great. Of the girls living in cities, 40 per cent planned to attend college, whereas one half of the city boys planned to attend college. Of the girls living in nonfarm areas, 37 per cent planned to attend college as compared with 43 per cent of the nonfarm boys. Only for the farm youth was there a tendency for slightly more girls than boys to attend college — 24 per cent and 20 per cent. Boys and girls differed regarding the frequency with which they planned to attend college and these differences appeared to be related to things other than differences in college aptitude.

Economic status of the family. The data presented in this volume, considered with the results of previous studies, leave little doubt that a family's economic resources determine in part whether or not its children attend college. Children coming from homes on a high economic level plan to attend college to a far greater extent than do children coming from homes lower on the economic ladder. If this were a perfect relationship, one could conclude that our educational system is a closed order to which only the economically privileged are admitted. But the correlations of the order of .10 reported in Chapter 15 between economic status and plans to attend college indicate that this is a far from perfect relationship. Many factors other than economic status help determine whether or not high school graduates plan to attend college.

Of children who had scores of 120 or higher on the A.C.E. Psychological Examination and who had fathers in top-level occupations, approximately 90 per cent planned to attend college; but of the children who had scores of 120 or above on this test and who had fathers who were factory laborers, only 55 per cent planned to attend college. The follow-up study revealed that children coming from high-level economic homes tended to carry out their plans to a greater extent than did children coming from homes low on the occupational ladder, so the discrepancy in college attendance between children of occupationally high-level parents and children of occupationally low-level parents is even greater than the differences revealed when plans are considered.

Examination of Figures 1 and 2 allows closer study of the relationships between plans to attend college, ability and high school achievement, and economic status, if we assume that paternal occupation provides an index of economic status.

Obviously, planning to attend college was less closely related to paternal occupation for the high-ability group, those students with A.C.E. scores of 120 or above, than for the group as a whole. Whereas 92 per cent of the high-ability sons of professional workers planned to attend college and 69 per cent of the high-ability sons of factory workers also had college plans — a difference of 23 per cent — 81 per cent of all the sons of professional workers planned to attend college as compared with 30 per cent of all the sons of factory workers — a difference of 50 per cent. Thus, although economic status is effective in determining who plans to attend college, it influences the plans of high-ability graduates to a lesser extent than it influences the plans of mediocre students. This was true for both the metropolitan boys and the nonfarm boys.

Although this generalization can be made for the girls also, the figures show a much closer relationship between economic status and plans to attend college, even for the high-ability girls. Of the high-ability daughters of professional workers in the metropolitan area, 88 per cent planned to attend college, but of the high-ability daughters of factory workers in this area, only 39 per cent planned to attend college, a difference of 49 per cent. Of all the daughters of professional workers in the metropolitan area, 72 per cent planned to attend college, whereas of the daughters of factory workers, only 19 per cent planned to attend college, a difference of 53 per cent.

Anderson and Berning found that of high school graduates in 1938, 84 per cent of those in the upper 10 per cent of their class who had fathers in the professions attended college, as compared with 57 per cent of those in the upper 10 per cent of their class who had fathers in the clerical occupations or in the skilled trades. This 57 per cent compares roughly with the 64 per cent who planned to attend college in 1950. In 1938, the study showed that 84 per cent of the high-ability children of professional men planned to attend college as compared with the more recent figure of 88 per cent. Comparisons of these figures suggest that during recent years there has been a tendency for more

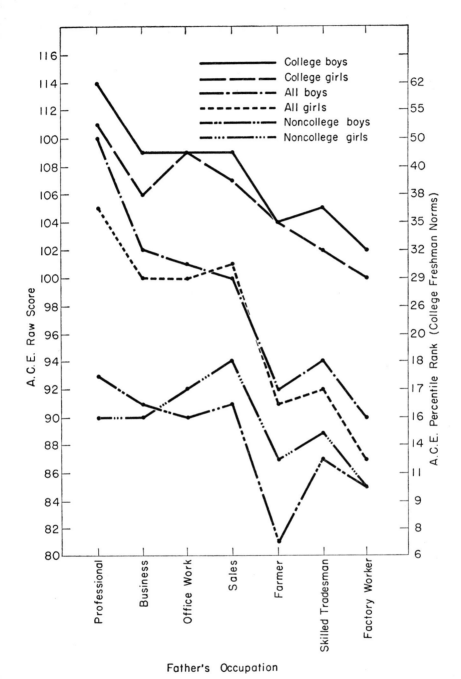

Figure 1. A.C.E. scores of children of men in different occupations according to plans of the children (metropolitan group)

61

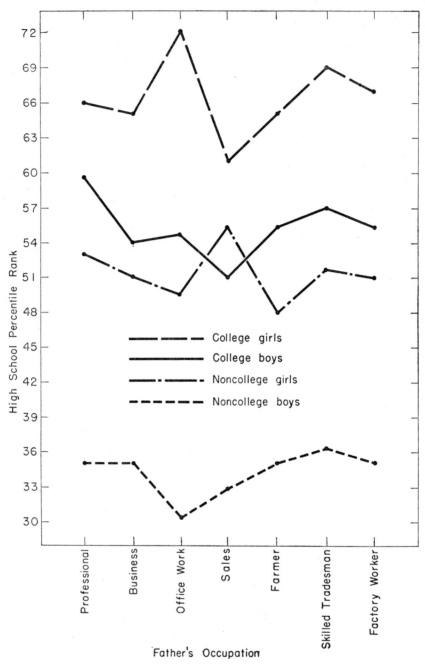

Figure 2. high school ranks of children of men in different occupations according to plans of the children (metropolitan group)

62

children to plan to attend college, for more children of high ability to plan to attend college, and for proportionately more high-ability children with fathers low on the occupational ladder to plan to attend college.

In general, the economic status of a family determines to a large extent whether or not children in that family will attend college, but for children of superior talent, this economic status does not provide as much of a limiting barrier as it does for children of lesser ability. In every group of high-ability students studied, with the exception of daughters of factory workers, more than 50 per cent were planning to attend college. Emphasis should be placed on the many high-ability students who are not planning to attend college, particularly those hundreds of high-ability students who come from homes low on the occupational ladder. But these results do demonstrate that contemplation of higher education is not restricted to the economically privileged. Rather, here is an avenue being considered seriously by a large number of persons from homes both high and low on the occupational ladder.

Cultural level of the home. Any approach to this hypothesis is confused by the demonstrated relationships existing between economic factors and the cultural level of the home. The analysis reported in Chapter 15 indicates that, if we use the instruments devised for this study, an economic status scale and a cultural status scale, a correlation of the order .65 exists between economic status and cultural status. This relationship is not fixed but varies in terms of the group studied and the area in which the group resides. Nevertheless, in every relatively heterogeneous group, the size of the relationship is large enough to make it extremely difficult to single out the effects of cultural status without also involving the effects of economic status.

The cultural status scale showed a correlation between cultural level of the home and plans to attend college in the range of .32. If we partial out the effect of economic status, this correlation drops to about .17. Comparison of the correlations between cultural status and plans to attend college with economic status partialed out, and between economic status and plans to attend college with cultural status partialed out, suggests that cultural status certainly is as important as, if not more important than, economic status in determining whether or not a high school graduate plans to attend college. Of course, we must always keep in mind the high correlation between cultural and economic status. The failure of high-ability students to plan to attend college is in general due not only to lack of funds but also to a complex pattern involving among other things low home cultural status.

In general, with both college aptitude and economic status held relatively constant, family attitudes and home cultural influences related to plans to attend college can be identified. A child coming from a home with many books will be more likely to plan to attend college than a child of similar ability coming from a home with similar economic resources but having few books. A family subscribing to many magazines is more likely to have a child who plans to attend college than an otherwise similar family subscribing to few or no magazines. Parents active in community organizations, particularly those related to schools, such as parent-teachers associations, are more likely to have children who plan to attend college than otherwise similar parents who do not participate in such community activities. Parents who have progressed far in school, particularly those who have attended college, are more likely to have children who plan to attend college than parents in similar occupations who have not attended college. This is true even when the children have comparable ability. Closely related to this is the parents' attitude toward college as perceived by the child. Children planning to attend college reported that their parents were more favorable to the idea of college than did children who had other plans.

College aptitude. Although none of the hypotheses of this study centered on college aptitudes, there were some interesting findings on this factor. College aptitude was found to be related to the sex of high school seniors, to the area of their residence (according to metropolitan, farm, or nonfarm areas), and to their after-high-school plans. Broad generalizations concerning intellectual differences between the sexes and between urban and rural youth cannot be based upon these data, for the selective factors determining high school attendance in each of these sex and area groups are unknown. For instance, more high-ability girls than boys may leave high school before graduation and this may explain the higher test scores of the boys in high school. Similarly, more high-ability farm children may leave high school before graduation, resulting in higher test scores for the metropolitan and nonfarm children than for the farm children who remain in high school.

The generalizations that may be based upon these data must be qualified, as are all the other generalizations in this study, by the sampling limitations. In this sample, the boys obtained slightly but statistically significantly higher mean scores on the A.C.E. Psychological Examination than did the girls. On the other hand, the girls consistently had mean high school percentile ranks that were statistically significantly larger than the means obtained by the boys. These sex differences in high school percentile ranks, in the reverse direction of the A.C.E. differences and of an order several times larger than the A.C.E. differences, were comparable to the sex differences usually reported for high school grades. They supported previous generalizations that girls find it easier to obtain good grades in high school, that they work harder, and that the teachers are influenced by their studiousness, docility, or charm.

Differences among means on the A.C.E. scores indicated that the high school seniors from the nonfarm areas were statistically significantly superior to the metropolitan and farm groups and the metropolitan group was significantly superior to the farm group. In light of the small absolute size of these A.C.E. differences, even though they were statistically significant, and in light of the large amount of overlapping, but little importance can be attached to these differences. It should be noted, however, that a significantly higher proportion of metropolitan seniors than of nonfarm seniors were planning to attend college, in spite of the tendency of the nonfarm seniors to have more college aptitude.

Of much more pertinence to this total study were the differences in college aptitude found among the groups with varying after-high-school plans. The mean A.C.E. scores and high school percentile ranks of boys and girls planning to attend college were significantly higher than those of the boys and girls not planning to attend college, and many more of the high-ability students were planning to attend college than were planning to take any other course of action. Yet, of the high-ability students, as defined here, one third were not planning to attend college and between 16 and 42 per cent of the students not planning to attend college actually obtained A.C.E. scores that exceeded the median score of the group planning to go to college.

On the other hand, between 10 and 15 per cent of the students planning to attend college had been such poor achievers in high school that only prediction of failure in college could be made.

Thus, although a substantial relationship appeared between plans to attend college and college aptitude, a large number of students who in spite of good college aptitude were not planning to attend college and a substantial number of students with questionable ability who were planning to attend college were identified. A perfect correlation between college aptitude and college attendance can never be obtained, and perhaps would be socially and educationally undesirable, but the conditions revealed here suggest too large a social and psychological waste.

Groups of graduates with varying plans. Another way of looking at the results of this study is through the plans of the Minnesota high school graduates. Approximately one third of them were planning to attend college and approximately the same number were planning to work after graduating from high school. Relatively small numbers of students were planning to attend other types of schools or to obtain other types of training. A relatively large number of farm youth were planning to work for their parents. These differences in plans were significantly related to the sex of the students, to the geographical areas from which they came, and to their abilities. Many more boys than girls were planning to attend college and relatively more girls were planning to work. Fewer farm youth than metropolitan and nonfarm youth were planning to enter college and relatively more farm boys were planning to work for their parents. Where a student lived and his sex had a direct relationship to his plans for after high school. The reader always must remember that these observed relationships were relatively small — a large amount of overlapping among groups was found.

High school seniors planning to attend college were a heterogeneous group of individuals coming from a large variety of home backgrounds. They differed widely in terms of parental education and occupations, economic and cultural environment, and physical surroundings.

Although disproportionate numbers of students planning to attend college were drawn from professional groups and high economic level groups, nevertheless a large proportion of the students planning on college came from other social strata. As we have already indicated, planning to attend college was not limited to certain economic classes, although economic and social conditions had a strong influence upon whether or not these youth planned to attend college.

Of the entire group of high school graduates, 9035 seniors — a substantial portion of our new labor force — were planning to work with no additional training. For them, jobs had to be found, on-the-job training frequently had to be provided, out-of-school community facilities were needed to serve recreational, social, cultural, and spiritual needs, and provisions had to be made to upgrade them as quickly as possible to the point where they could make a maximum contribution to society and themselves achieve a full life.

For the most part, these job-planners had no immediate plans for marriage; they were about eighteen years old when they graduated from high school; and they tended to come from unbroken homes. Their fathers were usually in skilled trades and in industry with relatively few coming from the homes of professional men or businessmen. For the most part, their fathers and mothers had at least an eighth-grade education and more than one fourth of them came from homes where the parents had some high school training. There was a general tendency for most of the children in a family to follow a common educational pattern, although of course there were many exceptions to this, as there are to all these generalizations.

The students planning to work usually came from homes where the income was derived primarily from wages, and they perhaps had been exposed to the insecurity that frequently accompanied this situation. Most of these young people said their families had at least the necessities of life, though many of them described themselves as being "hard up."

Almost one half of the girls in this group had taken courses directly related to their vocational plans but very few of the boys had obtained high school training that appeared to be directly relevant for their after-high-school plans. The girls seemed to be more sensitive to the need for taking courses in high school appropriate to their vocational plans, whereas the boys tended to select courses on the basis of immediate interest in the subject matter. The group planning to work seemed to have been relatively uninfluenced by counseling received from either professional counselors or teachers and, in fact, they reported they had not been influenced much by advice from parents.

Over one third of those who were planning to work said they would go to college if they had more money — 3029 made this comment, 1311 boys and 1718 girls. This number equals approximately one third of the total number of new college freshmen in Minnesota each year. About one half of the young people expressing interest in college, but unable to attend, said that they would need enough money to pay all their expenses and about one half said that they would need enough money to pay about 50 per cent of their expenses. In 1950, it was estimated that in Minnesota college cost $1000 per year.

About 10 per cent of the students planning to work said they could easily afford to go to college if they wanted to and another 20 per cent said they could barely afford it. Almost 40 per cent reported that they could not afford college, the remainder saying they could perhaps afford college but it would involve considerable sacrifice. Between one third and one half of the parents of these children wanted them to go to college in spite of the fact that their children were planning to go to work. Almost half of the parents were described by their children as being indifferent as to whether or not the children attended college. Very few of the children reported any parental opposition to college.

The youth planning to work were, for the most part, aiming at clerical jobs and jobs in the skilled trades, although a significant number were planning to enter either professional or semiprofessional occupations. The homes from which these high school students came tended to have fewer conveniences than the homes of those planning to attend college. In general, however, they all reflected a high standard of living in the sense that running water, electricity, mechanical refrigeration, and related conveniences were available in most homes.

The cultural background in these homes, as indicated by the number of books in the homes, was somewhat meager. Fewer than one half of the homes had more than fifty books, a far smaller proportion than was true for the students planning to attend college. Fewer magazines were available in these homes than in the homes of those planning to go to college.

A large proportion of the parents of the job-planning youth belonged to one or more organizations, almost half of the metropolitan group belonging to labor unions and to educational organizations such as the P.T.A. Again, however, figures for community organization membership were far smaller than similar figures for the college-planning groups.

The evidence here seems unquestionable that there is a close relationship between the type of life planned by the child and the type of home from which he comes. Again, it should be emphasized that there were no perfect relationships here, and in fact, there were not even any high correlations. There were many exceptions and there were always many individuals who behaved differently from what one would have predicted on the basis of a few simple generalizations. Often homes showed inconsistencies that made such predictions hazardous.

Immediate plans for marriage seemed to influence the girls to some extent in deciding whether or not they planned to attend college. Age appeared to be somewhat related to plans, but not to a great extent. Whether or not the father was living and an active member in the family seemed to make a difference in terms of what the children would try. A marked tendency was noted for the children of parents who had graduated from college to plan on college, but most of those who were planning to attend college came from the homes where the parents were not college graduates. The group of students planning to attend college, however, more frequently had parents who were college graduates than did those students who were planning to work. Of significance for educators is the fact that most high school seniors planning to attend college do not come from homes having a college background.

Most of the high-ability students planning to attend college took an appropriate curriculum in high school, but a small proportion of the students who did plan to attend college took high school curriculums that essentially were not preparatory for college.

The students who were planning to attend college reported that they were influenced in those plans by the belief that college would lead to their desired vocational goal. High-ability students who were planning to work indicated that their motivation was the desire to be independent from their family and the desire to make money. The latter group seemed to be more influenced by immediate advantage in their planned activities. Slightly more than one half of the high-ability students who were planning to work said they would attend college if they had more money. A successful scholarship program might increase the college freshmen class at Minnesota by approximately 400 superior students each year. An estimated cost of a scholarship program that would send students in all four college classes each year to college, giving each individual $500, would be $800,000. The results here, however, suggest that any effort to increase the proportion of high school seniors attending college would be unsuccessful unless we took into account the cultural and educational factors that help influence students' attitudes toward college as well as the economic factors determining college attendance.

In order to hold constant the effects of both college aptitude and fathers' occupations, a sub-sample was drawn from the group of high-ability students of those whose fathers were skilled tradesmen or factory workers. It was hoped that this would provide a group homogeneous on the basis of both paternal occupation and students' ability. The results demonstrated that even when a group is selected to be homogeneous in these ways, many significant differences can be found between the students who are planning to attend college and those who are not planning to attend college. The education of the parents, the number of books in the home, the magazines in the home, the family's attitude toward college, all seemed to be of great importance for this group.

If we hold family occupational level and student's college aptitude relatively constant, the importance of the factors related to family cultural background and to high school achievement stands out. High school achievement is probably closely related to these family background factors. A large number of high-ability students were found to come from the homes of skilled tradesmen and factory workers. Some of these students planned to attend college and some did not. Those who planned to attend college tended to have slightly higher ability than those who did not plan on college, and they tended to be superior students in high school. Those who planned on college tended to have greater access to books and magazines in the home and their parents tended to have more years of education.

Again, it must be emphasized that none of these relationships were perfect and that there will always be many many high-ability students coming from the homes of skilled tradesmen in which no literary materials are available and the parents are not educated who are nevertheless planning to attend college.

Special studies were made of other groups. The girls planning to enter nursing tended to come from homes that fell between the homes of girls planning to attend college and the homes of girls planning to work. They had more financial resources available to them than did the girls planning to work but not as many as had the girls planning to attend college. Similarly, the cultural backgrounds of their homes were superior to the backgrounds of the homes of girls planning to work but somewhat inferior to the cultural backgrounds of girls planning to attend college.

Differences among the metropolitan, nonfarm, and farm girls planning to enter nursing suggested that vocational interests affect these girls differentially and that perhaps nonfarm and farm girls often enter nursing not because of a basic interest in nursing but because it is a convenient and possible form of post-high-school training.

The girls who planned to attend business school and who came from metropolitan areas tended to be quite different in many respects from the girls planning to attend business school who came from farm and nonfarm areas. Among the latter were many who perhaps would have much preferred going to another kind of college, but who, because of financial limitations or other reasons, were unable to do so. The girls from the metropolitan areas, on the other hand, found other colleges more available, and if they decided to attend business school, this was perhaps because of a real preference for that type of training.

Some indication was found that in terms of both economic backgrounds and cultural backgrounds, girls who planned to attend business school tended to fall between the girls who planned to attend college and the girls who planned to work and in many ways they were quite similar to the girls who planned to become nurses.

The information obtained from the interviews suggested that the plans of youth conformed closely to the values held by their parents. The parents of children who planned to work saw college primarily in an economic context: college was a way to earn more money. As long as other avenues to a satisfactory income were available, college was not important. The parents of the students who planned to go to college, however, perceived college in terms of other values and the implied goals could be achieved only through the avenue of college.

The follow-up study revealed that in one or more of the four groups studied, age, source of family income, paternal occupation, mother's occupation before marriage, high school curriculum, reasons for after-high-school plans, family willingness to support college plans (both with money and with encouragement), and number of books in the home were all related to the extent to which after-high-school plans were carried through. Those factors that were related to stability of plans in every one of the four groups studied included age, source of family income, occupation of father, high school curriculum, and reasons for plans.

In the metropolitan group of boys and girls, those who planned on college and attended college were younger on the average than those who planned on college but did not attend college. The former group tended to come from homes where income was derived from fees and profits and where the father was in a profession or owned or managed a business, and they had taken a college preparatory course. When making plans for college, they expected more financial help from their families than those who did not realize their college-going plans.

In the nonmetropolitan group of boys and girls, those who planned on college and attended more often took college preparatory courses and less often took general courses than those planning on college but not attending.

In the group of nonmetropolitan boys and girls planning on working for someone other than parents, fewer of those who did work came from families having incomes derived from fees or profits than of those who did not work. Fewer of this former group had fathers who were farmers. In other words, both source of family income and occupation of father were related to realizability of work plans in the sense that a farmer father and income from fees and profits were inversely related to realizability of work plans. In this group, more of those following plans to work took vocational courses than of those who did not follow their plans to work.

For the most part, those factors determining the realizability of plans for the metropolitan group appeared to be somewhat different from the factors determining realizability of plans for the nonmetropolitan group. Similarly, some sex differences were apparent. These differences were suggested by the fact that many of the differences that were statistically significant for one group were not significant for another.

Nevertheless, some limited generalizations can be made for both boys and girls. First, there appeared to be a few factors related to realizability of after-high-school plans, regardless of what those plans were. For instance, having a mother who had been a teacher increased the probability that the student would follow his plans, whether they were to attend college or to work. Similarly, the younger a high school senior was when he graduated, the greater the probability he would follow his plans.

Another generalization concerned the relationship between realizability of plans and family background factors. Source of family income, occupation of parents, and family attitudes toward college all seemed related to whether or not high school seniors were able to realize their postgraduation plans. Just as these family factors have been found intricately related to the formulation of these plans, so were they related to whether or not students could fulfill these plans within a year after graduation.

Similarly, motivational differences, as revealed by the reasons students checked for making after-high-school plans, were related to the realizability of the plans. When a student motivated by the desire to make money plans on working, there is a greater probability that he will work than if he had been motivated by more social reasons — "everyone does it," or "to be with friends."

Finally, and perhaps most predictably, the high school courses taken by students appeared related to the extent to which they followed their plans. Quite naturally, those students who took vocational courses in high school were better prepared for jobs and found it easier to obtain jobs than students who had not taken such vocational courses. Similarly, the students who planned on college and who had taken college preparatory courses found it easier to attend college than those who had planned on college but had not taken college preparatory courses. Causal relationships must not be inferred hastily, because the conditions which resulted in a student who planned on college not taking a college preparatory course may also be the conditions resulting in a lessened probability that he will attend college.

As with all problems of this sort, the factors determining whether or not high school students actually follow their plans for after high school are extremely complex and depend in part upon the group being studied and the plans under consideration. Nevertheless, these factors can be studied systematically and knowledge of them should aid counselors in helping students develop plans and aid administrators and parents in making these plans realizable.

4

Some Interpretations

ONE can interpret in a variety of ways the results that have been presented, depending upon the emphasis desired. The figures do reveal a startling waste of human ability following high school graduation. On the other hand, these same figures indicate that a much larger proportion of talented than of intellectually mediocre youth seek college training. Access to a college education is determined in large part by economic factors but at the same time a large proportion of our college students come from homes that in no sense of the term can be called economically privileged. These results can lead one to view with alarm or to retreat into self-satisfied complacency, depending upon one's proclivities.

The most productive interpretation comes from neither an extremely optimistic nor an extremely pessimistic approach. Certain conditions have been found to exist. These conditions do not approach the ideal, but neither do they indicate catastrophic failures in the past. As with most social problems, a great deal of progress has been made and yet vast room for advancement remains. These are the facts; we must examine them closely with the hope that such examination will lead to the production of new ideas and to the initiation of new actions.

The interpretations made here rest upon certain assumptions that undoubtedly helped to determine the hypotheses originally posed and the experimental design of the study itself. The assumptions are these:

1. The quantity and the type of education and training required by individuals vary according to the individuals' abilities, interests, and personalities.

2. The community has an increasing need for educated and trained persons, a need that is not yet satisfied.

3. There is at present no danger of society being faced with an excess of educated and trained persons.

4. Access to educational facilities should not be determined on the basis of sex, race, religion, geographical location, or economic resources of the individual but rather on the basis of differential abilities and interests, acquired skills, and habits of application and industriousness.

5. Many persons potentially able to benefit from advanced training at present do not receive such training.

6. Factors of sex, race, religion, geographical location, and economic resources are now related to the extent to which individuals have access to advanced training.

7. The responsibility for seeing that as many qualified persons as possible receive advanced training belongs not only to the individual but also to high schools, colleges, local, state, and federal governments, business and industry, and all agencies of the community.

8. Our institutions of higher learning at present are unable to meet the needs of all highly talented individuals and some persons of exceptional ability will benefit from advanced training provided by institutions other than our colleges and universities as now organized. Not *all* high-ability students should attend college. Society has need for many of these persons in occupations not requiring professional preparation and a general education can be provided by means other than through a college education.

9. Attaining advanced training depends upon a number of conditions, and any program designed to increase the number of qualified persons receiving such training must be a many-faceted program if it is to be effective.

10. Any program designed to increase the number of persons obtaining advanced training must guarantee to each individual a maximum degree of self-determination as to the type of training to be acquired and the conditions under which it is to be obtained. Such self-determination, however, can lead to satisfactory social and personal adjustment only if decisions are made on the basis of all available information and after careful and mature deliberation.

A POINT OF VIEW

We have made certain generalizations in the preceding chapters concerning the phenomenon of college attendance and its dependency upon home conditions. Attitudes toward college attendance have been the principal content of this investigation, such attitudes being revealed by the plans students have regarding college. Too much emphasis cannot be placed on the fact that plans to attend college are not tantamount to attending college, but favorable attitudes toward college are an essential condition if college-attending behavior is to follow.

The follow-up study revealed a substantial relationship between attitudes as indicated by plans and actual behavior as revealed by attendance at college. The extent of this relationship between plans and behavior depended in part upon the economic status of the group studied, its cultural status, the sex of the individuals in the group, and the geographical area from which the group came. The relationship between plans and behavior is also probably dependent upon the length of the interval between the time at which the plans are ascertained and the time the behavior is studied. For instance, the relationship between plans and behavior will probably be quite low if the child is asked in the fourth grade whether or not he wants to attend college and if his actual attendance is then related to his plan. On the other hand, the relationship will be almost perfect if plans are ascertained the day before matriculation.

The generalizations that have been made will perhaps be most meaningful, and certainly most useful, if they can be placed within a conceptual framework. No attempt will be made here to construct a theory to explain the phenomenon of college attendance, but an attempt will be made to adopt a conceptual framework that may eventually lead to the development of such a theory.

A child may be regarded as a focal point existing since birth in an active field of forces, a field that never remains constant and one that is in perpetual interaction with the child. The forces within the field come from a great variety of sources; some of these maintain a constant direction and constant strength over a long period of years, other forces may change from day to day. It is the relative constancy of many of these forces that helps explain the demonstrated unity of personality.

The basic nature of the child helps in part to determine the characteristics of the forces with which we are concerned. For instance, if a child, because of the structure of his central nervous system, has the capacity to behave intellectually at a high level, perception of this fact by his parents and teachers will influence their attitudes and behaviors toward the child. These attitudes and behaviors constitute an important cluster of forces.

The child himself manifests a great variety of specific behaviors, perhaps thousands of behavioral acts are elicited each day. These behavioral acts can be grouped systematically according to a variety of categories. They could be grouped, for instance, upon the basis of common bodily structures — those motor acts involving the hands, perceptual acts involving the eyes, or emotional acts involving the gonads. These acts also could be categorized by the perceptual responses of observers, such as friendly acts, hostile acts, aggressive acts, or submissive acts. Or goals could provide the basis for categorizing these acts, goals perceived either by the child or by an observer.

The acts and related attitudes of primary interest here are those relevant for the gross and continuing behavior of "attending college." More explicitly, the exact behavioral act with which we are dealing is the statement "I am going to attend college," and the forces that have resulted in that act are the factors considered here in so much detail.

The forces that tend to direct a person toward college, and the strength of these forces, determine the certainty of his choice or his eagerness to be a college student. These forces come primarily from his family and secondarily from his age peers, from his teachers, and from other individuals and agencies within his community. A sufficiently strong force from his family usually is enough to direct a person toward college, but in the absence of such a force from his family, forces from these other sources, if strong enough, may also result in the individual attending college. If, however, the force from the family is actively in the direction away from college, then there is question as to whether or not it is possible for these other forces to counteract effectively the family force and to influence the individual to attend college.

The direction and strength of the force coming from the family are related to the economic status of the family, the cultural background of various family members, the experience the family has had with people who have attended college, the information the family has about college and other alternatives, and the values the family has relating to college and alternative plans. Perhaps also extremely important is the nature of the relationship existing between the child and his family. Thus, a child who rejects the family and the family's standards will react to forces differently from the child who maintains a cordial and warm relationship with his family.

The child's reaction to these forces within his field are for the most part learned reactions and it may be possible to apply well-founded principles of learning in considering these phenomena. By the time a student is in high school, and certainly by the time he is ready to consider college seriously, his reactions to the forces within his field have been determined by the many experiences he already has had and by the large repertoire of learned reaction patterns he has accumulated. If movement toward college results in approval from his parents, peers, and teachers, and if such approval has acquired a rewarding value for the student, the likelihood of college attendance increases. If the student anticipates that college attendance will provide greater social prestige, and if his needs are such that prestige is important, he will be favorably disposed toward college. If the student perceives college attendance as a means for postponing the cutting of closely established ties or maintaining need-fulfilling dependencies, he will move toward college. If the student has learned to perceive college as meeting certain needs for various pleasurable activities, both in and out of the classroom, movement again will be toward college.

On the other hand, if through contacts with his parents, teachers, and peers the student has attached negative values to education in general, including college, and if his consideration of college would lead to disapproval from these other persons, the likelihood of college attendance is diminished. Attending college might be perceived by the student primarily as involving a postponement of the acquisition of a higher standard of living, or it might be perceived by the student primarily as a continuation of an irksome dependency to which the student has learned to react negatively. In these cases movement will be away from college. College attendance might be perceived by the individual as enforced participation in activities that have acquired negative value — he may have learned to be bored by classroom activities, he may have acquired a distaste for group activities, or he may have learned to dislike sedentary activities involved with study. Again, movement will be away from college.

Thus, by perceiving the student as learning and operating within a field of forces, we may be able to relate to one another some of the seemingly disjoined results of the present analysis.

SOME IMPLICATIONS

When information is sought regarding a general problem, the application of the obtained facts is more difficult than their acquisition. Psy-

chologists know more about human behavior than they have been able
to apply in practical situations; educators also have been subjected to
this lag in application. Possession of information provides the possessor
with a feeling of security and a hope that by acquiring additional data
he has solved a problem. The most difficult step, however, involves the
application of the acquired knowledge to the problem originally approached.

All too often, acquired knowledge does not lead directly to relevant
and effective action and that is certainly true here. The obtained information, however, does allow us to make tentative conclusions that certain actions may lead to more effective utilization of our intellectual
resources.

The family, and parents in particular, are perhaps the most influential
factors determining whether or not children utilize their potentials. Like
still tends to beget like. Any program of action must be directed toward
the parents of high school students. Our first suggestion is that high
school counseling programs give much more attention to parents. Traditionally, the counselor in high school has dealt primarily with students,
secondarily with other high school teachers, and only in rare cases with
parents. Contacts with parents have usually been made when rather
drastic problems have presented themselves. When counselors have
worked with parents, they have been trying to solve crises. They have
not been attempting to develop systematically attitudes in parents that
will allow children to use their talents.

Periodic conferences between elementary teachers and parents are
now routine in many schools. Such conferences are also necessary between high school counselors and parents. In these conferences the
counselor would have the responsibility for seeing that the parent
thoroughly understood the capacity and interests of the child and the
resources and facilities available in the community for his education.
At present, high school counselors are hard pressed to deal with all the
students with whom they should work. Expanding their responsibilities
to include systematic work with parents would place an intolerable load
on these counselors unless the numbers of high school counselors were
greatly increased. But such work is important, for it may provide the
most direct means for influencing the attitudes of parents, the attitudes
that are here paramount.

Parents who are most active in community life contribute most of our college-going population. This should not be interpreted to mean that community participation results in children attending college. Rather, both college attendance and community participation can perhaps be traced back to other common factors. Possibly, however, increasing the extent to which parents participate in the community would bring about changes in parental attitudes toward college and toward other training programs with the general result that more of our capable students will attend college.

The relationships observed here between the amount of reading material in a home and the tendency of a child to attend college can be utilized also. Again, parents who have children more likely to attend college are the parents who also have more literature in their homes. Although we must recognize the hazards of making a causal interpretation, we might assume that if we placed more literature in the homes of talented children, this would increase the probability that those children will attend college. Counselors and teachers should take an active interest in seeing that books and periodicals are available in the homes of students coming from culturally restricted backgrounds.

Parents' attitudes toward college are influenced in part by the amount and the kind of information they have about college. Our interview study strongly suggested that parents know relatively little about college. Most of the parents of our high school graduates have never attended college and few of them have intimate acquaintances who are college graduates. Much information about college is obtained from movies, magazines, and newspapers. Only the "newsworthy" facts about college are made available to most parents and the newsworthy facts are rarely representative. High schools, colleges, and educational associations have a great responsibility to educate the general public, and parents particularly, regarding college and college life in America.

Finally, many children resist serious consideration of college because they feel that college involves a continuation of an undesired dependency upon the family. High school students who have already acquired a feeling of emotional and economic independence from the family are perhaps more likely to consider college than are more dependent children. Failure to attend college is frequently an indication of a revolt against the family, and if means can be developed for establishing independence from the family on the part of the child without affecting his willingness to maintain the minimum amount of dependency necessary for college attendance, an increasing number of children should be willing to continue their education. Similarly, the child's decision to attend college may be an expression of rebellion and an attempt to seek freedom at college.

It is questionable whether any program directed toward affecting the number of children attending college would be successful unless it worked actively in this area of the family. Making additional funds available through scholarship programs, whether these programs are government subsidized or financed by business or foundations alone, will have little effect other than to make it easier for those students now attending college, or planning to enter, to obtain higher education. Students' attitudes and motives are strongly related to family conditions and they can be changed only by bringing to bear upon family attitudes whatever influences can affect them.

Most scholarship programs at present are announced to high school seniors at the beginning of their last year in high school. The students who apply for these scholarships tend to be the ones who have already decided that they want to attend college. If scholarship programs are to be effective in increasing the number of qualified students attending college, *such programs should take into consideration not only the making available of funds, but also the creating of the desire to attend college.* Scholarship programs might well be announced to high school students long before the senior year, perhaps while the students are still in junior high school. Parents of qualified students in the eighth or ninth grade should be informed about scholarships and encouraged to have their children consider the possibility of attending college with the assistance of scholarship funds. Already a few programs grant scholarships to students long before their senior year in high school. Coupling this with intensive work with the families might well increase the number of qualified children continuing their education.

The school is the source of many of the most potent forces directing an individual toward or away from college. The results reported here, taken into consideration with previously available information, suggest several things for the schools to do if optimum use is to be made of our intellectual resources.

Perhaps most important, the counseling services available to high school students will have to be expanded, both in terms of number of counselors and quality of counseling provided. Few students reported they had been influenced directly by counselors or teachers in making plans for post-high-school careers. An effective counselor may operate in so subtle a fashion that the student is not aware of the influence the counselor has concerning a specific decision. Although this would be the merciful interpretation to make of our findings, an interpretation that unhappily is perhaps more accurate, is that the counselors available had so little time to work with students that students were for the most part uninfluenced by them.

A wise decision to attend college depends upon several things. First, the student must have attitudes favorable toward higher education and these attitudes usually are developed over a long period of time. Second, a student must have information about various alternatives open to him, including information about various kinds of colleges, specific colleges, and college programs. Finally, the student must have the skills necessary to evaluate this information so that he arrives at a wise decision. He must know how to approach a problem, how to gather and evaluate evidence, how to consider alternatives realistically, and how to arrive at a practical decision that leads to possible action.

These three steps of attitude development, information obtaining, and problem solving are all the concern of the high school counselor, although certainly every other individual in the school system is also concerned with these three functions. It is the counselor's primary responsibility, however, to see that high school students do develop attitudes that are healthy, that they do have information about alternatives, and that they do learn how to solve their individual problems. To do this effectively the high school counselor must have an opportunity to work frequently with individual students. He will not find it enough to see each student once or twice a year. Ideally, he should have an opportunity to see each student in a more or less formally structured situation at least once a month, and perhaps more often. At the least, the high school counselor should have an opportunity to conduct an interview with each student three or four times a year and at the same time to discuss with the student's teachers and parents the progress the student is making. Only by having many more well-trained counselors in our schools can the schools effectively influence the number of high-ability children who attend college.

Another closely related problem concerns the early identification of students who should attend college. A single test of college aptitude is insufficient to determine which students in a class are potentially college material. In the first place, single test scores are not completely reliable; second, a single test measures a rather specific kind of ability, and success in any endeavor depends upon several kinds of aptitudes and abilities. For instance, a student may do well on a test that is not timed, such as the Ohio Psychological Examination, and yet obtain a low score on a speed test, such as the American Council on Education Psychological Examination. If only the speed test were used, several talented people in each class would be missed because they are slow, and yet they have the intellectual ability to deal with problems at the college level. Thus in identifying talent, several types of tests must be utilized at various times. A test given at the beginning of the ninth grade provides evidence that should be considered in helping a student plan his career, but this is not sufficient evidence to help a student decide, without the use of any other information, that he should or should not attend college. A test given in the eleventh grade and another in the twelfth grade might present a picture considerably changed from that obtained with a single test in the ninth grade.

More attention should also be given to factors other than those closely related to intellectual ability. For instance, the matter of educational and vocational interest is extremely important in helping a student decided upon his post-high-school career. Given a minimum amount of ability, variations in interest can determine whether a person is a highly successful student in college or whether he is a borderline or failing student.

Another suggestion arising from these results is that the more flexible the curriculums of a high school are, the easier it will be for the individual student to adjust his plans according to his own needs and abilities. In many schools, students must decide at the beginning of the tenth grade whether or not they will prepare for college. A student may decide in the ninth or tenth grade that he will take a commercial course. After two or three years in that course, he may discover that another type of course would be more appropriate. Because of the rather rigid organization of most school curriculums, however, a student has difficulty making that kind of transition. Even when a school has provisions for such shifts, the attitudes of the students and of the teachers often are such that students tend to regard themselves as fixed in a given curriculum, once they have been in that curriculum for a year or more.

Then, too, high schools should have more and better information available to give to students about college and other post-high-school alternatives. This is a responsibility that involves the colleges as much as the high schools. College catalogs and bulletins in the past have been notoriously ambiguous. Information has been presented that the college staffs have assumed the high school teachers and students wanted. Little systematic effort has been made to determine the types of information actually required by high school students. In most college bulletins, perhaps one or two paragraphs are included describing the costs involved in attending a given college and ways of meeting those costs. In most public high schools, these are among the most important problems faced by students contemplating college and much more detailed information could be provided by the colleges to help high school students in their planning. Some colleges now publish bulletins presenting information about college in terms of occupations and professions being considered by high school students. Such an approach has been found to be of value to high school teachers, counselors, and students.

The high school shares with parents the responsibility for providing to each child an opportunity to work out his own dependency needs, for providing an opportunity to stand on his own feet. A high school that maintains a highly disciplined atmosphere and a rigid traditional curriculum, one manned chiefly by subject-matter-centered teachers, is preparing a group of students who by the time they complete high school are ready to revolt against all things academic. The students coming from such schools have a great need for independence, and they frequently see college only as a continuation of their dependency upon the high school and upon adults. A high school that has given students an opportunity to participate in the actual operation of the school, that has provided students with a feeling of independence, that has given students a chance to make decisions and to determine in part the programs in which they are participating, is helping to develop a feeling of independence that minimizes the adolescent rebellion against authority that so often results in failure to attend college. It has not been possible to determine here whether youth coming from schools with strong student government organizations are more likely to attend college than are other youth, but this reasonable hypothesis warrants further investigation.

Finally, the high schools have a very serious responsibility in developing within children an appreciation of the purposes of education. All too often, teachers in a high school, and the very community itself, fail to appreciate the broad variety of purposes behind our educational programs. Too many influential persons within a community regard preparation for an occupation as the primary and perhaps only function of education. Similarly, a smaller group of persons, but still a powerful minority, regard the extension of our cultural heritage as the primary function of education. Too few persons, and certainly not many students, have an appreciation of the many purposes that lie behind education. Youth must be given an appreciation of the broad purposes of education, in terms of the development of individual personalities, the advancement toward social goals, and the intrinsic satisfactions found in arriving at knowledge and truth.

All these suggestions directed toward the parent or toward the school have as their focal point the individual student. What must be done directly with students to increase their chances of making maximum use of the talents they possess?

Each student must be given an opportunity to understand and appreciate his own personality. He must have a realization of his own talents and of any special skills and abilities that he is fortunate enough to possess. Similarly, he must be given an opportunity to recognize his own limitations and to view himself as realistically as possible. Related to this, he must understand what his own motivations, his values and interests, are and what bearing this information has on his plans for the future.

This means that the student must have early assistance in selecting his goals and that such assistance must continue throughout his school career. This does not imply that the school or the teacher or the counselor provides the goals or specifies for the student what his goals shall be; it does imply that students should be placed in situations where they can consider a great variety of goals and that they should be given the skills needed in analyzing these goals and relating them to their own basic personality needs. A student who comes from an economically deprived home and who places an exaggerated value upon money should understand why he has developed that attitude and what the implications of the attitude are. In this sense, it is not the purpose of the school to indoctrinate students that *these* attitudes are good, or *those* attitudes are bad, but rather to help students understand *what* the attitudes are and *where* they come from, with the hope that such an understanding will eventually lead to the development of a healthy personality and a socially constructive set of attitudes.

CONCLUSION

The forces influencing the decisions of the 25,000 boys and girls we studied are complex and present a puzzle of causal relationships. The large mass of detailed information that has been accumulated here, and the few generalizations that have been justified, do enlarge to some extent our understanding of the phenomenon of college attendance.

The desire to attend college is closely related to our class structure. This class structure, in turn, can be conceptualized successfully in terms of economic status and cultural status. This conceptualization helps explain in part why some high school seniors plan to attend college and why others make alternative plans. Although such information does not lead directly to a course of action providing effective control over this phenomenon, it raises questions that must be discussed intelligently before any courses of action are finally adopted.

Whether or not a high school graduate attends college depends in large part upon the home from which he comes. The attitudes of the family toward things related to education, as shown by the books and magazines in the home, the community organizations in which the family is represented, and the education of the parents, are perhaps even more important than the family's financial resources. Children learn from their parents attitudes that may determine whether they want to attend college. Obviously if more qualified high school graduates are to attend college, any program of action must take into consideration the influence exerted by the family. Any program if it is to be effective in increasing the number of qualified students who attend college must attempt to influence the attitudes of both students and parents, as well as to reduce the economic barriers.

Part Two · Analysis of the Findings

5

Evaluation of the Data

THE data used in the analyses reported here must themselves be evaluated. Inasmuch as great weight is placed upon the information derived from the questionnaires, the reliability of that information should be considered carefully.

Three methods were available for evaluating the questionnaire data. First, the information pertaining to after-high-school plans reported in the original questionnaire was compared with the actual behavior of the student reported, again by questionnaire, one year after graduation from high school. This in one sense provided a summary statement of the validity of expressed after-high-school plans. The results of this comparison are presented in Chapter 16.

Another means of evaluating the data was provided by information obtained in the interview study. The parents interviewed were asked many questions which duplicated the questions asked of their children and by comparing the responses given by parents and children, we could estimate the agreement, or the reliability, of these two sources of information.

A third means of evaluating these data was provided by an independent study conducted in one of the Minnesota towns from which these high school students came. Dr. John Anderson and Dr. Dale Harris of the Institute of Child Welfare at the University of Minnesota were gathering information in the fall of 1951 pertaining to the family backgrounds of all school children in that town, a town other than the one in which the interview study was done. Much of the information they gathered through the use of questionnaires completed by both parents and children duplicated the information gathered in the present study and comparisons revealed the extent of agreement in response.

One must remember, of course, that since these various people were not questioned at the same time, lack of agreement did not necessarily mean that people were reporting the same facts differently. It was possible that the facts themselves could have changed. For instance, if parents reported only one automobile in the family whereas the child reported two, the actual number owned by the family might have changed in the interval between questionings. Some questions, however (for example, those pertaining to the education of father and mother and similar conditions), were not likely to have changed during a period of a few weeks or a few months.

Comparisons of information provided by students on the questionnaire and parents in the interview revealed a wide range of agreement and disagreement. Such comparisons were possible for 26 items of information. Table 1 lists the items and the percentage of agreement between the students and their parents.

Table 1. Percentage of Agreement of Students and Their Parents on Items of Questionnaire (N = 90 pairs)

Item	Percentage of Agreement
Father's occupation	82
Mother's occupation	97
Father's education	56
Mother's education	59
Plans for next year	90
Vocational objective	81
Parents' feeling about college	77
School or college student planned to attend	62
Payment of expenses for college	50
Effect of more money on educational plans	44
Reasons for plans	91
Parents' vocational wish for children	77
Magazines in the home	80
Organizations parents belonged to	88
Ownership of home	98
Number of people living in home	80
Number of cars in the family	92
Year and make of car(s)	69
Presence in home of:	
Central heating	87
Running water	100
Hot and cold water	91
Refrigerator	96
Telephone	98
Deep freezer	96
Television	96

Of the 25 items, there were 11 where 90 per cent or more of the parent-child pairs agreed in reporting information. There were 5 questions asked where agreement between child and parent was below 65 per cent. For example, in every case where a child said that the home had running water, the parent verified this; thus there was 100 per cent agreement. In the 90 child-parent couples, 86 of the parents agreed with their children in answering the question as to whether or not they had a mechanical refrigerator. In this case there was a 96 per cent agreement.

The children and their parents also agreed almost perfectly in reporting the mother's occupation, the child's plans for the next year, the reasons given for those plans, whether or not the family owned its own home, the number of cars in the family, and whether or not the family had hot and cold water, a telephone, a deep freezer, or a television set.

The parents and children did not agree as well in providing information about parental education, school or college the child was planning to attend, how much money the child would receive from the family for college, and whether or not the child would change his plans for college if he had more money.

Quite clearly the greatest agreement was found in answers referring to material possessions in the home and less agreement was found in the general area of attitudes. Nevertheless, in most of these cases the child perceived quite well how the parent felt about his plans and in turn the parent perceived quite well how the child felt about his own plans.

These figures suggest that although many of these data are not sufficiently reliable to be of great use in interpreting individual cases, their reliability is high enough to warrant the types of analyses reported here.

Comparisons between the students' questionnaire responses collected in this study and the data collected in the independent study by Drs. Anderson and Harris revealed some similarities and some differences. These are shown in Table 2. Data pertaining to the education of the father provided an agreement of 71 per cent and data on the education of the mother, 68 per cent. This agreement was considerably higher than the agreement found between parent and child. The number of books in the home provided an agreement of 77 per cent, the number of automobiles 66 per cent, running water 98 per cent, mechanical refrigerator 96 per cent, telephone 97 per cent, electric lights 99 per cent, television 99 per cent, the number of people living in the home 83 per cent,

Table 2. Comparison of Data Obtained in This Study and Data
Obtained in the Study by Anderson and Harris

Item	Number of Cases*	Percentage of Agreement	Estimate of Reliability
Education of father..........	107	70.86	.84
Education of mother.........	103	68.21	.83
Number of books............	117	77.48	.88
Number of automobiles......	99	65.56	.81
Running water..............	146	97.69	.98
Mechanical refrigerator......	144	95.36	.98
Telephone	147	97.35	.99
Electric lights	150	99.34	.99
Television	150	99.34	.99
Number of people living in home	126	83.44	.91
Number of rooms...........	100	66.23	.81

* The total number of families for whom data were gathered in both studies was 151. Not all the items, however, were answered by all the families in both studies.

and the number of rooms in the house, 66 per cent. In roughly estimating a reliability coefficient for each of these items, one arrives at coefficients ranging from .81 to .99.

The relatively high agreement, 77 per cent, in estimating the number of books in the home is somewhat surprising. It is easy to understand how people know whether or not they have one or two automobiles but very few people ever actually sit down and count their books.

In general it can be said that the data upon which these analyses were based were reasonably reliable so far as could be determined. Since the evaluation methods available to us indicated that very few, if any, of these data have reliabilities below .80, the responses to the questionnaires and the interviews appear to provide a reasonably good picture of the conditions as they truly were.

⚑ 6

Plans of High School Seniors

AFTER-HIGH-SCHOOL plans were available for 24,892 Minnesota high school seniors. Slightly over one third of this group were planning to work after graduating from high school and slightly over one third were planning to attend college. Less than 10 per cent of the total group planned on any one of these courses of action: working for parents, going to trade school, going to business school, going to some other school, doing postgraduate work in high school, entering military service, entering nurses' training, or following other plans.

The follow-up study reported in Chapter 16 revealed the extent to which students behaved after graduation according to previously made plans. Obviously not all students followed their plans, but these plans were one expression of a constellation of attitudes centering around higher education, previous educational and work experiences, and the working world. As expressions of attitudes, after-high-school plans were perhaps the single most important factor in determining what high school students did after graduation.

Of the entire group, 11,379, or 46 per cent, were boys. The number of girls graduating from high school in Minnesota has been slightly larger than the number of boys for several years. This sex difference was found not only for the total group, but also in each of the three geographical areas. Of the total group, 33 per cent of the students came from metropolitan schools, 30 per cent came from farm families, and 36 per cent came from smaller cities and towns. Thus the students were distributed almost equally by sex and among metropolitan, farm, and nonfarm homes.

Large differences that were both statistically significant* and of tre-

* In this and following chapters, statements regarding statistical significance are based on levels of probability derived from critical ratios, differences between means

mendous practical importance were found in the plans of these high school seniors when comparisons were made between the two sexes and among the three geographical groups.

PLANS TO WORK

For all three geographical groups, more girls than boys were planning on working immediately after high school graduation — 41 per cent against 30 per cent. This sex difference was reduced and in some cases eliminated when the students who planned to work for their parents were added to the students who planned to get jobs. Of all the male students, 42 per cent were planning either to get jobs or to work for their parents; of all the female students, 43 per cent had these plans. Of the boys living on farms, 63 per cent were planning to work for their parents or to get jobs, as compared with 50 per cent of the girls living on farms who had these plans. The male farm group was the only one of the groups that had a large number of students planning to work for their parents.

Of particular importance here was the large number of metropolitan girls — compared with the number of metropolitan boys — who planned on obtaining jobs. One third again as many girls as boys coming from metropolitan areas were planning to work.

PLANS TO CONTINUE EDUCATION

Of the total group, 51 per cent were planning to continue their education or training. The largest number of these were planning to attend college — 36 per cent of the total group.

Large geographical and some sex differences were apparent when the students planning to enter college were compared. Of the boys, 39 per cent were planning on college and of the girls, 34 per cent. College planning was more typical of boys than of girls among the youth coming from the metropolitan and non-farm areas, whereas college planning was more typical of girls than of boys among those from the farm areas. Only 20 per cent of the high school boys coming from farms were planning to attend college as compared with 50 per cent of the boys coming from metropolitan areas and 43 per cent of the boys coming from non-

or between percentages divided by the standard errors of the differences. Differences occurring no more than 5 per cent of the time through chance are described as "statistically significant."

farm areas. In Minnesota, then, college planning is a form of behavior more characteristic of students from metropolitan areas and small towns and is found relatively infrequently on farms. This was true of girls as well as boys, although the geographical differences were perhaps not quite so great for the girls.

Only 4 per cent of the total group — 7 per cent of the boys and 1 per cent of the girls — were planning to attend trade school after graduating from high school. These students were distributed rather evenly among the metropolitan, farm, and nonfarm areas.

A sex difference in the opposite direction was equally marked among the students planning to attend business school. These were characteristically plans of girls, 8 per cent of whom were planning to attend business school as compared with 2 per cent of the boys. Again there were relatively small and insignificant geographical differences.

Only 3 per cent of the total group were planning to attend other schools, including such institutions as schools of beauty culture, modeling schools, and schools to train airplane stewardesses. Of the total group of students, only 27 were planning to remain in high school to do postgraduate work. Of the total group of boys, 6 per cent were planning to enter military service, a somewhat greater number of the nonfarm boys having these plans than was true of the farm and metropolitan boys. Of the girls, 6 per cent were planning to enter nursing, with slightly fewer of the metropolitan girls than of the farm and nonfarm girls having these plans.

DIFFERENCES BETWEEN TWO GROUPS OF GRADUATES

The Anderson and Berning follow-up study, "What Happens to High School Graduates," allows us to make some comparisons between the plans of the high school seniors graduating in 1950 and the reported behavior of the high school seniors who graduated from Minnesota high schools in 1938. The method in the Anderson and Berning study differed from the method in the present study insofar as their data were collected through questionnaires sent to high school principals one year after the seniors graduated. Eighty-four per cent of the high schools responded, providing data on 22,306 students. In making these comparisons we must remember that the earlier study provided data on what high school students did; the present study provided data on what high school students planned to do. We must also remember, however, that our own limited follow-up indicated a fairly close relationship between plans and behavior: 36 per cent of the 1950 high school students planned to go to college, 35 per cent of those studied in the follow-up one year after graduation reported that they had actually attended college. This provides some grounds for assuming that the figures on plans of high school seniors, as they concern college attendance, are quite comparable to the figures on their actual behavior. Although the individual students who plan to attend college may not always be the ones who do attend, the total number of students who follow this course of action corresponds fairly well to the total number who so planned.

Of the 1938 high school graduates, 23 per cent attended college. This figure should be compared with the 36 per cent of the 1950 graduates who planned to attend college and the 35 per cent who reported they actually attended college. The increase amounts to almost 50 per cent. This means that for every two high school seniors who were going to college in 1938, three high school seniors were planning to attend college in 1950.

The earlier study did not provide figures for exact comparisons between specific geographical sections and between the sexes, but some figures were available for the metropolitan students. In 1938, 24 per cent of the high school seniors coming from Minneapolis, St. Paul, and Duluth attended college. Of the metropolitan students of 1950, 44 per cent were planning to attend college. Thus, the largest increase in the tendency to attend college is apparently that found in the metropolitan areas. The reader should note that the data of the 1938 study, as cited here, excluded the students coming from private schools, and these students tended to attend college more often than did the students from public high schools. The 1950 data include students from both public and private high schools. If one assumes that the tendency for private high school students to attend college is constant, regardless of the area in the state from which they come, and then adds the figures from the 1938 study for the private school students in the state to the 1938 figures for metropolitan students, the percentage of metropolitan public and private high school students attending college is increased from 24 to 28 (1472 Minneapolis, St. Paul, and Duluth high school seniors attending college plus 532 private school students attending college, this sum divided by 6013 Minneapolis, St. Paul, and Duluth high school seniors plus 1063 private school seniors).

In 1938, 35 per cent of the high school seniors were reported to be working full time one year after graduation. This is to be compared with the 36 per cent of the 1950 graduates who were planning to work. To this percentage should perhaps be added the 7 per cent planning to work for their parents. Thus a total of 43 per cent of the 1950 seniors planned to work. An additional 7 per cent in 1938 had part-time jobs and another 12 per cent were unemployed.

In 1938, 12 per cent of the total group of high school graduates were attending schools other than colleges and in 1950, 15 per cent of the high school seniors were planning to attend such schools (trade schools, business schools, other noncollegiate schools, high schools for post-graduate work, schools of nursing). Of the metropolitan students, 11 per cent were in other schools in 1938 as compared with 14 per cent of the metropolitan students planning to attend such schools in 1950.

On the basis of these figures, one might hypothesize that a large portion of the high school graduates who were unemployed one year after graduation in 1938 corresponded to the high school graduates who planned to attend colleges or universities in 1950. In other words, many of the 2696 unemployed high school graduates in 1939 would have been in college if conditions prevailing in 1950 had prevailed in 1939.*

* The data given in this chapter are summarized in a table included in an article by Ralph F. Berdie, "Why Don't They Go to College?" in *Personnel and Guidance Journal,* March 1953 pp. 352–56.

7

Relation of Plans of High School Seniors
to College Aptitudes

A SYSTEM of higher education designed to meet the needs of a large segment of our young population and to train people of many capacities for a variety of jobs should utilize a diversity of abilities and aptitudes. Instead of predicting a student's probable success in college on the basis of a single measure of college aptitude, we should make differential predictions for several collegiate training programs, basing the predictions on a variety of measures of different college aptitudes.

Unfortunately, our present system of higher education has not as yet achieved such a degree of differentiation, and predictions of success in college are usually based on one or a few highly related measures of college aptitude. Available in this study were two indices of college aptitude for most of the students: the total raw scores on the American Council on Education Psychological Examination, college edition, 1947 form, and high school percentile ranks.

These two measures have been used in Minnesota for several years to predict success in college. The correlation between the two measures approximates .50. The correlations between A.C.E. scores and college freshmen grades vary from .30 to .50. The correlations between high school percentile ranks and college freshmen grades vary from .40 to .55. Differences in relationships between predictors and grades are found among different colleges and among different years in the same colleges.

At best, these two predictors provide only a rough index of how well an individual student will do in college, but for purposes of comparing groups of students, as has been done in this study, these two types of data allow meaningful and educationally significant comparisons to be made.

A.C.E. SCORES

Test scores were available for 22,516 of the 24,892 students who expressed post-high-school plans. The means and standard deviations for these students are presented in Table 3.

The mean score for the total group was 96.15 with a standard deviation of 24.64. The mean score for the 9703 boys was 97.57 and the standard deviation 24.97; the mean score for the 12,813 girls was 95.07 and the standard deviation 24.34. The difference between the means of the boys and girls was statistically significant beyond the .01 level of probability.

The mean score of the metropolitan boys was 97.64 and the standard deviation 25.19, of the nonfarm boys 99.17 and 24.91 respectively, and of the farm boys 94.42 and 24.39 respectively. The differences between these means were all statistically significant beyond the .05 level of probability. The mean score of the metropolitan girls was 95.18 and the standard deviation was 24.72. Means and standard deviations for the nonfarm girls were 97.91 and 24.16 respectively, and for the farm girls 91.54 and 23.66 respectively. The differences between these means were all statistically significant beyond the .01 level of probability.

Thus the nonfarm boys and girls tended to obtain higher A.C.E. scores than did the metropolitan boys and girls and the metropolitan students tended to obtain higher scores than did the farm students.

These small but statistically significant differences between the sexes and among the geographical groups were dwarfed when compared with the differences found among the students who had different plans for after high school. The group with the highest mean score, 109.47, was the group of nonfarm boys planning on college, and the group with the lowest mean score, 85.62, was the group of metropolitan boys planning on going to other schools. The accompanying tabulation gives the mean scores for the boys and girls with differing plans without regard for geographical area. The differences among the means of the boys were all significant beyond the .05 level of probability, with the excep-

Plan	Mean A.C.E. Scores	
	Boys	Girls
College	107.91	105.21
Jobs	88.46	87.58
Other schools	90.06	91.09
Military service	90.71	
Nursing		98.17

Table 3. Mean Scores and Standard Deviations on the American Council on Education Psychological Examination for Boys and Girls with Different Plans Who Came from Different Areas.

Plan	Metropolitan Group			Nonfarm Group			Farm Group			All Groups		
	Mean	S.D.	N	Mean	S.D.	N	Mean	S.D.	N	Mean	S.D.	N
BOYS												
Job................	87.78	22.63	1,159	89.52	22.71	1,329	87.78	22.56	919	88.46	22.65	3,407
College...........	107.12	23.45	1,900	109.47	23.15	1,798	105.95	23.76	664	107.91	23.42	4,362
Other school......	85.62	23.59	416	92.93	22.92	491	91.41	22.01	324	90.06	23.14	1,231
Military service...	89.12	23.04	187	91.34	24.00	337	91.18	24.52	179	90.71	23.90	703
All plans, boys...	97.64	25.19	3,662	99.17	24.91	3,955	94.42	24.39	2,086	97.57	24.97	9,703
GIRLS												
Job................	87.53	23.06	1,792	88.97	22.77	1,844	86.31	22.53	1,933	87.58	22.83	5,569
College...........	105.19	23.13	1,739	107.59	22.69	1,807	101.04	22.65	1,024	105.21	22.98	4,570
Other school......	88.44	22.84	510	94.91	22.82	669	89.45	23.17	645	91.09	23.44	1,824
Nursing	94.70	23.50	208	100.72	21.72	355	97.54	24.09	287	98.17	23.12	850
All plans, girls.........	95.18	24.72	4,249	97.91	24.16	4,675	91.54	23.66	3,889	95.07	24.34	12,813
All plans, boys and girls...	96.32	24.97	7,911	98.49	24.50	8,630	92.54	23.97	5,975	96.15	24.64	22,516

tion of the difference between the means of boys planning on military service and of boys planning on other schools. The differences among the means of the girls were all statistically significant beyond the .01 level of probability.

For the boys and girls planning on college and jobs, the differences tended to favor the metropolitan students over the farm students, but the farm boys and girls planning on other schools and the farm girls planning on nursing tended to obtain higher mean scores than did the metropolitan youth with corresponding plans. The higher ability youth from cities and towns more often go to college than do those from farms, while the high-ability students from farms tend to go more often to other schools than do such students from cities and towns.

These figures left little doubt that there were some differences in test scores related to both sex and geographical area and much larger differences related to after-high-school plans. More educational significance, however, should be attached to the extent of overlapping, as shown in Tables 4 and 5, than to the differences in means that have just been discussed.

Of the boys planning on jobs, 19 per cent obtained scores that reached or exceeded the median score of the boys planning on college. Twenty per cent of the boys planning on other schools and 23 per cent of the boys planning on military service had scores that equaled or exceeded the median for the boys planning on college. Of the girls planning on jobs, 21 per cent reached or exceeded the median for girls planning on college and similar figures for girls planning on other schools and on nursing were 26 and 38 per cent respectively. Thus, almost one quarter of the students not planning on college did at least as well on this college aptitude test as did the average student who was planning on college.

Table 6 presents the percentages of students reaching or exceeding the median test score for each sex according to area and plan. To illustrate, of the 1159 metropolitan boys planning on jobs, 18 per cent obtained scores equaling or exceeding 109.7, the median score of all the 4362 boys planning on college. Of the 355 nonfarm girls planning on nursing, 49 per cent obtained scores equaling or exceeding 107.1, the median score of all the 4570 girls planning on college.

A raw score of 120 on the A.C.E. indicates that a student will be in approximately the upper 15–20 per cent of his high school class, as far as college aptitude is concerned, and that he will be in the upper quarter

Table 4. Distributions of Scores on the American Council on Education Psychological Examination for Boys with Different Plans Who Came from Different Areas.

A.C.E. Score	Boys Planning to Get a Job			Boys Planning to Go to College			Boys Planning to Go to Other Schools			Boys Planning to Enter Military Service		
	Metro-politan	Non-farm	Farm	Metro-politan	Non-farm	Farm	Metro-politan	Non-farm	Farm	Metro-politan	Non-farm	Farm
0–9	0	0	0	0	0	0	1	0	0	0	0	0
10–19	0	0	0	0	1	0	0	0	0	0	0	0
20–29	3	1	6	5	0	0	2	1	1	0	1	1
30–39	11	14	9	6	2	2	13	2	0	3	4	1
40–49	45	42	29	17	8	4	9	11	6	10	10	6
50–59	83	66	54	22	21	9	26	24	15	6	13	15
60–69	109	120	83	66	52	30	47	37	28	16	29	9
70–79	147	186	133	98	85	48	65	60	53	21	57	23
80–89	179	237	163	186	186	65	66	76	45	35	50	28
90–99	219	213	161	258	226	99	67	85	57	36	41	25
100–109	158	177	128	330	281	95	57	79	54	27	46	26
110–119	109	147	83	327	304	121	37	53	30	16	40	26
120–129	71	85	40	264	270	79	13	39	20	8	27	11
130–139	20	29	21	171	191	59	9	13	9	7	16	4
140–149	5	11	7	102	117	39	2	8	6	2	3	3
150–159	0	0	2	37	38	10	2	3	0	0	0	0
160–169	0	0	0	10	12	3	0	0	0	0	0	1
170–179	0	1	0	1	3	0	0	0	0	0	0	0
180–189	0	0	0	0	1	0	0	0	0	0	0	0
190–199	0	0	0	0	0	1	0	0	0	0	0	0
Total	1,159	1,329	919	1,900	1,798	664	416	491	324	187	337	179

Table 5. Distributions of Scores on the American Council on Education Psychological Examination for Girls with Different Plans Who Came from Different Areas.

A.C.E. Score	Girls Planning to Get a Job			Girls Planning to Go to College			Girls Planning to Go to Other Schools			Girls Planning to Enter Nursing		
	Metro-politan	Non-farm	Farm	Metro-politan	Non-farm	Farm	Metro-politan	Non-farm	Farm	Metro-politan	Non-farm	Farm
0–9	0	0	0	0	0	0	0	0	0	0	0	0
10–19	0	1	1	0	0	0	1	0	0	0	0	0
20–29	7	5	8	2	0	0	1	2	2	0	0	1
30–39	30	21	28	4	3	5	7	10	11	1	0	1
40–49	79	64	73	17	6	14	14	14	13	4	4	7
50–59	109	92	129	32	36	22	31	23	46	9	10	12
60–69	156	191	206	68	54	38	56	39	58	18	20	22
70–79	262	240	277	108	100	91	71	69	92	25	25	25
80–89	285	322	366	173	176	143	75	101	95	29	49	26
90–99	307	312	304	236	231	138	90	112	100	38	54	51
100–109	265	269	248	319	310	200	77	123	105	28	61	50
110–119	162	167	164	297	339	150	42	89	60	23	58	38
120–129	81	104	89	250	243	114	32	59	42	18	50	30
130–139	38	36	27	132	176	77	10	18	16	10	21	19
140–149	7	12	10	63	89	21	1	7	5	4	0	4
150–159	3	8	2	29	35	10	2	3	0	1	1	1
160–169	1	0	1	6	7	1	0	0	0	0	2	0
170–179	0	0	0	2	2	0	0	0	0	0	0	0
180–189	0	0	0	1	0	0	0	0	0	0	0	0
190–199	0	0	0	0	0	0	0	0	0	0	0	0
Total	1,792	1,844	1,933	1,739	1,807	1,024	510	669	645	208	355	287

103

Table 6. Percentage of Boys and Girls with Different After-High-School Plans and from Different Areas Who Obtained American Council on Education Psychological Examination Scores Equaling or Exceeding the Median Score of the Like-Sex Students Planning on College

Plan	Metro-politan Group	Nonfarm Group	Farm Group	All Groups
	BOYS			
Job	18	21	17	19
Other school.................	16	24	20	20
Military service..............	18	26	25	23
College	48	52	47	50
	GIRLS			
Job	21	22	19	20
Other school.................	23	32	24	26
Nursing	31	42	36	38
College	50	54	42	50

of Minnesota college freshmen. Of the 22,516 students for whom A.C.E. scores were available, 18 per cent had scores of 120 or above. Of the 9703 boys being considered for whom scores were available, 1906, or 19 per cent, had scores of 120 or above. Of the 12,813 girls for whom scores were available, 2033, or 16 per cent, had scores of 120 or above. Planning on college was typical of three out of every four high-ability boys as compared with fewer than two out of every four boys in general, regardless of ability; and, relatively, almost twice as many high-ability girls were planning on college as were girls in general, regardless of ability. The percentages with the various plans in the total groups and in the groups with scores of 120 and above are shown in the accompanying tabulation.

If we use this score of 120 or above to indicate a superior student, 9

	Boys		Girls	
Plan	All	Scores above 120	All	Scores above 120
College	45	74	36	62
Job	35	15	43	21
Other school	13	7	14	10
Military service	7	4		
Nursing			7	8

per cent of the boys planning to get jobs, 10 per cent of the boys planning to go to other schools, 12 per cent of the boys planning to enter military service, and 32 per cent of the boys planning to go to college were superior students. For the girls, 8 per cent of those planning to go to other schools, 19 per cent planning to enter nursing, and 28 per cent planning to go to college were superior students.

Of the boys planning on college, 11 per cent obtained scores no higher than the median score for boys planning on jobs. Of the girls planning on college, 22 per cent obtained scores no higher than the median for girls planning on jobs. The range of scores for students planning on college was somewhat greater than the ranges for other groups, because it was extended at the upper end and because some students planning on college obtained scores just as low as those in the other groups.

Table 7 presents, by sex and by area, the numbers and percentages of students who obtained scores of 120 or above and who planned to go to college, and corresponding data for the students who planned to obtain jobs. Of the college-planning students, 30 per cent obtained scores of 120 or above and of the students planning on working, 8 per cent obtained scores that high. If one is willing to accept a score of 120 as indicative of more than enough ability to do college work, it is quite apparent that the group planning to attend college contained a much higher percentage of the high-ability students than were to be found in the group as a whole or in the group planning to work.

In summary, after-high-school plans were closely related to college aptitude test scores. In turn, this relationship was associated with differences in sex and with differences in area, but sex and area differences in aptitude scores were of relatively minor importance when compared with the differences associated with plans.

Study of the overlap of test scores of groups with different plans revealed that no one type of plan for after high school was uniformly characteristic of either high- or low-ability students. Students with very high test scores usually planned on college, and students of high ability, as shown by scores of 120 or above, planned on college almost twice as frequently as did students in general, but a large number of high-ability students did not plan on college. Of the 1926 high-ability boys, 498 were not planning on college, and of the 2033 high-ability girls, 775 were not planning on college. Thus there were in Minnesota 1273 high-ability students not planning on college, or a number approximately double the

Table 7. Number and Percentage of Students Planning to Attend College, of Students Planning to Get Jobs, and of the Total Group of Students Having American Council on Education Psychological Examination Scores of 120 or above*

Area Group	Students Planning to Go to College			Students Planning to Get a Job			Total Group of Students		
	Total Number	Number with Scores above 120	Percentage with Scores above 120	Total Number	Number with Scores above 120	Percentage with Scores above 120	Total Number	Number with Scores above 120	Percentage with Scores above 120
BOYS									
Metropolitan	1,900	585	31	1,159	96	8	3,662	744	20
Nonfarm	1,798	632	35	1,329	126	9	3,955	867	22
Farm	664	191	29	919	70	8	2,086	315	15
All groups, boys	4,362	1,408	32	3,407	292	9	9,703	1,926	20
GIRLS									
Metropolitan	1,739	483	28	1,792	130	7	4,249	691	16
Nonfarm	1,807	552	31	1,844	160	9	4,675	873	19
Farm	1,024	223	22	1,933	129	7	3,889	469	12
All groups, girls	4,570	1,258	28	5,569	419	8	12,813	2,033	16
All groups, boys and girls	8,932	2,666	30	8,976	711	8	22,516	3,959	18

* For fewer than 2,500 of the students A.C.E. scores were not available. These students, of course, cannot be included here.

size of the largest freshman class entering any private college in Minnesota. Minnesota's colleges have far from exhausted the state's pool of high-ability people.

HIGH SCHOOL PERCENTILE RANK

A student's high school percentile rank indicates his relative standing in his high school graduating class. The grades upon which these ranks are based are the grades earned up through the first semester of the senior year. The percentile rank expresses where a student would stand if there were 100 students in his class. A percentile rank of 62 indicates that the student's high school average during his first three and one-half years in high school is superior to the averages of 62 per cent of his classmates, and that he is in the upper 38 per cent of his class.

Table 8 shows that when comparisons of mean high school percentile ranks were made between boys and girls coming from the same areas, and with comparable plans, in every case a statistically significant difference favoring the girls was found.

The area differences in mean high school rank were not large when comparisons were made between like-sex and like-plan groups coming from different areas. This is not surprising when one remembers that the high school percentile rank has a local point of reference. The distributions of high school percentile rank in various schools and in different areas should all be similar.

For each sex, and for each area, the group planning on going to college was the group with the highest average high school percentile rank and the groups with the lowest average high school percentile rank were the groups planning on jobs and military service. The group planning to go to other schools had mean high school percentile ranks between the means of the other groups; the girls planning on nursing had mean high school percentile ranks second only to the means of the girls planning on college.

The average boy planning on college had a rank of 57, the average girl a rank of 67. The median high school percentile rank for boys planning on college was 59.70, for girls planning on college 75.36.

Tables 9 and 10 present the distribution of high school ranks for these groups. Of the boys not planning on college, 18 per cent had high school percentile ranks equaling or exceeding the median for boys planning on college, and of the girls not planning on college, 25 per cent had high

Table 8. Means and Standard Deviations on High School Percentile Ranks for Boys and Girls with Different Plans Who Came from Different Areas

Plan	Metropolitan Group			Nonfarm Group			Farm Group			All Groups		
	Mean	S.D.	N	Mean	S.D.	N	Mean	S.D.	N	Mean	S.D.	N
BOYS												
Job	33.89	24.48	1,132	32.94	24.41	1,328	33.75	23.77	921	33.48	24.26	3,381
College	55.66	28.09	1,922	58.35	27.32	1,802	58.98	27.80	666	57.27	27.76	4,390
Other school	37.23	24.95	409	37.38	26.49	490	38.42	25.28	324	37.61	25.66	1,223
Military service	32.97	23.35	184	33.22	25.84	339	29.64	24.51	180	32.24	24.91	703
All plans, boys	45.69	28.48	3,647	45.08	28.85	3,959	42.16	27.97	2,091	44.68	28.56	9,697
GIRLS												
Job	50.39	26.72	1,784	48.47	27.43	1,839	48.08	27.36	1,950	48.95	27.20	5,573
College	66.57	26.64	1,741	69.70	24.22	1,811	66.44	24.77	1,027	67.78	25.33	4,579
Other school	52.23	27.52	507	56.76	26.56	668	56.30	27.00	649	55.37	26.99	1,824
Nursing	60.01	26.40	208	63.65	24.50	356	62.01	26.59	291	62.21	25.72	855
All plans, girls	57.73	27.83	4,240	59.04	27.57	4,674	55.29	27.73	3,917	57.46	27.75	12,831
All plans, boys and girls	52.16	28.77	7,887	52.64	29.01	8,633	50.72	28.51	6,008	51.96	28.80	22,528

Table 9. Distribution of High School Percentile Ranks for Boys with Different Plans Who Came from Different Areas

High School Percentile Rank	Boys Planning to Get a Job			Boys Planning to Go to College			Boys Planning to Go to Other School			Boys Planning to Enter Military Service		
	Metro-politan	Non-farm	Farm	Metro-politan	Non-farm	Farm	Metro-politan	Non-farm	Farm	Metro-politan	Non-farm	Farm
0–4	99	156	89	49	33	20	29	34	21	14	49	25
5–9	127	131	70	58	52	17	33	42	27	18	34	15
10–14	105	114	89	84	47	21	36	39	23	17	31	16
15–19	86	78	93	81	61	21	33	25	25	18	22	21
20–24	67	111	61	86	57	20	25	41	25	17	27	10
25–29	78	94	52	77	86	25	28	34	18	19	17	9
30–34	77	94	70	87	78	24	24	33	15	12	17	18
35–39	67	91	47	81	79	26	29	35	24	6	20	4
40–44	74	56	56	90	109	26	23	34	21	12	16	9
45–49	53	59	45	94	82	39	15	26	13	8	10	8
50–54	51	67	47	107	95	35	19	23	23	9	19	7
55–59	48	52	47	116	105	43	20	31	17	6	19	9
60–64	49	53	47	100	106	38	24	18	16	7	12	7
65–69	40	45	27	118	105	38	29	10	14	3	9	6
70–74	24	33	28	100	99	44	6	18	12	6	9	5
75–79	30	34	19	98	107	36	12	11	9	1	10	2
80–84	22	17	10	121	121	45	8	8	8	6	5	5
85–89	14	25	10	123	111	49	7	12	2	4	5	2
90–94	11	12	9	114	124	48	7	9	6	0	5	1
95–99	10	4	2	111	89	21	1	3	1	1	0	0
100	0	2	3	27	56	30	1	4	4	0	3	1
Total	1,132	1,328	921	1,922	1,802	666	409	490	324	184	339	180

Table 10. Distribution of High School Percentile Ranks for Girls with Different Plans Who Came from Different Areas

High School Percentile Rank	Girls Planning to Get a Job			Girls Planning to Go to College			Girls Planning to Go to Other School			Girls Planning to Enter Nursing		
	Metropolitan	Non-farm	Farm	Metropolitan	Non-farm	Farm	Metropolitan	Non-farm	Farm	Metropolitan	Non-farm	Farm
0–4	50	65	93	25	10	5	17	19	15	3	4	7
5–9	77	86	90	32	16	8	23	13	15	2	4	4
10–14	68	100	103	26	21	17	26	16	20	4	7	4
15–19	78	99	99	36	31	15	16	26	22	9	9	10
20–24	106	117	99	44	26	15	21	23	40	5	6	10
25–29	97	91	98	56	40	43	23	29	27	11	11	8
30–34	94	95	104	57	43	30	26	38	24	8	8	12
35–39	108	105	115	65	48	32	26	24	23	11	11	12
40–44	105	91	108	76	59	32	23	41	39	14	18	14
45–49	92	104	91	69	49	47	26	29	32	9	27	10
50–54	108	98	114	77	75	40	27	39	35	12	22	13
55–59	102	100	121	63	70	56	36	46	46	7	16	20
60–64	98	110	105	94	95	53	28	32	35	20	16	17
65–69	95	92	103	99	113	54	21	42	36	7	32	14
70–74	98	87	102	98	121	84	44	44	44	10	28	19
75–79	102	104	101	133	137	82	25	48	44	15	20	26
80–84	95	86	97	130	156	83	27	44	40	13	35	22
85–89	76	73	98	161	213	99	30	44	44	13	30	20
90–94	64	68	53	165	189	106	20	33	30	18	26	27
95–99	65	49	23	184	183	49	18	12	13	13	18	12
100	6	19	33	51	116	77	4	20	25	4	8	10
Totals	1,784	1,839	1,950	1,741	1,811	1,027	507	668	649	208	356	291

school percentile ranks equaling or exceeding the median for girls planning on college.

There were 229 boys and 96 girls in the lower 10 per cent of their high school classes planning on college and 807 boys and 327 girls in the lower quarter of their class planning on college. The low-ranking students planning on college tended to come from no one of the three areas in particular. A substantial number of high school students planning on college, approximately 13 per cent, had been poor performers, academically at least, in high school.

Only 40 of the 374 boys who were in the upper 5 per cent of their class were not planning on college but 362 of the 1022 girls in the upper 5 per cent of their class were not planning on college. Almost three times as many girls as boys were in the upper 5 per cent of their high school classes, but almost ten times as many of the girls as of the boys in this upper group did not plan on college.

🚩 8

Description of Those Who Planned
to Go to College

AN ATTEMPT will be made in this chapter and those following to describe groups of high school seniors who had differing plans.* By knowing more about the group planning on college, the group planning on working, and the groups with other plans, high school and personnel workers will be able to understand these young people better.

Of the 24,898 high school seniors who expressed some plan for the year following graduation, 8993 were planning on going to college. It is perhaps safe to generalize that of all high school seniors graduating in Minnesota in 1950, 36 per cent were seriously considering college.

SEX DIFFERENCES

As we indicated in Chapter 6 significant sex differences appeared regarding after-high-school plans for college. Of all the male students in the total group with after-high-school plans, 39 per cent were planning on college. Of all the female students, 34 per cent were planning on college. Sex differences were not consistent, however, when the total group was divided according to whether students lived in metropolitan areas, in nonfarm areas, or on farms. Of the boys who lived on farms, only 20 per cent were planning on attending college, whereas of the girls who lived on farms, 24 per cent were planning on college. Thus, although there was a tendency in metropolitan areas and in small towns

---

* Multilith copies of tables presenting the distribution of all variables reported in this study by sex, geographical location, and after-high-school plans can be obtained from the Student Counseling Bureau, University of Minnesota, Minneapolis, Minnesota. These distributions are available, first, for the entire group, and, second, for the group of students obtaining scores of 120 or above on the American Council on Education Psychological Examination.

for more boys than girls to plan on college, this tendency was reversed for farm students.

The differences regarding college plans among the metropolitan, non-farm, and farm groups were large. Of the metropolitan boys, one half were planning on attending college whereas of the farm boys, only 20 per cent were planning on college. Of the girls who came from metropolitan areas, 40 per cent were planning on college and of the girls from farms, 24 per cent were planning on college. About twice as many high school students coming from metropolitan areas were planning on college as were students coming from farms.

The students coming from nonfarm areas tended to resemble the metropolitan students to a greater extent in this regard than they resembled the farm students. Somewhat fewer of the nonfarm than of the metropolitan youth planned on college but these differences were not large. More than twice as many nonmetropolitan boys, however, were planning on college as were boys coming from farms. Thus, there was a general progression: more high school students from metropolitan areas were planning on college than were students from nonfarm and farm areas, and more students from nonfarm areas were planning on college than were students from farm areas. Rural life did not seem to be conducive to the development of attitudes favoring college attendance.

The median age of the college-planning students when they completed the questionnaire was approximately 17.5 years. The median age was 17.55 for the metropolitan boys, 17.59 for the nonfarm boys, and 17.31 for the farm boys. The median age was 17.47 for the metropolitan girls planning on college, 17.54 for the nonfarm girls, and 17.49 for the farm girls. Relatively few of these boys and girls, perhaps no more than 12 to 15 per cent, would be over 18 when they graduated from high school. Only twelve were married at the time they expressed their plans for college and only forty-three (twenty-two boys and twenty-one girls) said they planned to be married within the next year.

Students planning on college tended to come from unbroken homes. About 94 per cent said that their fathers were still alive and about 97 per cent said their mothers were still living. Fewer than 6 per cent said they came from homes where the parents were either divorced or separated. Thus approximately 90 per cent of the college-planning students came from unbroken homes.

OCCUPATION OF PARENTS

Parental occupation was one of the most significant factors related to plans for attending college. Of the college-planning youth coming from the metropolitan and nonfarm areas, approximately 15 per cent were from homes where the father was engaged in a profession and slightly over 25 per cent were from homes where the father owned or managed a business. Naturally, most of the fathers of the students who came from farms were classified as farmers, although a small proportion were classified in each of the other occupational groups.

In comparing metropolitan and nonfarm students planning on attending college, a few significant differences appeared in terms of parental occupation. For example, of the metropolitan boys planning on college, 21 per cent came from homes where the father owned or managed a business, whereas of the nonfarm boys planning on college, 31 per cent came from such homes. Of the metropolitan boys, 12 per cent had fathers who were office workers, compared with 6 per cent of the nonfarm boys. Similar geographical differences were found when the girls were compared.

In the metropolitan group planning on college, 19 per cent had fathers who were in the skilled trades and 12 per cent had fathers who worked in factories. Thus approximately one third of the Minnesota high school seniors planning on college came from homes where there was definitely not a college background, so far as could be inferred from the fathers' occupations.

EDUCATION OF PARENTS AND SIBLINGS

The inference about noncollege backgrounds was verified by the information available regarding the education of the fathers. Of the fathers of the metropolitan college-planning boys, 33 per cent had at one time or another attended college, 24 per cent were college graduates, 36 per cent were not high school graduates, and 22 per cent had gone no further than the eighth grade. The fathers' modal education for the group of metropolitan boys planning on college was high school graduation. In the nonfarm group, statistically significantly more of the students planning on college had fathers with no more than an eighth-grade education than was true for metropolitan students, but the percentage with fathers who were college graduates tended to be about the same as for the metropolitan group. Of the fathers of farm youth planning on college, 64 per cent had had no more than an eighth-grade education, only 9 per cent had attended college at all, and 4 per cent were college graduates. Here was perhaps one quite obvious explanation of why a much larger proportion of the metropolitan students planned on college than did the rural students: many more of the metropolitan students had fathers with high school and college educations.

Although the metropolitan, nonfarm, and farm youth planning on college were differentiated on the basis of their mothers' education, the differences, shown in the accompanying tabulation, were not as great as those for their fathers' education. The picture of the girls planning on college was very much the same as that for the boys with these plans.

	Education of Mothers	
	Some College Training	*None Beyond Eighth Grade*
Metropolitan boys	28%	19%
Nonfarm boys	32	25
Farm boys	26	44

In summary, metropolitan boys and girls planning on college tended to come from homes where the parents had had some college training more often than did farm boys and girls who were planning on college. Regardless of the area in which they lived, however, and regardless of sex, most high school students planning on college had parents who did not attend college and a large proportion of these students had parents with less than a high school education. For the most part, students planning on college today have developed attitudes toward college not as a result of parental college experiences but rather as a result of a variety of other factors. Our college population today is primarily a "first generation" population.

We made an attempt to arrive at the family pattern of education by asking about the education of older brothers or sisters. Slightly more than one half of the entire group of seniors had no older brothers and approximately the same number had no older sisters. Of the metropolitan group planning on college, over one half of the students who had older brothers indicated that those brothers had some college experience.

For the farm boys planning on college, the modal education of older brothers was high school graduation, whereas for the metropolitan and nonfarm boys planning on college, the modal education of older brothers was some college. Figures for the girls with older brothers were almost identical.

The modal education for older sisters of metropolitan boys planning on college was high school graduation. The nonfarm boys and the farm boys had more older sisters with advanced schooling than did the metropolitan boys. One might hazard a guess here that in a nonmetropolitan family where one or more daughters had gone to college there was an increased probability that their brothers would attend college also. Inasmuch as more boys go to college than girls, one might assume a priority. Perhaps boys are given the first chance for college in preference to girls in the family. If a girl is attending college, it may be because it is possible for her brothers also to attend college. Quite definitely there is a family pattern. The amount of education a child receives is in part determined by the amount of his parents' education, and there is a direct relationship between the amount of education a child has had or is planning and the amount of education obtained by his siblings.

LANGUAGE BACKGROUND

Approximately one third of the metropolitan and nonfarm students planning on college and almost one half of the farm students came from bilingual homes. For the most part, the second languages reflected the Scandinavian and Germanic backgrounds of these students. In the metropolitan area, 8 per cent of the boys and 7 per cent of the girls planning on college spoke German at home, whereas in the nonfarm area, 12 per cent of the boys and 13 per cent of the girls spoke German. In the farm group, 17 per cent of the boys and 16 per cent of the girls spoke German at home. Only 5 per cent of the metropolitan group planning on college and practically none of the nonfarm or farm youth came from Yiddish-speaking homes. These nationality backgrounds found expression not only in varying language patterns but also in varying family mores, social attitudes, and parental expectations.

FAMILY INCOME

The differences in the sources of family income for the college-planning groups are shown in accompanying tabulation.

Most of the students who planned on college came from homes where income was based on profit or a fixed salary. To the extent that wages are indicative of employment in a skilled or semiskilled trade, we can conclude that relatively few of the parents of the college-planning students were in skilled trades. Nevertheless, approximately 25 per cent of all the high school seniors planning on college did come from homes where income was derived from wages.

Not only was the source of family income related to after-high-school plans but the size of the family income was also important. Students

	Profits or Fees	Salaries	Wages
Metropolitan group	25%	42%	30%
Nonfarm group	34	37	24
Farm group	81	7	9

were not asked to estimate the size of the income but rather to categorize the family's way of living. Essentially, this was a question of how the child perceived the amount of money the family had in terms of the family's need.

Of the metropolitan youth planning on college, only 4 per cent indicated that their families were hard up or sometimes hard up and approximately 20 per cent indicated that their families had necessities although perhaps not much more. Approximately 65 per cent of the metropolitan students indicated that their families were comfortable, and 14 per cent indicated that their families were well-to-do. There were no significant sex differences. The figures for the nonfarm group were approximately the same as for the metropolitan group, as were the figures for the farm group.

Of all the students who planned on college, slightly over 60 per cent indicated that they came from economically comfortable homes and between 10 and 15 per cent indicated that they came from well-to-do homes. Only 4 or 5 per cent came from homes where there seemed to be a severe economic problem. The remaining 20 to 25 per cent came from homes having the necessities but not too many of the luxuries. In general, the students planning on college perceived themselves as coming from homes well above the subsistence level although a small minority came from homes economically insecure.

FINANCIAL AID FROM FAMILIES

Closely related to economic status of the home was the problem of how much money these students could expect from their families to help pay for their college expenses. Here was one of the few instances in this study where, although there were no significant differences between the metropolitan, nonfarm, and farm groups, there were significant sex differences.

Of the boys planning on college, between 10 and 15 per cent expected their families to pay all their expenses; but approximately one third of all the girls planning on college expected to receive such support from their families. Approximately one third of both the boys and the girls expected their families to pay most but not all their expenses. About 45 per cent of the boys expected their families to pay only some of their expenses, whereas only about 28 per cent of the girls expected this. Between 10 and 15 per cent of the boys expected no financial support from their families; only 5 per cent of the girls expected so little. In general, over one half of the students planning on going to college expected their families to pay most of their expenses and over 90 per cent of them expected their families to help them in some way; only a relatively small number planned on college with the expectation of no financial support from their families.

These figures indicate that girls are less willing than boys to attend college with little assurance from their families of financial help, or perhaps the families themselves are more reluctant to have their daughters attend college without such assurance. The prevailing belief, whether correct or incorrect, is that boys have less difficulty than girls in financing their own college education — or at least a large share of it. Some parents who might be reluctant to have their daughters leave home with $200, expecting to earn the rest of the money they would need while in college, would have no such reluctance when it came time for their sons to go to college.

FAMILIES' ATTITUDES TOWARD COLLEGE

The students were also asked to indicate how their families felt about their going to college. No consistent sex differences were present. Of the metropolitan boys planning on college, 15 per cent said their families insisted they go, whereas of the farm boys planning on college, only 4 per cent said their families insisted they go. Comparable figures for the girls were 10 and 4 per cent. Roughly, 80 per cent of all the students said their families wanted them to go to college. Five per cent of the metropolitan boys and 19 per cent of the farm boys said their families were indifferent. For the girls, comparable figures were 7 and 16 per cent. In the case of no group did more than 1 per cent of the parents show opposition to college-going plans, as inferred from the student's saying his family did not want him to go or would not allow him to go to college. This suggests infrequent overt conflict between a student and his parents over plans to attend college.

Perhaps another explanation may be found here of why relatively few farm youth are interested in college. Family attitudes — enthusiasm or indifference — can be expected to influence the attitudes of children, and farm youth perceived their families as being much less interested in college than did the students coming from other sections of the state. In general, however, parents of the students planning on college were well disposed toward college, well over three quarters of them wanting their children to attend an institution of higher learning.

HIGH SCHOOL CURRICULUMS

In considering the high school curriculums in which the college-planning students were enrolled, one must remember that not all high schools in the state had equally diverse curriculums and many of the metropolitan high schools had a greater variety of courses for the student to choose from than did most of the high schools in the nonmetropolitan area. No pertinent sex differences appeared in the curriculums chosen by college-planning students, but there were several significant geographical differences. For instance, of the metropolitan boys planning on college, 74 per cent took a college preparatory course in high school and only 19 per cent took a general high school course; of the farm boys, 45 per cent took a college preparatory course and 39 per cent took a general course. The nonfarm group falls between these other two groups. Figures were somewhat comparable for the girls: 74 per cent of the metropolitan girls planning on college took a college preparatory course and only 17 per cent took a general course, whereas 39 per cent of the farm girls planning on college took the college preparatory course and 42 per cent took a general course. Interesting to note is the fact that 14 per cent of the nonfarm girls planning on college and 18 per cent of the farm girls took a commercial course. Relatively few of the college-planning boys took shop courses, fewer than 4 per cent, although 11 per cent of the farm boys planning on college took an agricultural course.

The college-planning students tended to choose their high school courses because of vocational and interest factors. The most frequently given reason for selecting a high school course was that it fit vocational plans. (The girls especially indicated they were influenced by vocational plans.) Second in importance was that the course was interesting, and third, that the parents advised it. Only 5 per cent of the metropolitan boys planning on college indicated they took their course because it was the only one offered; but 17 per cent of the farm boys and girls planning on college reported this reason. Fewer than 10 per cent of the college-planning students attributed their choice of a high school course to counseling they had received from a high school counselor, and only about 5 per cent attributed their choice to teachers' advice or counseling. In other words, no more than 15 per cent of the high school seniors planning on college reported that counseling in the high schools was an important determinant, as they perceived it, in their selection of a high school curriculum. The sectional differences were perhaps due to more counselors being available in metropolitan areas than in nonmetropolitan areas. About 4 per cent of the students did not know why they had selected their high school curriculum. No important sex differences appeared in the reasons given for choosing courses.

OCCUPATIONAL GOALS

The students who were planning on college were asked to name the occupations they would like to be in at the end of ten years. Professional occupations were named by 60 per cent of the metropolitan and nonfarm boys and 50 per cent of the farm boys. Farming was named by 29 per cent of the farm boys but by only 1 to 2 per cent of the nonfarm and metropolitan boys. Five per cent of the boys were undecided. Twice as many metropolitan and nonfarm boys as farm boys named semiprofessional, clerical, and skilled trade jobs.

The figures for the girls are shown in the tabulation.

	Professional	Semiprofessional	Housewives
Farm girls	42%	13%	40%
Metropolitan girls	33	23	40
Nonfarm girls	36	16	40

The extent to which these occupational goals were influenced by parents was perhaps indicated by answers to the question "What occupation do your parents wish you to follow?" Approximately one third of the families of metropolitan and nonfarm boys hoped for professional jobs for their sons, as compared with 29 per cent of the families of farm youth planning on college. About twice as many metropolitan and non-farm parents hoped their sons would go into semiprofessional and clerical and skilled trades jobs as was true for the parents of farm youth. Hardly any of the metropolitan and nonfarm parents wished their children to become farmers, but 20 per cent of the farm parents wished their sons to become farmers. The girls from the farms indicated that 43 per cent of them had parents who hoped they would go into professional jobs, whereas the comparable figures for the nonfarm and metropolitan girls were only 34 per cent and 24 per cent. About 16 per cent of the girls indicated their parents hoped they would enter semiprofessional jobs as compared with about 6 per cent of the boys' parents. Almost one half of the parents of both boys and girls, according to their children, were undecided as to what occupation their children should enter.

In general, it appeared that the parents of boys set occupational goals considerably higher than did the parents of girls. The parents of boys coming from metropolitan areas had goals for their sons essentially little different from the goals set by parents of nonfarm boys; but parents of farm youth had somewhat different goals inasmuch as they hoped that many more of their sons would enter farming and that many more of their daughters would go into professional jobs. For the most part, the goals selected by the parents seemed to agree quite well with the goals selected by the children. In most cases, apparently, pressures that parents place on children to achieve certain occupational goals are not direct but rather are more subtle and indirect pressures that operate over a long period of time.

MATERIAL POSSESSIONS

Several questions were asked concerning the equipment available in homes, and some of the information elicited was helpful in understanding the ecology of the students planning on college. There were no significant sex differences in the answers to these questions.

Practically all the metropolitan and nonfarm students and almost two thirds of the farm students had running water in their homes. Almost all the metropolitan and nonfarm youth but only about one half of the farm youth had both hot and cold running water in their homes. Of the metropolitan boys planning on college, 97 per cent lived in homes with central heating; 90 per cent of the nonfarm boys and 68 per cent of the farm boys also reported central heating.

Most of these students reported mechanical refrigeration in their homes — 96 per cent of the metropolitan boys, 92 per cent of the non-farm boys, and 80 per cent of the farm boys. Almost all the metropolitan homes, 92 per cent of the nonfarm homes, and 78 per cent of the farm homes had telephones. More farm boys reported deep freezers available (either rented or owned) in their homes than did other boys: over 80 per cent of the farm youth compared with slightly fewer than one third of the metropolitan boys and almost one half of the nonfarm boys. Almost all the metropolitan and nonfarm youth and well over 90 per cent of those from farms had electricity in their homes.

The three groups did not differ on the basis of home ownership, with approximately 82 per cent of the college-planning students coming from families that owned their homes. The homes did differ in size, however, according to area, for the modal metropolitan student came from a six-room house, as did the nonfarm student, whereas the modal farm student came from an eight-room house. However, the farm youth had more people living in their homes. The modal number of people living in the metropolitan and nonfarm home was four; the modal number living in the farm home was five. Thus not only did the farm families have more rooms in their homes, but they also had greater need for those rooms. To obtain some idea of crowding within the house, this question was asked: "How many people sleep in your room besides yourself?" In approximately 60 per cent of the metropolitan and nonfarm homes, the student was the only one who slept in his bedroom, but in the farm homes only 48 per cent of the boys had bedrooms of their own. If this can be considered indicative of crowding, the homes of the farm families seemed to be somewhat more crowded.

Ownership of automobiles also gave an index of family status. Only 1 per cent of the farm families owned no car, whereas 11 per cent of the metropolitan and nonfarm families owned no car. Only 23 per cent of the metropolitan and nonfarm families owned two cars, whereas 42 per cent of the farm families owned two cars. Naturally, the automobile on the farm is actually part of a farmer's occupational equipment and must be so considered. The cars owned by the metropolitan families tended to be newer and more expensive than the cars owned by the nonfarm and farm families, but these differences, although statistically significant, were not large enough to warrant much attention.

Examination of these figures suggested that, in general, the differences between farm families and other families were in the expected direction. They were not nearly as large as they might have been several years before but, nevertheless, the farm youth did tend to have many fewer conveniences in their homes.

BOOKS AND MAGAZINES IN THE HOME

Significant differences were found in the number of books reported in the homes and the types of magazines read when comparisons were made between the metropolitan, the nonfarm, and the farm students planning on college. The metropolitan youth reported approximately twice as many books in their homes as did those from farms, while the nonfarm youth tended to fall between the other two groups. In terms of magazines, there were also significant differences. For instance, 43 per cent of the metropolitan students came from homes subscribing to the *Saturday Evening Post,* but only 26 per cent of the farm homes received that magazine. On the other hand, 35 per cent of the farm students came from homes subscribing to *Collier's,* but only 27 per cent of the metropolitan group did. More metropolitan students had access to *Reader's Digest, Holiday, Newsweek, Harper's, Fortune, Time,* and *Life* in their homes, whereas more farm youth had access to *Look.*

These results reflected the backgrounds of the researchers in the selection of magazines for the list. Since agricultural and farm magazines were not included, 71 per cent of the students from farms (compared with only 52 per cent of the metropolitan students) were unable to find specific titles and could indicate only that their families subscribed to other magazines. Nevertheless, in terms of the magazines included in the list, the differences were relevant. The farm and metropolitan groups did have varied cultural backgrounds, not only in terms of parental education, but also in terms of cultural stimulus found in the homes. This latter varied in kind as well as amount.

MEMBERSHIP IN ORGANIZATIONS

More than one half of the parents of the metropolitan students planning on college belonged to organizations similar to parent-teachers associations. The comparable figure for the farm group was only 37 per cent. Belonging to veterans' organizations seemed to be more typical of small-town parents than of metropolitan or farm parents, while membership in the Masonic Lodge tended to be a small town or metropolitan behavior. Memberships in labor unions and the farm bureau were distributed as one would expect. Memberships in ladies' aids appeared to be a nonmetropolitan sort of behavior, with the mothers of farm girls being most often represented in these groups. Study groups such as literary clubs seemed to be characteristic of the nonfarm mothers and fathers and sports clubs to be typical of metropolitan parents.

In summary, most of the families of these students belonged to at least one organization, the type of organization to which they belonged depending in part upon the place in which the family lived. The fact that 25 per cent of the metropolitan students planning on college had fathers belonging to labor unions supported the previous evidence that the youth planning on college came from a variety of occupational backgrounds and that a large proportion of our present-day college students are coming from what have been traditionally noncollege homes.

9

Description of Those Who
Planned to Get Jobs

OF THE 24,898 students who expressed post-high-school plans, 36 per cent, or the same percentage as that planning on college, indicated they were intending to get jobs after graduating from high school. This group did not include the 1648 students who were planning to work for their parents after graduation.

SEX DIFFERENCES

Relatively more girls than boys were planning on getting jobs, 38 per cent as against 32 per cent. This sex difference appeared in each of the geographic groups, as shown in the tabulation. (However, one should note that when the farm boys planning to work for their parents were added to the other boys planning to work, the figure was 63 per cent. The comparable figure for the two groups of girls was 50 per cent.) Thus, the sex difference noted among those who were planning on college was reversed here for those planning on getting jobs.

	Girls Planning to Work	Boys Planning to Work
Metropolitan group	41%	30%
Farm group	46	28
Nonfarm group	38	32

GEOGRAPHICAL DIFFERENCES

For the boys, regional differences regarding work plans were not as large as were the regional differences regarding college plans. For the girls, there was a rather marked difference between the farm girls and the nonfarm girls: only 38 per cent of the nonfarm girls planned on working while 46 per cent of the farm girls planned to get jobs. Even here, however, the differences among the girls were not as large as they were when comparisons were made among those planning to go to college.

AGE

The median age of the students planning on working was 17 years, but nearly one quarter of the boys and almost 20 per cent of the girls with these plans were 18 years of age or over. When compared with the groups planning on college, almost twice as many of the job-planning students were 18 or over. The median age for metropolitan boys planning on jobs was 17.69, as compared with the median age of 17.55 for the metropolitan boys planning on college. There were no meaningful differences between the median ages of the three groups of boys planning on jobs but there was a general tendency for the girls planning on jobs to be somewhat younger than the boys planning on jobs, just as there was a tendency in the metropolitan and the nonfarm groups for the girls planning on college to be somewhat younger than the boys planning on college. The most striking difference in respect to age, however, was in terms of the significantly greater proportion of 18-year-olds who were planning on working, when compared with the proportion planning on college.

MARITAL STATUS OF STUDENTS

Of the students planning on college, between 99 and 100 per cent were single and not engaged. This was also true for the boys planning on jobs, but of the girls who planned to work, 5 per cent of the metropolitan group, 5 per cent of the nonfarm group, and 4 per cent of the farm group were engaged. Thus immediate marital prospects may have had some influence in determining after-high-school plans for a small number of the girls but for the boys this did not seem to be a matter of great importance.

STATUS OF THE HOME

Of the metropolitan and nonfarm boys planning on working, 12 per cent reported their fathers were no longer alive; this was about half again as many as reported by those boys from these areas who planned on college. In all geographical groups there was a trend for the students planning on working to report more frequently than students planning on college that their fathers were dead: 10 per cent of the job-planners compared with 6 per cent of the college-planners.

The "get a job" groups and the "go to college" groups did not show a difference in terms of whether or not their mothers were living. Approximately 4 per cent of the boys and girls, regardless of where they came from or what their plans were, reported that their mothers were no longer alive. The effect of a student's father upon after-high-school plans could be in terms of both economic opportunities and attitudinal influences. But the apparently negligible effect of the mother's death on such plans suggested that perhaps the decided influence of the father's death was due more to financial than attitudinal considerations. Obviously, this is only speculation.

When the metropolitan and nonfarm groups planning on jobs and planning on college were compared as to whether or not they came from broken homes, almost twice as many of the students planning on working came from broken homes as did students who were planning on college. Between 10 and 12 per cent of the students planning to get jobs had parents who were separated or divorced and between 4 and 6 per cent of the students planning to go to college had parents who were separated or divorced. In the farm groups, however, these differences did not appear and the number of broken homes in this group was consistently smaller; only between 2 and 4 per cent of farm children came from homes where the parents were divorced or separated. For the metropolitan and nonfarm groups, separation of the parents had an influence that might have been somewhat equivalent to the death of one or both parents, but this influence apparently was considerably less for farm youth.

OCCUPATION OF PARENTS

Among the metropolitan boys planning on working, the largest percentage had fathers who were skilled tradesmen and an almost equal number had fathers who worked in factories. Approximately two thirds of the boys planning to get jobs came from homes at these occupational levels. For the nonfarm youth planning on working, the figures were almost the same, although slightly more came from factory workers' homes than from skilled tradesmen's homes. Naturally, almost all of the students living on farms who were planning on working came from homes where the father was a farmer. Almost 10 per cent of the farm group, however, came from homes where the father was a factory worker.

No significant sex differences appeared here, for nearly two thirds of the metropolitan girls planning on working came from skilled trades-men's and factory workers' homes and the figures were almost the same for nonfarm girls. Of the farm girls, 86 per cent came from homes where the father was a farmer.

Fewer than 4 per cent of the students planning on working came from homes where the father was in a profession. In absolute figures, 96 of the boys and 98 of the girls planning on working came from professional homes. Relatively, about four times as many of the students planning on college came from professional homes as did those who were planning on jobs. Thus, for example, only 4 per cent of the metropolitan boys planning on jobs came from professional homes, whereas 17 per cent of those planning on college came from professional homes.

Of the metropolitan boys planning on jobs, 9 per cent came from homes where the father owned or managed a business; for the nonfarm group planning on jobs, 17 per cent came from similar homes. Figures for the girls were somewhat comparable.

In examining these figures, one must remember that even though most of the children from professional homes plan on college, our col-lege-planning population is still predominantly from nonprofessional homes and includes large numbers of students from skilled tradesmen's and factory workers' homes. At the same time, these are the homes that also produce most of the young people who directly enter the labor force at the termination of high school.

When we considered the occupation reported for the mothers before marriage, we found that the mothers of only about 5 per cent of the students planning on jobs had been teachers; this was roughly about one half as many proportionately as of the students planning on college. Between three quarters and four fifths of the mothers of metropolitan and nonfarm youth and practically all the mothers of farm families were reported to be housewives, regardless of what their children were planning.

EDUCATION OF PARENTS AND SIBLINGS

The modal education of fathers of the students planning on working was completion of the eighth grade, regardless of the students' sex or geographical area. Of the metropolitan boys planning on working, 14 per cent had fathers with less than an eighth-grade education; the com-parable figure for the farm boys was 24 per cent. Comparisons between the fathers of children planning on college and the fathers of children planning on working showed significant differences in the expected direction. There were no sex differences apparent for paternal education.

The picture for maternal education was approximately the same as for paternal. The modal education for the mothers of the students planning on working was completion of the eighth grade. But almost twice as many mothers of metropolitan students planning on jobs were high school graduates as was true for the mothers of farm students planning on jobs. Throughout this analysis the differences in education between parents living in nonfarm and metropolitan areas and parents living on farms was most striking.

Approximately one half of the students planning to get jobs had an older brother. About one half of these older brothers were high school graduates and between 10 and 20 per cent had some college training, the remainder having less than a high school education. The accompanying tabulation gives the figures for one geographical group. Again, the familial educational pattern seemed to bear a close relationship to after-high-school plans.

	Siblings Not Graduating from High School	
	Brothers	Sisters
Metropolitan boys planning on jobs....	12%	9%
Metropolitan boys planning on college..	3	2

LANGUAGE BACKGROUND

Of the metropolitan boys, 13 per cent spoke German in their homes and 16 per cent spoke a Scandinavian language; of those living on farms, 17 per cent spoke German and 20 per cent spoke a Scandinavian language. Figures for the girls were approximately the same. When compared with those planning on college, more of the students planning to work came from bilingual homes.

FAMILY INCOME

Of the metropolitan boys planning on working, 65 per cent said their family income came from wages, 20 per cent reported salaries, and only 10 per cent reported professional fees or business profits. For the metropolitan and nonfarm groups, approximately twice as many of the students planning on working as of the students planning on college reported income based on wages. The typical high school student planning on college came from a home where the income was derived from a salary; the typical high school student planning on working came from a home where income was derived from wages. There were no apparent sex differences in this regard.

Over one half of the students planning on jobs reported they came from homes that were comfortable or well-to-do and only 10 to 12 per cent came from homes described as being "hard up" or "sometimes hard up." Perhaps children coming from destitute homes tended not to reach their senior year in high school; we may have had much economic screening going on before the senior year. Some differences in economic status were apparent when comparisons were made between the job-planning and the college-planning groups. More of the college-going group described the family income as "comfortable" and fewer of the college-going group said they had the necessities but not many of the luxuries.

HIGH SCHOOL CURRICULUMS

The typical male student planning to find a job had taken a general course in high school regardless of the area in which he lived. The typical female student planning on a job had taken a commercial course in high school. Fewer than 15 per cent of the students planning on jobs were in a college preparatory course.

It is interesting to note that one half of the girls planning on working had taken courses providing some direct occupational preparation in high school, whereas fewer than 20 per cent of the boys planning on working had taken vocationally relevant courses. Even in the farm group, only 17 per cent of the boys planning on working had taken agricultural courses in high school in spite of the fact that a large percentage of them planned to do agricultural work.

When the reasons presented for taking high school courses were examined, we found that the metropolitan boys planning on working reported they were most influenced by thinking certain courses would interest them. For instance, 34 per cent of these boys said they selected a course because it sounded interesting, whereas only 26 per cent of the the boys planning on college gave that as a reason; 47 per cent of the college-planning boys said that the course fitted their vocational plans whereas only 25 per cent of the job planners gave that reason. This trend was partially reversed with the girls. More girls planning on jobs said that they selected a course because it fitted their vocational plans than said they selected a course because of interest factors. The fact that boys and girls chose different courses perhaps bears this out. Of the students planning on working, only 10 per cent selected their high school curriculum on the basis of parental advice and fewer than 10 per cent selected their course on the basis of a counselor's advice. The students planning on college appeared to be more influenced by advice given by counselors or parents.

FINANCIAL STATUS

The students who were planning on working were asked if they would attend college if they had more money. Approximately 44 per cent of the boys and 35 per cent of the girls said they would. There were no significant regional differences, although there was a tendency for more students from nonfarm areas than from other areas to say they would go to college if they could better afford it. The students who said they would go to college if they had more money were asked how much more money they would need; approximately one half of these indicated they would need enough money for all their expenses and the remainder said they would need enough money for about one half of their expenses. There were no significant sex or regional differences here.

When asked if they could afford to go to college if they so desired, 11 per cent of the metropolitan boys said that they could afford it, 20 per cent said they could barely afford it, and 31 per cent said it would involve great sacrifice. Thirty-eight per cent said they could not afford college. There were no significant sex or regional differences. Thus, approximately one tenth of the job-planning group could afford to go to college if they wanted to and slightly over one third considered that they could not possibly afford to go to college.

ATTITUDES OF PARENTS

About 50 per cent of the metropolitan and nonfarm boys planning to get jobs reported their parents wanted them to go to college and the remainder reported that their parents were for the most part indifferent. Only a negligible number of parents opposed college plans. Of the farm boys planning to work, 36 per cent reported their families wanted them to go to college and over 59 per cent indicated their families were indifferent. There were large sex differences here, since 60 per cent of all the girls planning to work reported their parents were indifferent as to whether or not they attended college and only 32 per cent indicated their parents wanted them to go to college. Almost twice as many of the girls as of the boys planning on working reported that their parents did not want them to go to college. Apparently family attitude toward college attendance was in part directly dependent upon the sex of the child.

OCCUPATIONAL PLANS

Regarding future plans and aspirations, 37 per cent of the metropolitan boys and 32 per cent of the nonfarm boys planning on working after high school expected to be in clerical occupations or skilled trades within ten years. Almost one half of the farm boys hoped to be farmers at the end of the ten-year period. Fourteen per cent of the metropolitan boys named a professional occupation in response to this question and 13 per cent named a semiprofessional occupation. Fewer than 7 per cent of all boys planning to work named any of the following: farming, semiskilled trades, skilled trades, or unskilled labor. Between 5 and 10 per cent of the total male group planning on working were undecided when faced with this question.

Between 60 and 70 per cent of the girls hoped to be housewives within ten years, more of the girls from farms than of the metropolitan girls hoping to be housewives. The largest single group of metropolitan girls planning on jobs hoped to be in semiskilled trades; the largest single group of nonfarm girls planning on working hoped to be in semiprofessional jobs. Few aspired to professional work.

When students were asked what their parents hoped they would do, almost half reported they did not know what occupations their parents wished them to follow. Seventeen per cent of the metropolitan boys planning on working said their parents wanted them to enter a professional occupation and 22 per cent of the metropolitan group said their parents wanted them to enter a clerical occupation or a skilled trade. Possibly these parental attitudes as perceived by children influenced the children in what they actually did; family aspirations may provide one reason why many students planning on jobs actually do attend college.

MATERIAL POSSESSIONS

For the remaining variables, no significant sex differences were apparent with the exception of answers to the question "How many people sleep in your room besides yourself?" Of the farm group more of the girls than of the boys planning on working had rooms of their own and this sex difference was reversed for the metropolitan boys and girls planning on jobs. Also, regardless of plan, more farm girls than boys had their own rooms.

The accompanying tabulation indicates the geographical differences in home equipment among the students planning to work.

	Metropolitan	*Nonfarm*	*Farm*
Central heating....................	90%	76%	60%
Running water	88	83	42
Hot and cold running water.........	88	86	32
Electric or gas refrigerators..........	90	80	67
Telephones	97	79	71
Deep freezers	16	33	73
Electric lights....................	99	99	87

Three quarters of the families of metropolitan and nonfarm students planning on working owned their own homes and 85 per cent of the farm families were reported to own their own homes.

The metropolitan and nonfarm youth planning on working reported the modal number of people living in their homes was four but the modal number of people living in farm homes was five. The farm homes, on the other hand, tended to have more rooms than either the metropolitan or the nonfarm homes, the typical metropolitan and nonfarm student coming from a home containing six rooms.

Practically all the families of farm youth planning on working owned cars, but between 17 and 25 per cent of the families of metropolitan and nonfarm children did not own a car. Almost one half of the farm families owned more than one car; fewer than 25 per cent of the families of metropolitan or nonfarm students owned more than one car. The cars owned by these families tended to be approximately the same average age and to have the same average value.

BOOKS AND MAGAZINES IN THE HOME

Of the metropolitan students planning on working, 8 per cent reported they had fewer than ten books in their homes and more than one quarter reported they had fewer than twenty-five. Only 20 per cent reported they had one hundred or more books in their homes and only 44 per cent reported they had more than fifty books in their homes. Of the nonfarm youth, 13 per cent reported fewer than ten books in their homes and 43 per cent reported they had fewer than twenty-five. Thirty per cent indicated they had more than fifty books in their homes. The figures for the farm children tended to resemble those for the non-farm children.

Almost one half of the metropolitan students planning on working came from homes subscribing to the *Reader's Digest*, and almost one third had access in their home to the *Saturday Evening Post, Life*, and *Better Homes and Gardens*. The figures for the farm and nonfarm groups were approximately the same for the *Reader's Digest* but relatively fewer of these homes subscribed to the *Saturday Evening Post* and to *Life*. *Collier's* and *Look* seemed to be as popular in farm and nonfarm homes as in metropolitan homes. Fifty per cent more of the metropolitan homes subscribed to the *American Magazine* than did the farm homes.

MEMBERSHIP IN ORGANIZATIONS

Almost one half of the metropolitan parents belonged to a parent-teachers association, but only one third of the nonfarm and farm parents belonged to such organizations. Twice as many of the nonfarm as of the metropolitan and farm groups had fathers belonging to veterans' organizations. Almost none of the students planning on working had fathers belonging to Rotary clubs and only 5 per cent had fathers belonging to the Masonic orders. Forty-two per cent of the metropolitan group and 25 per cent of the nonfarm students planning on working had fathers belonging to labor unions. On the other hand, almost one half of the farm boys and girls planning on working reported their fathers belonged to the Farm Bureau. With the exception of membership in labor unions, there was a tendency for the parents of students planning on college to belong to more organizations, regardless of what they were, than did the parents of students planning on jobs.

High-Ability Students: Those Who Planned to Go to College and Those Who Planned to Get Jobs

IN PREVIOUS chapters rather complete descriptions were presented of groups of students having differing after-high-school plans, those who planned on attending college and those who planned on getting jobs. In these descriptions some comparisons were made within the different groups; the purpose of the descriptions was to provide a comprehensive picture of each group with specific plans. In the present chapter the purpose is somewhat different. Here we shall compare two small groups of students, those with relatively high ability who planned to attend college and those with similar ability who planned to work.

In the entire group of 24,898 students expressing after-high-school plans, 711 who were planning on getting jobs had scores on the American Council on Education Psychological Examination of 120 or above and 2666 who were planning on going to college had scores in this range. Since there were 9035 students in the entire group planning on getting jobs and 8993 planning on college, 7.9 per cent of the job-planning group and 29.6 per cent of the college-planners had A.C.E. scores of 120 or more.

AGE

The median age of the high-ability students at the time they completed the original questionnaire was 17.5. In every case where comparisons between geographical and "plan" groups were made, the boys tended to be slightly older than the girls. When comparisons were made between the boys planning on college and the boys planning on jobs, the latter were slightly older than the others, but in the case of similar

135

comparisons between the girls, these age differences were not consistent for all geographical groups. When the high-ability students were compared with the total groups of students from which they came, in every case the high-ability students on the average were slightly younger than the entire group except for the farm boys planning on college; this high-ability group was slightly but not significantly older than the entire group of farm boys planning on college. None of the differences in median age was large.

In the high-ability group there were significantly more students who were 16 years of age at the time they completed the questionnaire than there were in the entire group. This was true for both the students planning on college and the students planning on jobs.

MARITAL STATUS

As with the entire group, the group with high A.C.E. scores had for the most part no immediate plans for marriage. Fewer than 1 per cent of the boys in this group reported they were either engaged or married. However, the possible influence of forthcoming marriage on the determination of after-high-school plans was shown when the high-ability girls planning on jobs were compared to the high-ability girls planning on college. Of the high-ability metropolitan girls planning on working, 8 per cent were engaged to be married, whereas of the high-ability metropolitan girls planning on college, only two tenths of 1 per cent were engaged to be married. Differences were in the same direction but not quite of the same magnitude for the nonfarm and farm high-ability girls. Obviously, the causal nature of this relationship is not clear — did the girls become engaged and then decide they would not go to college or did they decide to find jobs and then become engaged?

STATUS OF THE HOME

Several comparisons suggested the influence of the home in determining whether or not high-ability students attend college. Of high-ability metropolitan boys planning on college, 94 per cent reported their fathers were alive, whereas only 88 per cent of the boys planning on jobs reported their fathers were alive. Thus more than twice as many of those planning on jobs as of those planning on college had fathers who were deceased. This relationship was substantially the same for the high-ability nonfarm boys, but for the high-ability farm boys, 96 per cent of those planning on college and 96 per cent of those planning on jobs had living fathers. The situation was essentially the same for the girls — whether or not the father was living had a relationship with the plans of the metropolitan and the nonfarm girls but not with the plans of the farm girls.

The survival of the mother seems to have had no relationship to the after-high-school plans of the high-ability students. Approximately 97 per cent of all students, regardless of sex, plan, or area, reported their mothers were alive.

The percentages of boys in the various areas coming from broken homes are given in the accompanying tabulation. Differences were in

	College	Jobs
Metropolitan boys	3%	10%
Nonfarm boys	4	14
Farm boys	4	7

the same direction for the girls as for the boys. For example, almost three times as many nonfarm girls planning on jobs came from broken homes as did girls who were planning on college.

For high-ability pupils in high schools, a home where the father was dead or where the parents were separated or divorced decreased the probability of the student's attending college and increased the probability that he would plan on working immediately after leaving high school.

OCCUPATION OF PARENTS

As with the entire group, for the high-ability students the occupation of the father had a relationship to after-high-school plans, as shown in the accompanying tabulation.

	High-Ability Metropolitan Boys		High-Ability Metropolitan Girls	
	College	Jobs	College	Jobs
Professional homes	23%	8%	22%	4%
Skilled tradesmen's homes	17	31	16	35
Factory workers' homes	9	16	6	26

In this high-ability group, the students planning on working came predominantly from the homes of skilled tradesmen and factory workers, and the students planning on college tended significantly more often to come from the homes of professional workers. Large numbers of college-planning students, however, came from the homes of skilled tradesmen and factory workers.

For the high-ability students the occupation of the mother before marriage was also related to after-high-school plans. Of the metropolitan boys planning on jobs, only 4 per cent reported that their mothers had been teachers before marriage; but of the boys planning on college, 18 per cent, or more than 4 times as many, reported their mothers had been teachers. These differences were reduced to a two-to-one ratio for the nonfarm and the farm boys. The sizes and the significances of these differences held for the girls too. Having a mother who had been a teacher greatly increased the probability that a high-ability student would plan on attending college after high school.

EDUCATION OF PARENTS

As one might have expected, the education of the parents was related to the after-high-school plans of the high-ability youth. The modal paternal education for the high-ability students planning on jobs was completion of the eighth grade; the modal paternal education for the high-ability students planning on college was college graduation for the metropolitan boys, high school graduation for the nonfarm boys, and eighth-grade graduation for the farm boys. Of the metropolitan boys planning on college, 23 per cent reported fathers who had graduated from college in contrast to only 4 per cent of the metropolitan boys planning on jobs who reported fathers who were college graduates. Of the nonfarm boys planning on jobs 51 per cent reported fathers who had finished the eighth grade or less, whereas of the nonfarm boys planning on college, only 26 per cent reported fathers with eighth-grade educations or less. The differences for the farm groups were not nearly as large as they were for the metropolitan and nonfarm groups.

There were few differences between the metropolitan boys and girls and between the nonfarm boys and girls, but the farm girls seem to have had their plans influenced to a greater extent by the father's education than did the farm boys. Of the farm boys planning on working, for instance, 54 per cent reported their fathers had finished the eighth grade or less and of those planning on college, 43 per cent so reported. Similar figures for the farm girls were 56 and 35 per cent.

The education of the mother differentiated the groups similarly. For the metropolitan boys planning on college, 17 per cent reported mothers who were college graduates, whereas only 3 per cent of those planning on jobs reported mothers who had graduated from college. Approximately one quarter of the metropolitan youth reported their mothers had graduated from high school whereas fewer than one fifth of the farm students reported this much maternal education.

We must again emphasize the fact that in spite of the close relationship between parental education and plans of the child, there were many, many exceptions. Children coming from homes with a relatively low educational status frequently aspired to college, and not infrequently children coming from homes with a high educational level decided to work rather than to attend college, although they may have had adequate ability for college work.

Data concerning the education of older brothers and sisters also revealed a tendency for the establishment of family educational patterns. The high-ability students planning on college tended to have older brothers and sisters who had more education than did those planning on working.

LANGUAGE BACKGROUND

For the high-ability group, a bilingual home background had some relationship to after-high-school plans. Of the metropolitan boys planning to work, 13 per cent came from German-speaking homes, but of the boys planning to go to college, only 7 per cent came from such homes. This difference appeared also for the metropolitan girls. Approximately one quarter of the high-ability farm students came from homes where a Scandinavian language was spoken, but this bore no apparent relationship to college-going plans. For the farm youth who had high ability, a bilingual background was not related to whether a student was planning on college or a job. The difference based on language background was most pronounced for the metropolitan groups and second for the nonfarm groups. In general, in the metropolitan or nonfarm areas, speaking German or a Scandinavian language in the home had a slight negative influence on college plans and slightly increased the probability of a student's planning on working after he graduated from high school.

FAMILY INCOME

Differences between the job-planning and college-planning groups were large in regard to variables directly related to income. Of the metropolitan boys planning on college, 24 per cent reported family incomes from fees or profits, 49 per cent reported their family incomes came from fixed salaries, and 25 per cent reported incomes from wages. Of the metropolitan boys planning on jobs, 13 per cent reported incomes from fees or profits, 25 per cent reported incomes from fixed salaries, and 60 per cent reported incomes from wages. These differences were approximately the same for the metropolitan girls and the general tendency was the same for the nonfarm students.

Reports of adequacy of income also bore a relationship to after-high-school plans for the high-ability group. Of the metropolitan boys planning on jobs, 47 per cent reported they had necessities or less; the same status was reported by only 22 per cent of the metropolitan boys planning on college. Fourteen per cent of the metropolitan boys planning on college but only 1 per cent of those planning on jobs reported they were well-to-do. Differences were of the same magnitude for metropolitan girls, and the general tendencies were the same for the farm youth. One difference was truly astonishing. Of the farm boys planning on college, 67 per cent reported they were comfortable but not well-to-do, whereas only 3 per cent of the farm boys planning on jobs reported this. Similar figures for farm girls were 66 and 47 per cent. The way the child perceived his family income appeared to be highly related to his after-high-school plans.

REASONS FOR PLANS

The group planning on college was differentiated from the group planning on working on the basis of the reasons given for making plans. Of the boys planning to go to college, approximately 80 per cent gave as a reason "preparation for a vocation," and approximately one third expressed a desire for a liberal education. Of the boys planning on working, approximately one third indicated they wanted to earn money and approximately one third gave as a reason the desire to be independent. All students seemed to be motivated by the desire to make money, but the college-going students appeared to be looking further ahead into the future.

Approximately one third of the students planning on college gave a liking for school as their reason; this was rarely given by those planning on jobs.

Interesting to note was the fact that almost one third of the students planning on working said they made these plans because they could not afford any others. Thus financial motivations, along with a motivation to be independent, were extemely important for those who were planning to work. The desire for vocational preparation and a liberal education appeared to be quite important for the students planning to go to college. Incidentally, the girls reported more interest in obtaining a liberal education than did the boys.

HIGH SCHOOL CURRICULUMS

The differences in high school curriculums between the students planning on jobs and the students planning on college were obscured by the differences between the sexes and among the geographical areas. As one would expect, there was a direct relationship between the high school courses in which students were enrolled and their plans for after high school, although this relationship was far from perfect. The courses chosen by metropolitan boys are indicated in the accompanying tabulation. The largest group of the nonfarm boys who were planning on

	Commercial	College Preparatory	General
Metropolitan boys planning on college	2%	86%	10%
Metropolitan boys planning on jobs	15	37	41

jobs took the general course; one third of them, however, took the college preparatory course. Of the college-planning, nonfarm, high-ability students, 80 per cent took the college preparatory course and 17 per cent took the general course. Fewer than 10 per cent of the nonfarm boys planning on jobs took shop or technical courses, although 24 per cent of the farm boys planning on jobs took commercial, agricultural, or shop or technical courses.

Of the metropolitan girls planning on college, 87 per cent took the college preparatory course as compared with 46 per cent of the farm girls planning on college who took this course. Of the other farm girls planning on college, 42 per cent took the general course, and 13 per cent took the commercial course. Only 4 per cent of the metropolitan girls planning on college took the commercial course. Approximately one half of the girls planning on working took vocational courses in high school as compared with a much smaller proportion of the boys. One might question the extent of the difference between the college preparatory course and the general course provided in most high schools. Perhaps in many high schools these two curriculums might well be combined.

Large differences regarding the reasons given for choosing their high school courses were found between those who planned on jobs and those who planned on college. Of the metropolitan boys planning on college, 56 per cent said they had selected their high school courses because they best fitted their vocational plans; only 22 per cent of the metropolitan boys planning on jobs presented this reason. On the other hand, 41 per cent of the metropolitan boys planning on jobs, but only 26 per cent of the boys planning on college, gave the reason "It was the most interesting." The metropolitan students appeared to be more influenced by counselors than were the farm or nonfarm students, although even here fewer than 15 per cent of the metropolitan students planning on college indicated that a counselor's advice was a factor they considered. Parents' advice, particularly for those who were planning on college, was more important than advice from other souces in determining what courses the students took in high school.

If one may generalize from these rather meager data, it appears that the students planning on college were most influenced in selecting high school programs by what they thought would be most pertinent occupationally, whereas those planning on jobs were more influenced by what they thought would be most interesting.

FINANCIAL SUPPORT FOR COLLEGE

Between 8 and 16 per cent of the boys planning on college and between 22 and 35 per cent of the girls indicated their families would pay all their college expenses. Thus approximately twice as many girls as boys hoped to have all their support come from their family. The metropolitan students expected more help from their families than did the nonfarm students, and the nonfarm students expected more help than did the farm students. Only 5 per cent of the girls expected to be completely self-supporting; the comparable figure for the boys was about 12 per cent. Both sex and geographical differences regarding the extent to which financial help was expected from the family were large.

The high-ability students planning on obtaining jobs were asked if they would go to college if they had more money. There were no important sex or geographical differences here. Of the 711 high-ability pupils planning on jobs, 411 — 58 per cent — said they would attend college if they had more money. Approximately one third of the metropolitan and nonfarm boys who were willing to change their plans indicated they would need enough money for all their expenses; about one half of the farm boys and one half of all the girls also indicated they would need enough money for all their expenses. Roughly, about one half of all the groups indicated that if they were to attend college they would need enough money to pay for about one half of their expenses. Only a small proportion indicated they would need money for less than one half of their expenses.

If we assume that the average student in this group of 411 would require approximately three quarters of the funds necessary for college if he were to attend and that the cost of college for the average student is $1000 a year, we could compute the amount of money needed if all these people were to be sent to college. In order to send these 411 students to college for one year, $308,250 would be necessary.

Each year approximately 7000 freshmen in Minnesota enter college. Approximately 2800 of these freshmen eventually graduate. Of the 7000 freshmen, about 25 per cent, or 1750, obtain A.C.E. scores of 120 or above. A large proportion of the freshmen who graduate come from these high-ability students. If we assumed that the 411 students not going to college for lack of funds were added to the 1750 high-ability students who now attend college, and that 80 per cent of these 411 would graduate, the total number of college graduates in the state would be increased by 12 per cent $(.80 \times 411 = 329; \quad 329 \div 2800 = 12\%)$. Each class of 411 such students would require about one third of a million dollars a year and four such classes in college at one time would cost about one and one third million dollars a year. Thus, we could estimate that a scholarship program in Minnesota amounting to slightly over one million dollars a year could increase the number of college graduates each year by about 12 per cent.

Of all the high-ability students who were not going to college, fewer than 10 per cent indicated they could easily afford college and approximately 25 per cent indicated they could barely afford college. Between 35 and 40 per cent of the students planning on jobs indicated they could not afford college at all and an almost equal number indicated that attending college would involve a great sacrifice. These figures suggested that lack of money was not the only important factor in determining whether or not high-ability students planned on attending college. Here were a substantial number of high-ability youngsters who, as they perceived their situations, could afford to go to college and yet had decided not to attend college but to obtain jobs.

FAMILY ATTITUDES

Only 4 per cent of the metropolitan boys planning on college indicated their families were indifferent to college, although 25 per cent of the metropolitan boys planning on working said their families were indifferent. Practically all the parents of the metropolitan and nonfarm youth who were planning on college either insisted that their children go or wanted them to go to college.

The differences found here suggested that the attitudes of a student's family toward college were an important determinant in deciding whether or not he planned on college. If high-ability students believed their families wanted them to attend college, this increased the probability of their attending. On the other hand, if the student perceived his family as being indifferent toward college, this diminished the probability of his attending. One must remember, of course, that the student who had decided not to attend college could have had his perception of his parents' wishes influenced by this decision and therefore saw his family as not favoring college.

OCCUPATIONAL PLANS

Of the high-ability metropolitan boys planning on college, 70 per cent expressed a desire to enter an occupation at the professional level and 16 per cent were aiming at a semiprofessional occupation; of the high-ability boys planning on jobs, only 24 per cent were aiming at professional occupations and 20 per cent at semiprofessional occupations. Thirty per cent of the metropolitan boys planning on jobs were aiming at clerical jobs and skilled trade jobs. The figures for the nonfarm boys were roughly the same, but for the farm boys they were quite different. Of the farm boys planning on college, 18 per cent were planning to go back into farming when they finished college. Of the farm boys planning on jobs after high school, 45 per cent were hoping eventually to become farmers and only 16 per cent were aiming at professional jobs.

Of the girls, many who were planning on college were hoping to obtain a professional-level job. Of the metropolitan girls planning on college, 37 per cent were aiming at a professional job and 20 per cent at semiprofessional jobs, whereas of the metropolitan girls planning on working, 19 per cent were aiming at either professional or semiprofessional jobs. These two groups of girls had different marriage plans, according to their reports. Of the metropolitan girls planning on working after high school, 56 per cent were looking forward to being housewives within ten years, whereas only 38 per cent of the college-planning girls were looking forward to the housewife's career. Figures were roughly comparable for the job and college groups in both nonfarm and farm areas.

These figures suggested that plans for the year following graduation from high school, as expressed by these students, should be distinguished from long-term plans, inasmuch as a large percentage of the students who were planning on working during the year following graduation eventually planned to enter a profession, usually a profession involving college training. For instance, 24 per cent of the 96 metropolitan boys planning on working the year after graduation said they were planning eventually on entering professions, thus indicating that they perhaps hoped to go to college at some time even though their immediate plans for the next year did not involve college.

The occupational ambitions parents had for their children more or less followed the ambitions the children themselves expressed. The parents of those planning on college hoped that their children would enter professional occupations to a greater extent than did the parents of children planning on going to work after high school. More than one half of the youth reported that their parents were undecided or the youth themselves were undecided as to what the parents' hopes for their children were.

MATERIAL POSSESSIONS

The high-ability students planning on going to college on the average had more material possessions in their homes than did the students planning on working after graduating from high school. No important or consistent sex differences appeared in this respect, although there was a rather marked geographical trend. The metropolitan students tended to have more mechanical equipment and conveniences in their homes than the nonfarm students, and the nonfarm students tended to have more than the farm students. We interpreted the relatively consistent but small differences between the students planning on jobs and those planning on college as reflecting for the most part differences in economic status and as closely related, in all probability, to the previously discussed facts involving family income and occupation of the father.

Of the metropolitan high-ability students planning on college, 97 per cent reported they had central heating in their homes, whereas only 87 per cent of those planning on working so reported. The respective figures for nonfarm boys were 89 and 75 per cent and for farm boys 59 and 46 per cent.

Practically all the metropolitan students had running water in their homes but there were marked differences between the job and college groups in the nonfarm and farm areas, with the college-planning groups tending more frequently to report running water in their homes.

Of the metropolitan boys planning on college, 98 per cent reported hot and cold running water in their homes, whereas of the metropolitan boys planning on working, only 88 per cent reported they had this convenience. The respective figures were 88 and 71 per cent for the nonfarm boys and 50 and 31 per cent for the farm boys.

The metropolitan students planning on college and those planning on jobs were not differentiated on the basis of having mechanical refrigeration in the home but the nonfarm students and the farm students were so differentiated, with the college-planning groups more frequently reporting mechanical refrigeration.

The same differentiation appeared when the groups were compared on the basis of having a telephone in the home: almost all the metropolitan students had telephones, but more college-planners than job-planners in both nonfarm and farm areas had telephones.

Twice as many of the high-ability metropolitan students planning on college had deep freezers as was true for the high-ability metropolitan students planning on jobs. This difference was in the same direction although not quite as large for the nonfarm and the farm groups. It was interesting to note that this was one convenience that appeared almost twice as often on the farms as it did in the metropolitan areas, although it was certainly recognized that on the farms the deep freezer had more economic utility than it had in the city.

Practically all the metropolitan and nonfarm students reported electric lights in their homes, but the farm youth who planned on college and those who planned on working were differentiated in this respect.

The metropolitan and the nonfarm students with different plans were also differentiated according to whether or not their families owned their own homes, but the farm students were not.

For the metropolitan youth, there were no significant differences between the job-planning and the college-planning groups in terms of the number of people living in the home, but the farm students planning on college had slightly more people living in their homes than did the farm students planning on working. In the metropolitan and the nonfarm groups there was a slight and significant tendency for the youth planning on college to have somewhat larger homes than the youth planning on jobs. The high-ability students planning on college and those planning on jobs did not differ in terms of the numbers who had bedrooms of their own.

When the groups having different plans were compared on the basis of the number of cars in the family, there was a tendency for the families of the college-planning groups to have more cars and a slight tendency for these cars to be newer and more expensive. These differences were statistically significant.

In general, these data regarding equipment in the home and possessions of the family reflected the previous generalizations concerning the effect of economic status on plans of high school seniors.

BOOKS AND MAGAZINES IN THE HOME

Marked differences were found between the job-planning and the college-planning groups in terms of the number of books in the home. Of the high-ability metropolitan students planning on college, 59 per cent reported they had 100 or more books in their homes, whereas of the high-ability metropolitan students planning on jobs, only 27 per cent indicated a like number of books. The differences were in the same general direction for the nonfarm and farm boys and for the metropolitan and nonfarm girls. The differences were not nearly so large, however, for the farm girls: 21 per cent of the farm girls planning on jobs and 28 per cent of the farm girls planning on college reported they had 100 or more books in their homes.

Similar differences were found in respect to the availability of magazines in the home. Forty-six per cent of the metropolitan boys planning on college had the *Saturday Evening Post* in their homes and 71 per cent had the *Reader's Digest*, as compared with 29 and 48 per cent of the job-planning groups. The differences were in the same direction for the other male groups and for the female groups. The college-planners and job-planners were also differentiated on the basis of *Time, Life,* and *Newsweek.* They did not seem to be differentiated on the basis of whether or not their families subscribed to the *American Magazine, Collier's,* or *Look.*

MEMBERSHIP IN ORGANIZATIONS

Marked differences between the job-planning and college-planning groups were found when comparisons were made on the basis of organizations to which the parents belonged. For instance, 68 per cent of the metropolitan boys planning on college reported their families belonged to parent-teachers associations, but only 54 per cent of the job-planning groups reported this. The difference was of an equal size but reversed in direction when membership in labor unions was considered.

In general, the job-planning students and the college-planning students in the high-ability group appeared to be differentiated both on the basis of cultural and educational factors and on the basis of economic and material factors.

High-Ability Students from
Workmen's Homes

SOCIAL, economic, cultural, and intellectual factors related to college attendance are so complex that the interrelationships among these factors are difficult to identify. Of various methods that can be used to estimate the relative importance of some of these factors, one promising method consists of holding one or more factors relatively constant and observing conditions related to variations in the remaining factors. Essentially, that is the method used in this part of the study.

Of the 17,366 boys and girls coming from metropolitan and nonfarm areas, between 20 and 25 per cent came from the homes of skilled tradesmen and approximately the same number came from the homes of factory workers. In the total sample of metropolitan and nonfarm students were 940 high school seniors with A.C.E. scores of 120 or above who came from the homes of skilled tradesmen or factory workers (559 had fathers who were skilled tradesmen and 381 had fathers who were factory workers). By studying this group intensively, we felt additional information could be obtained regarding the factors influencing decisions to attend college.

Here was a group of relatively high-ability students coming from a rather restricted occupational background. It was not assumed that workmen's families constituted a wholly homogeneous group. In fact, it was assumed that great variability existed among the homes of workmen, and the purpose of this particular analysis was to determine the extent to which these differences among the homes of these men were related to the plans of their children.

The total group of high-ability students from these occupational groups was divided according to sex and according to whether the students lived in metropolitan or nonfarm areas. For obvious reasons, the youth living on farms were not included in this analysis. Each of these groups was then divided according to whether or not the students indicated that they planned to attend college after graduating from high school.

As shown in the accompanying tabulation, there was a significant tendency for more of the high-ability metropolitan boys than of the high-ability nonfarm boys in this group to plan on college. Approximately the same proportion of metropolitan and nonfarm girls planned on college. Within each sex and geographical group, comparisons then were made between the students planning to attend college and the students not planning to attend college.

	Total Number	Those Going to College	
		Number	Per cent
Metropolitan boys............	203	146	72
Nonfarm boys..............	271	154	57
Metropolitan girls...........	205	100	49
Nonfarm girls..............	261	130	50

A.C.E. SCORES

Although the total group had been made relatively homogeneous in ability by selecting only those who had A.C.E. scores of 120 or above, there nevertheless was a possibility that the college-planning students would differ on the basis of their A.C.E. scores from the students who were not planning to attend college. Therefore, the mean A.C.E. scores of the college and noncollege groups were compared. For the metropolitan boys planning to attend college, the mean A.C.E. score was 132.88 and for the metropolitan boys not planning to attend college, the mean A.C.E. score was 129.74. Although this is not a large difference between means, it is a statistically significant one, with a critical ratio of 2.53. The critical ratio of the difference between the means of the nonfarm boys was 3.89, the critical ratio of the difference between the means of the nonfarm girls 2.50. The critical ratio between the means of the metropolitan girls planning to attend college and of those not planning to attend college was 1.41. Thus, in three of the four groups there was a significant tendency for the college-planning students to obtain somewhat higher mean A.C.E. scores than the students not planning to attend college. Even with such a relatively homogeneous group, differences in ability were related to plans to attend college.

HIGH SCHOOL ACHIEVEMENT

The college and noncollege groups were also differentiated on the basis of achievement in high school. For both sexes and in both geographical areas, the differences between means of high school percentile rank for the two groups were statistically significant. The differences between the boys planning on college and those not planning on college, however, were far greater than the differences between the similar groups of girls. The mean percentile ranks and the critical ratios of the differences between the means are shown in the accompanying tabulation.

	Mean Percentile Rank	Critical Ratio
Metropolitan boys		
College group	76	6.05
Noncollege group	51	
Nonfarm boys		
College group	76	6.2
Noncollege group	58	
Metropolitan girls		
College group	85	2.15
Noncollege group	79	
Nonfarm girls		
College group	86	2.32
Noncollege group	82	

Undoubtedly, many of the students were planning to attend college because of the availability of college scholarships. These scholarships are usually based more on high school grades than they are on test scores and this might be one of the explanations of why some high-ability high school students with relatively poor grades in high school do not plan to attend college. Often high school counselors may interpret poor grades in high school as being indications of poor academic motivation and counselors, teachers, and parents may advise students, regardless of test scores, not to attend college if they have not obtained good grades in high school.

Certainly, students who lack interest in school may receive low grades, regardless of intellectual ability, and this lack of academic interest which resulted in low grades may also result in the student's decision that college would merely be a continuation of an uninteresting high school career.

MARITAL PLANS

Whether or not girls are planning to attend college seems in part to be dependent upon their plans for marriage. Of the 230 girls planning to attend college in this group, only one indicated she was planning on being married during the following year, whereas of the 236 girls not planning to attend college, 13 were planning on being married the next year. Although this is a small difference, it is statistically significant with a critical ratio of 2.0. This difference was also reflected in the fact that more of the noncollege-planning girls than of the college-planning girls said they were engaged to be married.

AGE

There were no consistent or significant age differences between the students planning to attend college and those with other plans. The median age for each group was very close to 17.5 years.

STATUS OF FAMILY

The status of the students' families was related to the plans of the students. Although there were no differences between the students planning to attend college and those with other plans in terms of whether or not their parents were living, there were significant differences in terms of whether the parents were separated or divorced. Of the nonfarm male students planning to attend college, 5 per cent came from broken homes, whereas of the nonfarm boys not planning to attend college, 16 per cent came from broken homes. The critical ratio of this difference was 2.9. A corresponding critical ratio for the nonfarm girls was 3.06. The differences in this respect for the metropolitan students were not statistically significant — actually for the metropolitan boys the difference was in the reversed direction.

OCCUPATION OF PARENTS

As with ability, even in such a homogeneous group, paternal occupation was related to whether or not students were planning to attend college. The difference here was significant only for the metropolitan girls, where 71 per cent of the college-planning girls came from homes of skilled tradesmen as compared to 57 per cent of the noncollege-planning girls. The critical ratio for this difference was 2.13.

The mother's occupation before marriage was significantly related to plans to attend college for only the metropolitan boys. This was a rather peculiar sort of relationship. Of the metropolitan boys planning to attend college, 28 per cent said they did not know what their mother's occupation was before marriage, whereas of the metropolitan boys not planning on college, 50 per cent did not know their mother's occupation before marriage. Twice as many of the college-planning students as of the noncollege-planning students had mothers who had been teachers before marriage, but these differences were not statistically significant. The differences did reach statistical significance when the present occupation of the mother was considered. Of the nonfarm boys planning to attend college, 5 per cent had mothers who were teachers when the students completed the questionnaires, but only 1 per cent of the nonfarm boys not planning on college reported their mothers were teachers. The critical ratio here was 1.99. The corresponding critical ratio for the metropolitan girls was 2.07. Thus, there was evidence that the occupation of the mother prior to marriage and the mother's actual occupation at the time the student was in high school had a significant although small relationship to students' plans for after high school. The relationships between plans and maternal occupations other than teaching were unknown.

EDUCATION OF PARENTS

The education of the parents was also significantly related to the plans of these seniors. Of the metropolitan boys planning to attend college, 44 per cent had fathers who were high school graduates; only 25 per cent of the metropolitan boys not planning to attend college had fathers who were high school graduates. The critical ratio of this mean difference was 2.64. The corresponding critical ratios for metropolitan girls and nonfarm girls were 2.65 and 3.24 respectively, but the critical ratio for the nonfarm boys was less than 1. Fifty-five per cent of the mothers of the metropolitan boys planning to attend college were high school graduates as compared with 39 per cent of the mothers of the metropolitan boys not planning to attend college. The critical ratio for this difference was 2.01 and corresponding critical ratios for the metropolitan girls and nonfarm girls were 4.38 and 2.05 respectively. Again, the differences in maternal education between nonfarm boys planning to attend college and those with other plans were not significant. Thus, the evidence was quite conclusive that parents of college-planning students coming from workmen's homes and having relatively high ability tend to have more education than parents of similar students who are not planning to attend college.

Another cultural variable related to after-high-school plans is the language spoken in the home. An analysis of the languages other than English spoken in the homes of students planning to attend college and not planning to attend college revealed significant differences only for the metropolitan girls. Of the girls planning to attend college, 71 per cent spoke only English in their homes, but of the girls not planning to attend college, only 54 per cent spoke only English. Of the college-planning girls, 11 per cent spoke a Scandinavian language in their homes, whereas of the noncollege-planning girls, 29 per cent spoke such a language. Thus, for the metropolitan girls, a Scandinavian language background was inversely related to plans to attend college.

FAMILY INCOME

Figures reflecting the economic status of the family revealed some differences between the students planning to attend college and the students with other plans. There was a tendency, statistically significant for the male students, for more of the students planning to attend college to come from homes where the income was derived from fixed salaries and for more of the students not planning to attend college to come from homes where the income was derived from wages. These trends were in the same direction but were not statistically significant for the girls. The critical ratios for the metropolitan boys and nonfarm boys were 2.24 and 2.09 respectively.

Students were also asked to report on the adequacy of their family incomes. No significant differences were found among the students planning to attend college and the students having other plans. Over one half of the students described their incomes as allowing them to live comfortably and about one third reported that they had the necessities but not many of the luxuries.

HIGH SCHOOL CURRICULUMS

Significant differences were found in terms of the educational background of the students themselves. These differences were in the expected direction. Among the metropolitan boys, significantly more of the noncollege-planning group took commercial courses in high school (critical ratio $= 2.70$), significantly more of the college-planning group took the college preparatory course (84 per cent compared with 37 per cent of the noncollege-planning group), and significantly more of the noncollege-planning group took the general course in high school (12 per cent compared with 40 per cent of the noncollege-planning group). Significantly more of the nonfarm boys planning to attend college took the college preparatory course and significantly more of the nonfarm boys not planning to attend college took the general course.

Among the girls, significantly more of the group not planning on college took the commercial course in high school than did the girls planning on college. For the metropolitan group, 6 per cent of the college-planning girls and 39 per cent of the noncollege-planning girls took the commercial course; in the nonfarm group, 15 per cent of the college-planning girls and 46 per cent of the noncollege-planning girls took the commercial course in high school. Significant differences were also found among the girls taking the college preparatory courses and the general courses in high school; these differences were in the expected direction.

Only a few differences were found among the college and noncollege groups pertaining to the reasons given for taking their high school courses. More of the metropolitan students planning to attend college reported they selected their high school course on the basis of advice from a counselor than was true for the students not planning on college, the critical ratios for the boys being 1.88 and for the girls 2.85. Significantly more of the boys planning to attend college than of the boys not planning to attend college gave as a reason for selecting their high school course that the course they selected best fitted their plans. For instance, 53 per cent of the metropolitan boys planning to attend college gave this reason as compared with 25 per cent of the metropolitan boys not planning to attend college.

Thus, there were significant differences between the college-planning and the noncollege-planning students in terms of their high school backgrounds. The students planning to attend college tended to take appropriate high school curriculums and there was a tendency for them to select these curriculums more frequently on the basis of a counselor's advice and perhaps with a slightly better appreciation of how this selection of a course fitted in with their long-term plans than the noncollege-planners did.

FINANCIAL SUPPORT IN COLLEGE

Information was also available concerning plans of the college-going students for financing their educations. Approximately 5 per cent of the boys and approximately 12 per cent of the girls expected their families to pay all their college expenses. Of the boys, 16 per cent expected to pay all their expenses themselves; 9 per cent of the girls expected to pay all of their expenses themselves. In general, the girls expected more financial aid from their families than did the boys. The sons and daughters of these skilled tradesmen and factory workers expected less financial help from their families than did the total group of students planning to attend college.

Between 48 and 58 per cent of the youth not planning to attend college indicated that they would attend college if they had more money. Thus, of the high-ability children of skilled tradesmen and factory workers who were not going to college, somewhat more than one half would go to college if they had more financial support. There were here 165 students with A.C.E. scores of 120 or above whose primary reason perhaps for not attending college was lack of funds; and there were 145 who, it can be inferred, had reasons other than lack of money.

Of the students who would go to college if they had more money, approximately one half said they would need enough money to pay about one half of their expenses. The following indicated that they would need enough money to pay all their expenses if they were to attend college: 28 per cent of the metropolitan boys, 36 per cent of the nonfarm boys, 45 per cent of the metropolitan girls, and 53 per cent of the nonfarm girls. Thus, there were interesting sex and geographical differences in the amount of money needed.

Approximately 10 per cent of the students not planning to attend college said they could afford college if they wanted to attend and approximately one third reported that they could not possibly afford college. About one quarter of these students indicated that they could barely afford college if they wanted to go. This again suggests that the reasons for not attending college are far from being purely financial.

FAMILY ATTITUDES

Reported family attitudes significantly and consistently differentiated between the students going to college and those not going to college. For both sexes and in both geographical areas, statistically significantly more students planning to attend college reported their families wanted them to go and statistically significantly more of the students not planning to attend college reported their families were indifferent to college. We do not know whether or not each child accurately perceived his parents' attitudes; but regardless of the accuracy of this perception, the reported perception itself had a close relationship to whether or not the student planned to attend college.

REASONS FOR AFTER-HIGH-SCHOOL PLANS

Some indication of students' motivations for attending college was found in the check list on the questionnaire. Among the reasons given for making after-high-school plans there were many statistically significant differences between the students planning to attend college and the students not planning to attend college. For both sexes and in both geographical areas, statistically significantly more of the students planning to attend college gave "preparation for a vocation" and "desire for a liberal education" as reasons for their after-high-school plans. For each sex and in each geographical area, statistically significantly more of the students not planning to attend college gave these reasons: "to make money quickly," "to be independent," and "only thing I can afford." For the nonfarm boys and the metropolitan girls, significantly more of the noncollege-planning students gave as a reason "a foregone conclusion"; but significantly more of the nonfarm college-planning girls presented this as a reason. Statistically significantly more of the college-planning students said that they liked school and so were planning to continue.

To summarize the reasons for making after-high-school plans, the students planning to attend college were more influenced by long-range needs, both for vocational preparation and for a liberal education. Liking for school also appeared to have an influence here. The students not planning to attend college were more influenced by immediate pressures, including the desire to make money quickly and the desire for independence from their families. The financial resources of the students were also obviously influential in determining their plans.

VOCATIONAL GOALS

The vocational goals of these students also varied significantly. Many of the boys and girls planning to attend college hoped eventually to have professional jobs and the students not planning to attend college were more often aiming at clerical or skilled trades jobs. The college-planning students demonstrated an upward occupational mobility.

The occupational wishes of the parents for their children corresponded to the occupational goals of the children themselves, with the parents of the college-planning youth hoping their children would eventually be in professional jobs and parents of noncollege-planners hoping their children would be in clerical or skilled trades jobs.

MATERIAL POSSESSIONS

Some significant differences were found between the college-planning and the noncollege-planning students in terms of material comforts in the home. Significantly more of the nonfarm girls planning to attend college reported they had central heating in their homes than did the non-college-planning girls. Significantly more of the metropolitan boys planning to attend college than of the metropolitan boys not planning to attend college reported they had both hot and cold running water in their homes. Significantly more of the nonfarm girls who were planning to attend college than of the nonfarm girls not planning to attend college had mechanical refrigeration and telephones. No statistically significant differences were found regarding the presence in the home of running water, a deep freezer, electric lights, or television, or regarding home ownership.

No significant differentiating trend was found in terms of the number of people living in the home or in terms of the size of these homes. No significant differences were found among the students having bedrooms of their own and no significant differences among the students having no car or having more than one car. These groups apparently were similar on the basis of automobile ownership.

BOOKS AND MAGAZINES IN THE HOME

Differences were found among the groups on the basis of the number of books reported to be in their homes. Forty-one per cent of the metropolitan boys planning to attend college reported 100 or more books in their homes as compared with 26 per cent of the metropolitan boys not planning to attend college. The critical ratio of this difference was 2.03. Comparable percentages for the metropolitan girls were 35 per cent and 23 per cent with a critical ratio of 1.98. Of the nonfarm girls planning to attend college, 62 per cent had fifty or more books in their homes, but of the nonfarm girls not planning to attend college, only 45 per cent had this many books. In general, there was a consistent and significant difference between the students planning to attend college and those not planning to attend college on the basis of the number of books in their homes.

Only one magazine appeared to consistently differentiate between students planning to attend college and students not planning to attend college. Significantly more of the students planning to attend college reported that their families subscribed to the *Reader's Digest*. For instance, 62 per cent of the metropolitan boys planning to attend college said their families read the *Reader's Digest*, but only 45 per cent of the metropolitan boys not planning to attend college reported this. Significantly more of the nonfarm girls planning to attend college had access to *Life* magazine (43 per cent compared to 22 per cent of the noncollege-planning girls). Significantly more of the metropolitan and nonfarm girls planning on college had access to *Better Homes and Gardens*.

Thus, the reading material available in the homes, in terms of both books and magazines, appeared to be related to whether or not students coming from relatively homogeneous groups planned to attend college.

MEMBERSHIP IN ORGANIZATIONS

Parental membership in organizations was also related to plans for college for this group. More of the college-planning students had parents belonging to parent-teachers associations than did the noncollege-planning students. This difference was statistically significant for the nonfarm boys and for the metropolitan girls. Significantly more of the metropolitan boys planning to attend college than of the metropolitan boys not planning to attend college had mothers who belonged to ladies' aids and to card-playing groups. Significantly more of the college-planning nonfarm girls had parents who belonged to labor unions. Thus, college plans for the high-ability group from workmen's homes were related to a parent's activity in the commmunity and in occupational organizations.

✍ 12

Girls Who Planned to Enter Nursing

Of the 13,513 girls who reported after-high-school plans, 857 (6 per cent) indicated they were planning to enter nurses' training. Unfortunately, the questionnaire provided no means of distinguishing between the girls who planned to enter directly into nurses' training and those who planned to enter college before specializing in nursing. It might be assumed that the latter group would indicate on the questionnaire their intention to go to college, and here we will make this somewhat questionable assumption, and view the girls who checked "enter nursing" as girls who planned to enter nursing with no college preparation. By geographical group, 5 per cent of the metropolitan girls, 7 per cent of the farm girls, and 7 per cent of the nonfarm girls were planning on nursing. Of the 11,379 boys who reported after-high-school plans, only 4 reported plans to take nurses' training.

AGE

At the time the questionnaires were distributed, the median age of the girls planning on nursing was 17.5 years. The ages of the girls planning on nursing were not significantly different from the ages of the girls having other plans and there were no significant age differences among the girls from cities, farms, or towns who were planning on nursing. Fewer than 1 per cent of the girls planning on nursing indicated they were also planning on being married the following year.

STATUS OF HOME

The fathers of 8 per cent of the metropolitan girls planning on nursing, 13 per cent of the nonfarm girls, and 4 per cent of the farm girls were dead. Approximately 4 per cent of the girls planning on nursing had mothers who were deceased; there were no area differences here. Of the metropolitan girls planning on nursing, 14 per cent had parents who were separated or divorced, whereas only 7 per cent of the nonfarm girls and 2 per cent of the farm girls came from broken homes. The girls from metropolitan homes planning on nursing, as was true for the metropolitan girls with other plans, tended to come from somewhat less stable families than the girls from the other areas.

OCCUPATION OF PARENTS

The modal paternal occupation for the metropolitan girls planning on nursing was "skilled trade." Almost one third of these girls came from homes where the fathers were in a skilled trade and approximately one quarter came from homes where the fathers were factory workers. One quarter of the nonfarm girls planning on nursing came from homes where the fathers were in a skilled trade and one quarter came from homes where the fathers owned or managed a business. In the metropolitan group, in terms of fathers' occupations, the girls planning on nursing resembled more closely the girls planning on jobs than they did the girls planning on college. Among the nonfarm girls, however, there was a greater tendency for the girls planning on nursing to resemble the girls planning on college. Of the metropolitan girls planning on nursing, 20 per cent came from professional homes or from homes where the father owned or managed a business, while of the nonfarm girls planning on nursing, 30 per cent came from such homes. The main difference was that there were more nonfarm girls from homes where the father owned or managed a business. Perhaps nursing was a more acceptable occupation to the middle-class families in towns than to the middle-class families in cities. The metropolitan girls planning on nursing tended to come mainly from the homes of laboring families.

The pre-marriage occupation of the mother was also related to nurses' training plans. Teaching was the occupation where the relationship was clearest: 11 per cent of the metropolitan girls planning on nursing, 16 per cent of the nonfarm girls, and 23 per cent of the farm girls had mothers who had been teachers. Having a mother who was a teacher was perhaps of most influence upon college plans, but certainly there was a significant influence here also upon plans to be a nurse.

EDUCATION OF PARENTS AND SIBLINGS

The modal education of the fathers of the metropolitan girls planning on nursing was "some high school education." Only 8 per cent of these girls had fathers who were college graduates and only 5 per cent more had fathers with some college training. The modal paternal education for the nonfarm and the farm girls planning on nursing was "completion of the eighth grade." In general, on the basis of paternal education, the girls planning on nursing more closely resembled the girls who planned on jobs than they did the girls who planned on college in that they tended to come from homes that did not have college backgrounds. This was borne out by the figures available for the mothers as well as by the figures for the fathers.

Of the mothers of metropolitan girls planning on nursing, 8 per cent were college graduates and 11 per cent had some college training but had not graduated. Figures for the mothers of nonfarm girls planning on nursing were quite similar, but relatively more of the farm girls planning on nursing had mothers with a college background. The modal education of mothers of metropolitan, nonfarm, and farm girls planning on nursing was "some high school education."

The older siblings of the girls planning on nursing tended to have college backgrounds to about the same extent as did the siblings of youth planning on college. More of the older siblings of the girls planning on nursing, however, had only high school educations, when compared with the siblings of the girls planning on college. There was some indication that the older sisters of the girls planning on nursing tended to attend college less often than did older sisters of the girls planning on college.

LANGUAGE BACKGROUND

A Scandinavian language was spoken in the homes of 23 per cent of the metropolitan girls planning on nursing, whereas only 11 per cent of the metropolitan girls planning on college and only 16 per cent of the metropolitan girls planning on jobs came from such homes. Language patterns in the home perhaps have some relationship to plans for nursing.

FAMILY INCOME

Closely related to the occupation of the father was the source of family income. Fifty-two per cent of the metropolitan girls planning on nursing came from homes where the source of income was wages, as compared with 65 per cent of the metropolitan girls planning on jobs and 28 per cent of the metropolitan girls planning on college. The family income was derived from a salary in the homes of 29 per cent of the metropolitan girls planning on nursing, as compared with 22 per cent of the metropolitan girls planning on jobs and 44 per cent of the metropolitan girls planning on college. In both the metropolitan and nonfarm groups planning on nursing, there was a tendency for the girls to come from homes lying between the homes of girls planning on jobs and the homes of girls planning on college (in terms of source of family income).

Of the metropolitan girls planning on nursing, 30 per cent said they had the necessities in their homes and 59 per cent described their homes as comfortable. Comparable figures for the metropolitan girls planning on jobs were 27 and 60 per cent and for the metropolitan girls planning on college, 16 and 68 per cent. On this basis, the metropolitan girls planning on nursing considered themselves to be more like the metropolitan girls planning on jobs than like the metropolitan girls planning on college. This tendency was not apparent, however, for the nonfarm girls, who tended to regard themselves, on the basis of how they reported their family income, as more similar to the nonfarm girls planning on college than to the nonfarm girls planning on jobs.

It thus seemed that the girls planning on nursing tended to come from homes not as high on the economic scale as the homes of the girls planning on college but somewhat higher on the economic scale than the girls planning on jobs. And there were significant differences in economic backgrounds among the girls planning on nursing coming from metropolitan areas, nonfarm areas, and farms.

REASONS FOR CHOICE

When asked their reasons for selecting nursing, approximately 83 per cent of the girls stated they regarded their plans primarily from a vocational point of view. About 10 per cent considered that nurses' training would provide them with a liberal education and about 15 per cent claimed they had made such plans in order to be independent. Between 10 and 16 per cent indicated they had chosen nursing because it would allow them to make friends and helpful connections. Approximately 18 per cent of the nonfarm and farm girls and 7 per cent of the metropolitan girls said they were influenced because they liked school. Possibly girls who like school would go to one of several schools if such schools were available, as they tend to be in metropolitan areas; but in nonfarm and farm areas, girls who like school go to whatever school is most easily available and that may frequently be a nurses' training school. In general, the expressed motivation of the girls planning on nurses' training was primarily vocational.

HIGH SCHOOL CURRICULUMS

Approximately one half of the metropolitan and nonfarm girls planning on nursing took college preparatory courses in high school. Significantly fewer of the farm girls than of girls from other areas took the college preparatory course and relatively more took the general course in high school. Approximately 11 per cent of the girls planning on nursing took a commercial course in high school. The primary reasons given for selecting the course taken in high school were that it fit vocational plans and that it was interesting. Fewer than 10 per cent of the girls planning on nursing selected their high school course on the advice of a counselor and only 4 per cent indicated they had the advice of a teacher. What little advice the girls did remember tended to come from parents.

FINANCIAL SUPPORT

Almost 40 per cent of the girls planning on nursing reported they would attend college if they had more money. In the geographical groups, 40 per cent of the metropolitan girls, 39 per cent of the nonfarm girls, and 33 per cent of the farm girls said they would go to college if they had more money. There was some evidence here that the farm girls entering nursing might eventually be more satisfied with nursing than would the girls from the other two areas. Of the girls planning on nursing and coming from metropolitan areas who would be willing to go to college if they had more money, approximately one quarter said they needed enough money for all their expenses and two thirds said they needed enough money for half of their expenses. The nonfarm girls and farm girls estimated they would need slightly more money than the metropolitan girls if they were to change their decisions and attend college.

Approximately one quarter of the girls planning on entering nurses' training said they could not afford college; about one fifth said they could easily afford college. The girls planning on nursing were for the most part somewhat better able to afford college than were the girls planning on jobs.

Approximately one third of the girls planning on nursing reported that their parents were indifferent to college and almost two thirds reported that their families wanted them to attend college. The parents of the farm girls planning on nursing appeared slightly more indifferent to college than did the parents of the metropolitan and nonfarm girls planning on nursing.

OCCUPATIONAL GOALS

When the girls were asked to name the occupation they hoped to be in after ten years, 74 per cent of the metropolitan girls and 60 per cent of the nonfarm and farm girls indicated they hoped to be in a semiprofessional job (that is, nursing), 35 per cent of the nonfarm and farm girls and 20 per cent of the metropolitan girls said they hoped to be housewives. Perhaps this indicated that the metropolitan girls planning on nursing had stronger vocational motivations than did the nonfarm or farm girls. Perhaps the farm and nonfarm girls were taking nurses' training because it was the most easily available post-high-school training, whereas the metropolitan girls, who had other training resources available, were taking nurses' training because of a genuine vocational interest.

Parental approval of the choices of the girls planning on nursing was indicated inasmuch as two thirds of the girls reported that their parents hoped the girls would enter nursing. Approximately one quarter of the parents, according to the girls, were not decided as to what occupation the girls should enter.

MATERIAL POSSESSIONS

As with the students planning on college and planning on jobs, figures were available showing the number of girls planning on nursing who had certain kinds of equipment in their homes. The homes of more girls planning on nursing than of those planning on jobs had central heating, but central heating was to be found in the homes of fewer girls planning on nursing than of girls planning on college. The same was true for the nonfarm and farm girls in terms of whether their homes had running water, hot and cold running water, mechanical refrigerators, and (for the nonfarm girls) telephones. More of the metropolitan and nonfarm girls planning on nursing had access to a deep freezer than was true for the girls planning on jobs, but fewer had access to freezers than was true for the girls planning on college. Figures on ownership of the home also indicated that, if this is considered as an index of economic status, the girls planning on nursing tended to be somewhat superior to the girls planning on jobs but somewhat inferior to the girls planning on college.

BOOKS AND MAGAZINES IN THE HOME

Of the metropolitan girls planning on nursing, 31 per cent indicated they had 100 or more books in their home, whereas only 18 per cent of the nonfarm girls and 13 per cent of the farm girls planning on nursing reported this many books. Quite consistently, the girls planning on nursing tended to have more books in their home than did the girls planning on jobs but fewer books than did girls planning on college.

The figures showing the availability of various magazines within the home did not suggest any relationship between access to magazines and plans to enter nursing. The differences previously described among the homes in the metropolitan, nonfarm, and farm areas were apparent here too, however.

MEMBERSHIP IN ORGANIZATIONS

More of the girls planning on nursing had parents who belonged to parent-teachers associations than was true for girls planning on jobs, planning on college, or planning on other schools. There was a tendency for the girls planning on nursing to resemble the girls planning on college insofar as their parents belonged to ladies' aids and community organizations more frequently than parents of girls planning on jobs, and to resemble the girls planning on jobs insofar as more of their parents belonged to labor unions than was true for the girls planning on college.

✒ 13

Girls Who Planned to Attend Business School

OF THE 13,513 girls reporting plans for after high school, 1015 (8 per cent) indicated they planned to attend business school after graduation. Six per cent of the metropolitan girls and 8 per cent of the farm and non-farm girls planned on business school. Since only 2 per cent of the boys planned to attend business school, no detailed description of the characteristics of these boys will be provided here.

AGE
The median age of the girls planning on going to business school was 17 years. Approximately 10 per cent were 16 years old and another 10 per cent were 18 years old at the time they completed the questionnaire.

MARITAL PLANS
Only 26 of the 1015 girls planning to attend business school indicated they were going to be married during the next year. Only 21 of the 26 indicated they were engaged, so apparently some were planning to be married without going through the formality of an engagement.

STATUS OF THE HOME
Approximately 93 per cent reported their fathers were alive and 97 per cent reported that their mothers were alive. Ninety-three per cent reported they came from homes that were not broken by divorce or separation; only 2 per cent of the farm girls planning to attend business school came from broken homes.

OCCUPATION OF PARENTS
Almost one third of the metropolitan girls who planned to attend business school had fathers who were skilled tradesmen, 28 per cent had fathers who were factory workers, and only 12 per cent had fathers who

owned or managed a business. Of the nonfarm girls, however, 21 per cent had fathers who were skilled tradesmen, 29 per cent had fathers who were factory workers, and 25 per cent had fathers who owned or managed a business. Thus, the nonfarm girls planning to attend business school tended to a greater extent to come from the homes of businessmen, whereas the metropolitan girls planning on business school tended to come from the homes of laboring men.

Only 5 per cent of the metropolitan girls planning to attend business school had mothers who had been teachers before marriage, but 12 per cent of the nonfarm and farm girls had mothers who had been teachers.

EDUCATION OF PARENTS

The modal paternal education for girls planning to attend business school was completion of the eighth grade. The post-eighth-grade education for fathers in the various geographic groups is shown in the accompanying tabulation.

	High School Graduation	Business or Trade Schools	Some College Training
Metropolitan	14%	13%	8%
Nonfarm	11	10	6
Farm	6	5	3

The modal education of the mothers of these girls was completion of the eighth grade with slightly more of the mothers than of the fathers having had some high school training or having completed high school. Approximately 10 per cent of these girls had mothers with some college training; the differences found in the metropolitan, nonfarm, and farm areas for fathers who went to college were not found for the mothers who went to college. The girls planning to attend business school did not tend to have mothers who had been to business school to any greater extent than did the girls planning to work or planning to become nurses; the girls planning to attend college tended to have mothers who had attended business school to a greater extent than did the girls planning to attend business school. Attending business school was perhaps one step upward in our socio-educational hierarchy.

LANGUAGE BACKGROUND

Of the girls planning on business school, 15 per cent of the metropolitan group, 23 per cent of the nonfarm group, and 34 per cent of the farm group came from homes speaking a Scandinavian language. The respective figures for German-speaking homes were 10 per cent, 13 per cent, and 18 per cent. In general, the trend here was for more girls from farm areas to come from foreign-language-speaking homes than was true for nonfarm girls and, in turn, more nonfarm girls came from foreign-language-speaking homes than did metropolitan girls.

FAMILY INCOME

Of the metropolitan girls planning to attend business school, 57 per cent came from homes where the income was derived from wages and 28 per cent came from homes where the income was derived from fixed salaries. The figures for the nonfarm girls were 42 per cent and 31 per cent. Seventy per cent of the metropolitan girls planning to attend business school reported they came from comfortable but not well-to-do homes, and the figures were approximately the same for the nonfarm and farm girls. Approximately 20 per cent of the girls planning on business school indicated they came from homes that had the necessities but no luxuries, and approximately 5 per cent reported they came from homes that were "hard up."

REASONS FOR PLANS

Approximately 76 per cent of the girls planning to attend business school had made these plans because they wanted to prepare for a vocation and slightly over 40 per cent indicated they wanted to make more money than they could if they began to work immediately. Sixteen per cent indicated they were influenced by the desire to become independent. Liking school was the reason for planning to attend business school given by 5 per cent of the metropolitan girls, 14 per cent of the nonfarm girls, and 19 per cent of the farm girls.

HIGH SCHOOL CURRICULUMS

Of the girls planning on going to business school, 61 per cent had taken a commercial course in high school and approximately 25 per cent had taken a general course. Only 9 per cent had taken a college preparatory course. Thus, most of the girls planning on business school had had related experiences in high school. Apparently very few of them had selected a high school curriculum leading directly to college.

The reasons given for selecting high school curriculums suggested the vocational thinking of these girls. Of the metropolitan girls, 52 per cent said they had taken their high school course because of vocational reasons; this was also indicated by 65 per cent of the nonfarm girls and 54 per cent of the farm girls. One third of the girls planning to attend business school said they had selected their high school course because they considered it the most interesting and 18 per cent said they took the course because they thought they would do best in it. Twelve per cent of these girls said they were influenced by their parents' advice and 7 per cent of the metropolitan girls had selected their high school course because of a counselor's advice. Only 2 per cent of the nonfarm girls and only 1 per cent of the farm girls said they had been influenced by counselors. About 2 per cent of the girls had been influenced, so they said, by advice of teachers.

ATTITUDES TOWARD COLLEGE

Of the metropolitan girls planning to attend business school, 30 per cent said they would go to college if they had more money; 46 per cent of the nonfarm girls and farm girls said they would go to college if they had more money. Of the metropolitan girls who said they would go to college if they had more money, 23 per cent said they would need enough money for all their expenses and 70 per cent said they would need enough money for about one half of their expenses. The figures were roughly the same for the nonfarm and the farm girls, although these latter two groups indicated that they perhaps needed slightly more financial assistance than the metropolitan girls.

Of the girls planning to attend business school, approximately one quarter said they could afford college easily if they wanted to attend. Fifteen per cent of the metropolitan girls, 24 per cent of the nonfarm girls, and 27 per cent of the farm girls said they could not afford college. Apparently the nonfarm girls who go to business school are influenced to a greater extent by lack of financial resources available for college than are the metropolitan girls. The metropolitan girls are often able to go to college but decide otherwise.

ATTITUDES OF PARENTS

The parents of the girls who planned on going to business school had attitudes toward college that varied according to whether or not they lived in metropolitan areas. Of the metropolitan girls planning on business school, 41 per cent had parents who were reported to be indifferent to whether or not the girl went to college, whereas of the farm and non-farm girls, only 28 per cent had parents who were indifferent. Significantly more of the nonfarm parents than of the metropolitan parents wanted their daughters to attend college. This could also be interpreted as indicating that the metropolitan girls were more likely to be planning to do what they and their parents really wanted them to do than were the other girls.

OCCUPATIONAL GOALS

Almost one fifth of the girls planning on business school wanted to be in some semiprofessional occupation ten years after graduation and another one fifth hoped to be in clerical work or a skilled trade. Approximately one half of the girls hoped to be married and to be housewives at the end of ten years. There were no significant area differences regarding these plans.

Almost one quarter of the parents hoped their daughters would be in some semiprofessional job and approximately one third of the parents hoped their daughters would be in clerical or skilled trade jobs. Another one third of the parents were undecided as to what their daughters should be doing.

MATERIAL POSSESSIONS

Information about material resources in the home indicated that the girls planning to attend business school tended to fall between the girls planning to attend college and the girls planning to work. The geographical differences are shown in the following tabulation.

	Metropolitan Girls	Nonfarm Girls	Farm Girls
Central heating............	95%	80%	60%
Running water	99	90	52
Hot and cold running water..	93	73	39
Mechanical refrigeration.....	94	85	73
Telephones	98	85	69
Deep freezers	20	40	79
Electric lights	99	99	91

Seventy-five per cent of the metropolitan girls planning to attend business school reported that their families owned their own homes as compared with 79 per cent of the nonfarm girls and 86 per cent of the farm girls. The metropolitan and the nonfarm girls tended to be similar in terms of the number of people reported living in the home, whereas the farm girls tended to report that more people lived in their homes. Related to this was the fact that the farm girls reported their homes were larger in terms of number of rooms than did the metropolitan and nonfarm girls. The extent to which girls in these three areas had rooms of their own did not vary according to areas.

Metropolitan and nonfarm girls tended to be similar on the basis of the number of cars the family owned, but significantly more of the farm-area girls who were planning on going to business school came from two-car families. There was a slight tendency for the metropolitan girls to report cars of a slightly greater value than those of the nonfarm or farm girls.

BOOKS AND MAGAZINES IN THE HOME

The metropolitan girls tended to have more books in their homes than the nonfarm girls and, in turn, the nonfarm girls tended to have more than the farm girls. One quarter of the metropolitan girls planning to attend business school reported they had more than 100 books in their homes, whereas only 10 per cent of the farm girls and 14 per cent of the nonfarm girls reported this.

Significant differences appeared between these three groups on the basis of magazines available in their homes. Almost one third of the metropolitan girls reported their families subscribed to the *Saturday Evening Post*, but only 19 per cent of the nonfarm girls and 15 per cent of the farm girls reported that this magazine was available in their homes. The girls from the three areas who were planning to attend business school tended to be similar in terms of availability of the *Reader's Digest, Liberty,* and *Collier's.*

MEMBERSHIP IN ORGANIZATIONS

Differences were also found in terms of the organizations to which the parents of these girls belonged. One quarter of the girls from the nonfarm area who were planning to attend business school reported their parents belonged to veterans' organizations, whereas only 14 per cent of the metropolitan girls and 8 per cent of the farm girls reported this. Of the farm girls planning to attend business school, 64 per cent reported that their mothers belonged to ladies' aids as compared with 48 per cent of the nonfarm girls and 17 per cent of the metropolitan girls.

⨀ 14

Parental Attitudes toward College

by BEN WILLERMAN

THE exact degree to which parental attitudes influence students' decisions to attend college is unknown. In light of the complexity of this relationship, we perhaps will never have a precise description of how parents influence their children as they are planning their post-high-school career. Certainly such a relationship exists over a long period of time and any study that does not consider the developing parent-child attitudes will provide an incomplete picture of these phenomena.

In order to obtain information that would throw light upon the reliability of the questionnaires completed by the high school seniors in this study, interviews with parents in one town were arranged to provide data comparable to that secured from their children. Indexes of agreement were then computed between the responses of parents and of children and these have been reported in Chapter 5. In addition to the questions directed toward establishing the reliability of the data obtained from the students, questions were also asked concerning the parents' attitudes toward their children's postgraduation plans, the parents' perceptions of the factors influencing the child's decision (in particular the conditions related to college-going), and the parents' attitudes about college.

The attitudes and beliefs of the parents of college-planning children and those of the parents of work-planning children were compared with two purposes in mind: first, to determine whether there was an association between parental attitude and college-going and, second, to use the parents as informants about the child's attitudes toward college or work and about the parents' own financial situation.

The interviewers were ten women, all of whom had previous experience doing open-ended interviewing for polling agencies. The interview used here was a fixed-question, free-answer type interview; the interviewers were given several hours of special training for this type of interview and were given an opportunity to practice using the interview schedule developed.

Approximately one half of the parents interviewed were fathers and one half were mothers, only one parent of each child being interviewed. The selection of the father or mother was made randomly. Appointments were made in advance with the parents who returned postcards indicating the times they would be available. There were 93 high school seniors in the town selected who had parents living in the town; parents of 90 (97 per cent) were interviewed.

Of the parents interviewed, 29 reported that their children planned to attend college and 28 reported that their children planned to obtain a job after graduation from high school. These 57 parents provided the basis for the information reported in this chapter. Of the remaining 33 parents interviewed, 11 had children who expected to attend other types of schools, 18 had children who were undecided about their plans, 3 had children who were entering military service, and 1 had a child who was getting married.

GENERAL ATTITUDES TOWARD COLLEGE

Acquiring a college education was valued by almost all parents. Only two parents said that college was not worth while. Some parents qualified their approval of higher education by remarks indicating that the ability and interests of the child should determine the usefulness of a college education.

The specific reasons for considering higher education as desirable varied considerably. These reasons, however, could be categorized into either an "economic benefit" category or a "personal development and general education" category. The parents of college-planning children and the parents of work-planning children did not differ in the frequency with which they gave reasons falling into the first category, "economic benefits." Twice as many of the parents of the college-planning group, however, gave reasons falling into the second category. Thus, parents of college-planning children and parents of work-planning children both perceived college as a path toward economic security and advancement. The parents of the college-planning group apparently placed additional emphasis on noneconomic advantages.

ATTITUDES TOWARD CHILDREN'S PLANS

The questions probing parents' attitudes toward their children's plans revealed that, for the most part, parents expressed approval of their children's decisions, regardless of whether the children had decided to attend college or to work. But, while all the parents of college-planning children expressed complete approval of their child's decision to enroll in college, about one third of parents of children planning to work would have liked their children to continue in school, despite their approval of plans to work. Here was additional evidence that college was viewed as attractive. Whatever the conflicts were between parent and child centering around attending college or beginning to work, probably few conflicts occurred as a result of parents not wishing their children to attend college.

WHAT PARENTS THOUGHT THEIR CHILDREN'S REASONS WERE

Parents were asked how their children came to make their decisions to work or to attend college. More of the parents of the college-planning group than of the work-planning group reported that the children's decisions were based upon a positive attraction. Of the parents of college-planning children, 23 said that something about college attracted their children, whereas of the parents of work-planning children, only 16 gave this as a reason. Nine parents reported their children's decisions to go to work were made through default — the children were unable to finance a college education.

Parents occasionally mentioned the influence of family members, teachers, friends, and ministers upon the students. Ten of the parents of college-going children indicated such influences, as contrasted with only 2 of the parents of the work-planning children.

Of the parents of children planning to work, 16 reported that their children had considered college, and 11 of the 16 claimed that lack of money prevented the children from attending college. Only 5 of these parents, however, believed that their children were disappointed because of their inability to attend college.

PARENTAL ATTITUDES TOWARD FINANCING COLLEGE

Of the parents of college-going children, 13 expected to pay their children's total college expenses (excluding living expenses), 10 expected to pay some of these expenses, and only 5 expected their children to pay all these expenses. Sixteen of these parents expected to pay all of their children's living expenses, 4 expected to pay some of their children's living expenses, and 9 expected their children to pay all their own living expenses. Only 4 of the parents reported that they expected their children to provide the money for both their school costs and their living expenses. Sixteen reported that they had money saved for the purpose of financing their children's education.

In order to estimate the extent of sacrifice anticipated, the parents were asked, "How hard will it be on you financially having (him, her) go to college?" One half of the parents replied "hard" or "not too easy." None of the parents complained about the sacrifice involved, all indicating that it was worth while.

REASONS FOR CHOOSING THE COLLEGE

Many different reasons were presented by the parents for the choices of the colleges which their children were to attend. The principal reasons were these: educational reputation of the institution, closeness to home, smallness of the college, affiliation of the college with the parents' church, and family tradition.

PARENTS' ATTITUDES TOWARD VOCATIONAL CHOICE

The parents of the children planning on college were asked whether their children were going to college to prepare for a particular career. Twenty-one of the 29 parents replied in the affirmative. Only 4 of the 21 parents disapproved of the occupations chosen by their children. The parents of the children planning to work also tended to approve of the children's choices of a job, with only 2 of these parents disapproving of the job chosen by their children.

SUMMARY

Perhaps the most important finding resulting from this study is the difference between the parents of college-planning children and parents of noncollege-planning children in their perceptions of the advantages of a college education. Although both groups of parents were equally cognizant that a college education is ultimately financially rewarding, the parents of the children planning to attend college emphasized the values of general education to the personal development of the student.

If we assume that parental attitudes are somehow partially responsible for the decisions to attend college, we can advance a plausible interpretation of these results. If a parent thinks of a college education primarily in terms of its contribution to the future economic welfare of his child, he may seriously consider alternative means which promise financial rewards. In other words, he may not perceive college as a necessary path for the goals he has for his child if good job opportunities are present. However, a parent who values the results of a general education is almost bound to perceive college as a necessary path for the goals he has for his child.

There is also evidence that the college-planning students had careers in mind which require a college degree. If this is a fact, their tendency to regard college as a necessary means to their goals is strengthened. Although we do not have comparable data from this particular study about the career choices of the students not planning to attend college, it is probable that their choices did not usually require a college education.

We may imagine that within the homes of college-planning students, to a greater extent than for those not planning to attend college, there is a climate of positive valuations of college education and of expectations that the children will attend college.

✒ 15

Socioeconomic Status
and After-High-School Plans

by WILBUR L. LAYTON

ARE the after-high-school plans of a high school senior related to his socio-cultural environment? When the economic status of a student is held constant, is his socio-cultural status related to his plans to attend college?

Sixty-one items obviously related to socioeconomic status were included in the questionnaire. Some of these items, such as "Source of family income," measured predominantly economic status. Some items, such as "Number of books in the home," measured predominantly socio-cultural status. Other items, such as "Organizations father or mother belong to," measured both factors to some degree.

An adaptation of Mosier's method* of "scaling by reciprocal averages"

* See "Measurement in Rural Housing, A Preliminary Report," *Educational and Psychological Measurement*, 2:139–52 (1942); *Evaluating Rural Housing* (Gainsville, Fla.: University of Florida, 1942); and "Machine Methods in Scaling by Reciprocal Averages," *Proceedings of the Research Forum* (New York: IBM Corporation, 1946), pp. 35–39.

This method results in a set of weights with the following properties: "1. the reliability of each item and the internal consistency of the weighted inventory are maximized; 2. the correlation between item and total score is maximized and the product moment correlation coefficient becomes identical with the correlation ratio; 3. the relative variance of the distribution of scores (coefficient of variation) is maximized; 4. the relative variance of item-scores within a single case is minimized; 5. the correlation between an item and total score is proportional to the standard deviation of the item-weights for that item; 6. questions which bear no relation to the total score variable are automatically weighted so that they exert no effect on the scoring.

"The method is particularly fitted for dealing with large numbers of items with discrete and qualitative, rather than quantitative, responses. The assumptions underlying the method seem to be: (1) that there exists some variable which is measured was used to obtain an economic scale and a socio-cultural scale†. Scores on the economic status scale and the cultural status scale were computed for the students earning a raw score of 120 or above on the A.C.E. Psychological Examination. These students, subdivided by sex and by the three geographical areas, constitute the group subjected to the analysis reported in this chapter.

RELATION OF THE SCALES TO COLLEGE PLANS

The economic and cultural scores for the groups classified by sex and geographical area were correlated with plans to attend or not to attend college and a correlation was also computed between the two scales for each of the groups. Table 11 presents these coefficients of correlation. The correlations between economic scores and college plans and between cultural scores and college plans were similar for the nonfarm and metropolitan boys. The correlation between cultural status and college plans for the metropolitan girls was higher than for nonfarm girls, but the correlations between economic status and college plans for these two groups were quite similar. The correlations between the economic and cultural scales for the six groups differed, being lowest for the farm groups and highest for the nonfarm groups.

These differences may be explained in this way: In smaller towns, families with the highest economic status tend to dominate the socio-cultural life of the community. In these towns professional and semi-professional occupational groups are the leaders in terms of income. Education and hence cultural status help determine economic status since greater than average education is demanded in these occupations. Therefore, one would expect a high degree of relationship between economic and cultural status in nonfarm areas.

in common by the majority of the items included in the questionnaire; (2) that this is the variable which it is desired to measure; (3) that it is possible to assign weights to the items on an a priori basis which bear some recognizable relation to the optimum weights. (This last assumption is convenient, but not necessary. If assumption (1) holds, a random distribution of initial weights should eventually produce the optimum weights.)" ("Machine Methods in Scaling by Reciprocal Averages.")

† The weights derived for the two scales may or may not be specific to the populations on which they were derived. New weights should be derived for other groups upon which the scales are to be applied. Further study may demonstrate whether or not these weights can be applied generally.

Separate scales were developed for each of the three geographical areas, metropolitan, farm, and nonfarm. A random sample of 500 students was drawn from each of the three areas. After the scales were determined, the samples were returned to the total group and were used in the further analyses.

Table 11. Coefficients of Correlation between Economic and Cultural Scores and College Plans for Boys and Girls with Raw Scores of 120 or above on the American Council on Education Psychological Examination in the Three Geographic Areas

Variables Correlated	Boys			Girls		
	Farm (N = 397)	Nonfarm (N = 899)	Metro-politan (N = 734)	Farm (N = 497)	Nonfarm (N = 897)	Metro-politan (N = 699)
Economic score and college plans (r point biserial)	.11	.31	.31	.22	.34	.38
Cultural score and college plans (r point biserial)	.15	.32	.32	.25	.39	.46
Economic score and cultural score............	.54	.79	.68	.44	.77	.68

In the metropolitan areas, skilled tradesmen and small businessmen tend to have relatively high economic status but do not have and are not required to have concomitant educational backgrounds and cultural status in their occupations. These groups tend to cause the correlation between economic and cultural status in metropolitan areas to be lower than that in small towns. This phenomenon is even more apparent among the farm groups. In these groups financial success may depend relatively less upon education, and hence cultural status, than in the other groups. Economic status in farm groups depends more upon skill in farming and farm management which at the present time are not necessarily learned through formal education. Consequently, the farmer's contact with "culture" is not apt to be highly related to his economic status.

A scrutiny of the weights assigned to the various items in the two scales indicated that the items concerned with the organizations to which parents belonged received approximately the same weights for both the economic and cultural scales. Therefore, we decided to remove these items from each scale and then compute the correlations of the scales with college plans and with each other. This was done for a sample of 102 girls and 94 boys from the nonfarm area. Table 12 presents the

Table 12. Coefficients of Correlation between Economic and Cultural Scores, with Common Items Eliminated, and College Plans for Nonfarm Boys and Girls

Variables Correlated	Boys (N = 94)	Girls (N = 102)
Economic score and college plans (r point biserial)	.31	.28
Cultural score and college plans (r point biserial)	.43	.32
Economic and cultural scores	.44	.37

correlations found. Although the correlations between the economic and cultural scores dropped considerably, perhaps as a result of the removal of the common items, the correlations between the two scales and college plans changed only slightly. Therefore the remainder of the investigation was completed using the original items for both scales.

In order to test the hypothesis that the cultural score discriminated the college-planning group from the noncollege-planning group, we computed the mean cultural scores for these groups after they had been classified by economic score. Tables 13, 14, 15, present these data. Our hypothesis was supported by the data. When we held economic scores constant, there were noticeable differences in mean cultural scores between the college-planning and noncollege-planning groups, with the latter group having lower mean scores. For the farm-area boys and girls, the differences in mean cultural scores were not nearly as great as for the other two areas. This was reflected also in the semi-partial

Table 13. Mean Cultural Scores by Economic Score Intervals for Farm-Area Boys and Girls with Raw Scores of 120 or above on the American Council on Education Psychological Examination and Classified into College-Planning and Noncollege-Planning Groups

Economic Scores		Boys				Girls		
	N	College	N	Noncollege	N	College	N	Noncollege
110–119..	2	42.50	3	43.33	3	46.33		
100–109..	17	35.59	17	33.47	20	37.80	9	29.33
90–99 ..	39	29.49	33	27.00	50	28.44	40	24.38
80–89 ..	53	24.02	39	21.95	55	24.51	54	21.04
70–79 ..	22	22.64	39	20.38	43	22.86	55	18.80
60–69 ..	29	20.66	33	17.85	26	19.46	57	18.53
50–59 ..	13	16.62	19	16.05	16	17.13	29	18.24
40–49 ..	12	19.58	17	14.12	8	17.75	23	16.78
30–39 ..	4	11.25	6	14.33	2	18.00	6	20.00
20–29 ..								
10–19 ..							1	5.00
Total and average	191	24.64	206	21.66	223	25.14	274	20.09

Table 14. Mean Cultural Scores by Economic Score Intervals for Metropolitan-Area Boys and Girls with Raw Scores of 120 or above on the American Council on Education Psychological Examination and Classified into College-Planning and Noncollege-Planning Groups

Economic Scores		Boys				Girls		
	N	College	N	Noncollege	N	College	N	Noncollege
100–109..	3	61.00			2	63.00		
90–99 ..	28	52.71			28	56.00	1	49.00
80–89 ..	67	44.96	4	33.00	68	44.88	3	42.00
70–79 ..	124	37.94	14	28.14	121	36.81	19	25.32
60–69 ..	180	31.06	38	23.16	136	30.17	58	23.55
50–59 ..	134	21.87	54	19.93	78	27.83	67	20.12
40–49 ..	41	22.20	28	20.18	37	23.76	45	18.22
30–39 ..	8	16.63	9	20.00	10	21.70	19	17.58
20–29 ..			2	18.50	2	13.00	2	16.50
Total and average	585	32.38	149	21.91	482	34.43	214	21.29

Table 15. Mean Cultural Scores by Economic Score Intervals for Nonfarm-Area
Boys and Girls with Raw Scores of 120 or above on American Council on
Education Psychological Examination and Classified into College-
Planning and Noncollege-Planning Groups

Economic	Boys				Girls			
Scores	N	College	N	Noncollege	N	College	N	Noncollege
110–119..	12	85.17			5	81.80		
100–109..	23	71.17	2	86.00	22	74.00	2	58.50
90–99 ..	58	60.78	7	56.00	56	60.41	8	52.63
80–89 ..	105	50.26	12	43.58	98	50.44	27	38.50
70–79 ..	157	38.48	47	32.57	138	37.54	67	34.55
60–69 ..	144	29.61	58	27.02	114	32.43	92	26.07
50–59 ..	70	26.47	76	23.00	75	27.73	69	21.97
40–49 ..	38	22.29	48	20.40	34	21.00	52	20.65
30–39 ..	18	19.00	14	18.79	7	20.00	26	17.23
20–29 ..	6	15.00	1	9.00	3	17.33	5	17.80
10–19 ..	1	8.00						
Total and average	632	39.41	265	27.11	552	40.26	348	27.05

correlations which indicated the relationship between economic scores
and college plans and between cultural scores and college plans.

Table 16 presents the semi-partial correlations and multiple correlations between college planning and economic and cultural scores for
the high A.C.E. groups from the nonfarm, metropolitan, and farm areas.*
When the economic score was partialed out from the cultural, and the
cultural score was partialed out from the economic, the correlation with
the criterion, college planning, dropped considerably. For the girls in
the three groups there remained a significant correlation between cultural status and college planning after the economic score was partialed
out. However, this was not true for the boys in the three groups, and
when the cultural score was partialed out from the economic score and
the latter was correlated with the criterion, college planning, the correlations dropped to almost zero for all groups. This supports the hypothesis that cultural status is important when one holds economic score con-

* A coefficient of semi-partial correlation indicates the relation between two
variables when a third variable is partialed out (held constant statistically) from
one of the variables but not the other. In the more familiar coefficient of partial
correlation, the third variable is partialed out of both original variables.

The coefficients of semi-partial correlation were computed to give further information on the relation of cultural and economic scores to each other and to
college plans.

Table 16. Semi-Partial and Multiple Correlations between College Plans and Economic and Cultural Scores

	Boys			Girls		
Item	Farm	Nonfarm	Metro-politan	Farm	Nonfarm	Metro-politan
Correlation between economic score and college plans with cultural score partialed out of (held constant in) college plans	.03	.06	.10	.11	.05	.08
Correlation between cultural score and college plans with economic score partialed out of college plans	.09	.08	.12	.16	.14	.21
Correlation between economic score and college plans with cultural score partialed out of economic score	.04	.10	.12	.12	.07	.10
Correlation between cultural score and college plans with economic score partialed out of cultural score	.10	.12	.15	.17	.20	.27
Multiple correlation between college plans and economic and cultural scores	.15	.33	.35	.28	.40	.47

stant. When one holds cultural status constant, economic status has very little relationship with college-going for any of the three major groups. For all groups the multiple correlations are somewhat higher than the semi-partial correlations.

RELATION OF THE SCALES AND FATHER'S OCCUPATION TO COLLEGE PLANS

Next the relation between economic and cultural status and college plans, with the father's occupation held constant, was determined. This analysis was made for each of the three areas and the two sexes. For the farm area this analysis was possible for only the occupational group "farmer." The results are presented in Tables 17, 18, and 19, and graphed in Figures 3 and 4. (The results for the farm area were not graphed.) These data are presented in terms of standard scores which have a mean of 50 and a standard deviation of 10. The standard scores were computed from the distribution for each of the major groups that were presented.

The metropolitan area. There was wide variation in the means on the economic scale for the college-planning metropolitan boys classified by father's occupation (Table 17 and Figure 3, top half). Students whose fathers owned or managed their own businesses had the highest mean economic score. The next highest mean economic score belonged to those students whose fathers were professional men. Somewhat lower, by about four standard score points, was the mean for students whose fathers engaged in sales work. A wide discrepancy in mean economic score existed between students whose fathers owned or managed their

Table 17. Mean Economic and Cultural Scores by Father's Occupation for Metropolitan Boys and Girls with Raw Scores of 120 or above on the American Council on Education Psychological Examination and Classified into College-Planning and Noncollege-Planning Groups (Means Expressed in Standard Scores with a Mean of 50 and Standard Deviation of 10)

Father's Occupation	College Group			Noncollege Group		
	N	Economic Score	Cultural Score	N	Economic Score	Cultural Score
BOYS						
Profession	129	56.46	57.78	12	48.03	50.29
Owns or manages business	114	58.87	55.75	24	51.45	44.62
Office work	64	49.20	50.32	13	44.20	43.65
Sales	72	52.22	52.11	10	48.32	47.06
Owns or manages farm	11	51.89	44.50	3	49.39	36.12
Skilled tradesman	93	43.56	44.00	35	41.53	42.20
Factory worker	52	43.29	45.41	24	41.17	41.05
Other occupations	27	49.28	51.77	8	45.45	44.17
No data	21	42.81	47.16	20	35.59	42.20
GIRLS						
Profession	99	50.49	60.04	13	50.97	51.56
Owns or manages business	112	58.95	55.33	22	51.86	44.67
Office work	56	51.30	51.40	17	46.26	44.99
Sales	56	51.45	55.21	19	47.12	46.05
Owns or manages farm	6	52.74	44.91	5	46.92	36.15
Skilled tradesman	71	52.65	46.89	59	43.04	42.65
Factory worker	29	40.15	43.14	44	41.52	40.69
Other occupations	24	49.97	49.61	7	39.57	45.49
Retired or pensioned	5	45.25	54.47	2	46.85	43.25
No data	24	42.40	48.92	25	37.91	39.60

Table 18. Mean Economic and Cultural Scores by Father's Occupation for Nonfarm Boys and Girls with Raw Scores of 120 or above on the American Council on Education Psychological Examination and Classified into College-Planning and Noncollege-Planning Groups (Means Expressed in Standard Scores with a Mean of 50 and Standard Deviation of 10)

Father's Occupation	N	College Group		N	Noncollege Group	
		Economic Score	Cultural Score		Economic Score	Cultural Score
BOYS						
Profession	110	57.74	58.45	23	52.08	52.26
Owns or manages business	179	57.94	56.31	51	51.03	48.24
Office work	47	52.72	52.44	13	47.87	47.94
Sales	45	54.15	51.94	14	47.22	45.50
Owns or manages farm.....	16	50.01	49.82	4	46.21	46.15
Skilled tradesman...	81	41.75	45.89	76	42.77	43.75
Factory worker.....	72	41.57	43.59	44	40.01	41.28
Other occupations...	33	51.08	49.93	19	43.79	43.07
Retired or pensioned	9	50.74	49.63			
No data..........	40	57.74	46.92	19	40.12	41.72
GIRLS						
Profession	105	58.52	60.42	14	48.12	51.60
Owns or manages business	157	58.21	63.04	68	53.14	48.67
Office work	28	48.62	52.18	20	48.12	48.85
Sales	49	52.49	52.74	26	52.91	49.02
Owns or manages farm....	12	48.07	44.35	8	44.94	44.22
Skilled tradesman...	75	45.31	47.14	76	43.00	42.71
Factory worker.....	55	44.07	45.98	60	39.51	41.00
Other occupations...	35	49.10	51.47	31	46.09	45.15
Retired or pensioned	2	43.88	46.56	11	45.75	45.32
No data	32	45.53	48.86	30	40.08	47.27

own businesses and those whose fathers were skilled tradesmen and factory workers. This was a difference of approximately eighteen standard score points. Also worthy of note was the fact that the mean economic scores of students whose fathers engaged in office work was almost exactly the mean for the entire group of boys who planned to attend college.

The patterns of the mean economic scores for the college-planning and the noncollege-planning groups were almost identical. However, the mean economic scores for the noncollege-planning boys were lower than those of the college-planning boys. The largest discrepancy between mean economic scores for the two groups was for the boys whose fathers were in the professions. The next highest discrepancies in mean economic scores were between college-planning and noncollege-planning boys whose fathers were in the categories "owns or manages own business" and "office work." Although the mean economic scores for all groups of college-planning boys were above the group mean (college and noncollege groups combined), only one of the means for the noncollege-planning group was above the group mean.

A high degree of relationship between economic status and cultural status appeared for all groups of college-planning boys except for the

Table 19. Mean Economic and Cultural Scores for Farm Boys and Girls with Raw Scores of 120 or above on the American Council on Education Psychological Examination and Classified into College-Planning and Noncollege-Planning Groups (Means Expressed in Standard Scores with a Mean of 50 and Standard Deviation of 10)*

Item	Boys	Girls
College-planning group		
Number	149	191
Mean economic score	53.29	53.56
Mean cultural score	51.65	52.72
Noncollege-planning group		
Number	172	229
Mean economic score	50.24	49.65
Mean cultural score	48.70	47.68

*Only a few of the fathers in this group were engaged in occupations other than farming; hence, the other occupations were not included.

group whose fathers were farmers and for those for whom no data on the father's occupation were available. For the group whose fathers were farmers, the mean cultural score was far below the mean economic score. The relationship between economic and cultural scores was not as great for the noncollege-planning boys as for the college-planning boys.

Further evidence to support the importance of cultural status in determining college plans is the fact that the mean cultural scores for the college-planning groups were higher than those for the noncollege-planning groups. The largest difference was for the group whose fathers owned or managed their own businesses. The smallest discrepancy was for the group whose fathers were skilled tradesmen. The mean cultural scores for five of the college groups were above the total group mean

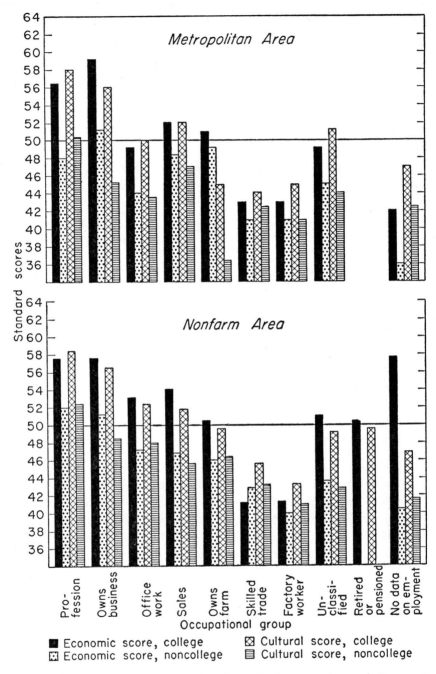

Figure 3. Mean economic and cultural standard scores of metropolitan and nonfarm boys grouped by father's occupation

188

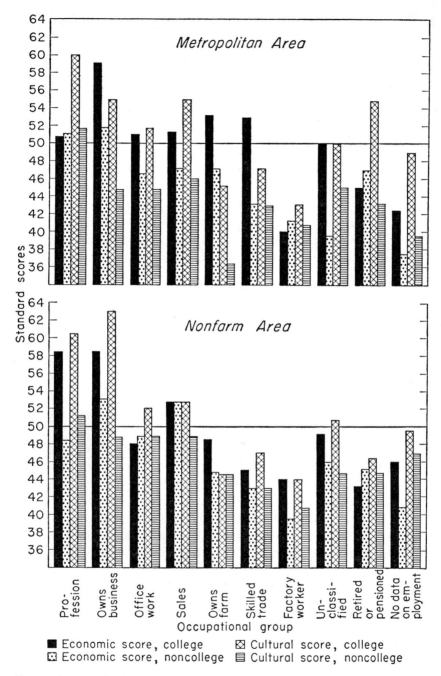

Standard scores

Metropolitan Area

Nonfarm Area

Occupational group

Pro- fession | Owns business | Office work | Sales | Owns farm | Skilled trade | Factory worker | Un- classi- fied | Retired or pensioned | No data on em- ployment

■ Economic score, college   ⊠ Cultural score, college
⊡ Economic score, noncollege   ⊟ Cultural score, noncollege

Figure 4. Mean economic and cultural standard scores of metropolitan and nonfarm girls grouped by father's occupation

whereas for only one of the noncollege groups did the mean cultural score even equal the total mean.

When one examines all the patterns of the mean scores for the metropolitan boys (in Figure 3), it is apparent that there is a complex relationship between economic and cultural scores and college plans. For example, there was a discrepancy in favor of the college-planning group in both scales. However, on the economic scale this difference was most pronounced for the three higher occupational groups, the "professional" group, the "owns or manages own business" group, and the "sales" group. In the cultural scale, there appeared to be approximately the same discrepancy for every occupational group except for the skilled trades and factory worker occupations. Perhaps some other variable was operating here to account for the lack of discrepancy. Such a variable might be a status-seeking drive on the part of these students, so that as many of them would come from low cultural status homes as would come from high. This would make the mean cultural status score of the college-planning group identical, or approximately so, with that of the group which was not planning to go to college.

For the metropolitan girls, the general patterns of mean scores (see Figure 4, top half) were very similar to those for the boys. However, for the college and noncollege girls whose fathers were factory workers or in the professions there was almost no difference in mean economic scores. For these two groups the cultural status score differentiated the college-planning from the noncollege-planning girls. For girls whose fathers were in a profession there was a difference of 8.5 standard score points between the mean cultural status scores of the group planning to attend college and the group not planning to attend college. The mean cultural score for the college-planning girls whose fathers were factory workers was only 2.5 points above the mean cultural score for girls whose fathers were similarly employed and who were not planning on going to college.

The pattern of mean cultural scores for the girls planning to go to college was generally similar to that for the boys planning to go to college. For the girls, but not for the boys, the mean cultural status score for those whose fathers were professional men was much higher than the mean economic score for the same group. This was not true for the girls whose fathers were in the skilled trades or farming. For these girls the mean cultural score was much lower than the mean economic score.

This discrepancy did not hold for the college-planning boys whose fathers were in the skilled trades.

The pattern of mean cultural scores for noncollege-planning girls was similar to that of the college-planning girls, but the scores were not as high. The noncollege-planning boys and girls had lower mean cultural as well as lower mean economic scores than did the college-planning boys and girls. For four groups of girls in Figure 4 the mean cultural status score was much above the comparable mean economic score. These were the girls whose fathers were professional men, salesmen, factory workers, retired or pensioned, or for whom there were no data about the father's occupation. For most of the groups the cultural scores differentiated the college group from the noncollege group much better than did the economic scores. For the daughters of skilled tradesmen, the economic score as well as the cultural score differentiated the two groups. For daughters of factory workers, the difference in mean cultural scores was in the expected direction but was relatively small. The economic score did not discriminate for this group. For the girls whose fathers owned or managed their own businesses, the mean cultural score was below the mean economic status score for both the college-planning and the noncollege-planning groups. Hence, the higher the cultural score the greater the likelihood of the girl's planning on college.

The nonfarm area. The bottom half of Figure 3 shows the high degree of correlation between the economic and cultural scores for the boys in the nonfarm area since the economic and cultural patterns for the college and noncollege groups almost coincide. In every case, except for the skilled trades and factory worker occupations, the mean economic score for the college-planning boys was much higher than the mean economic score for the noncollege-planning boys. The mean cultural score for the boys planning on college was higher than the mean cultural score for those not planning on college. This again supports the hypothesis that the cultural score is an important determiner of college-going. This was particularly true in the skilled trades and factory worker occupations, for which the economic score does not discriminate but the cultural score does.

For the nonfarm group of girls, the mean economic scores of the college-planning girls exceeded the mean economic scores of the noncollege-planning girls for all occupational groups except sales and those retired or pensioned. However, only in the professional and factory worker occupations were there very large differences between the mean economic scores for the girls planning on college and those of girls not planning on college. For the nonfarm group of girls as a whole, the cultural score discriminated between those planning to go to college and those who were not. The exception was those whose fathers were farmers; the mean cultural scores coincided for the two groups. For the girls whose fathers were in the professions the difference between the mean cultural score for the college and noncollege groups of girls was much greater than the difference in the mean economic scores for the two groups. For the office work, sales, skilled trades, and "other" occupations, the cultural score discriminated between the girls planning on college and those who were not. (See bottom half of Figure 4.)

The farm area. For the farm-area groups there were so few students living on farms whose fathers were not engaged in farming that we have presented only the mean economic and cultural scores for the boys and girls broken down into college and noncollege groups (see Table 19). For the boys there was very little difference in mean economic and cultural scores for the college and the noncollege groups, although the differences were in the hypothesized direction. The difference in the mean scores for the girls planning on college and the girls not planning on college was also quite small although again in the expected direction.

▶ 16

The Follow-up

THE sample drawn for the follow-up study consisted of 2735 persons, of whom 1283 were from the metropolitan areas and 1452 were from the nonmetropolitan areas of the state. As Table 20 shows, the sample was almost equally divided between boys and girls, with 1329 boys and 1367 girls in the sample, not including the 39 cases to whom questionnaires were not delivered because of wrong addresses.

Table 20. Sex and Geographic Area of Those to Whom
Questionnaires Were Sent*

Item	Boys	Girls	Total
Metropolitan group			
Returns	562	553	1115
Non-returns	66	65	131
Nonmetropolitan group			
Returns	478	528	1006
Non-returns	223	221	444
Total			
Returns	1040	1081	2121
Non-returns	289	286	575

* Questionnaires sent to 39 persons were undelivered because of wrong addresses. These have not been included in this table.

Of the 2735 questionnaires mailed, 77 per cent were returned. Table 21 shows the returns from metropolitan and nonmetropolitan areas and the type of return. Slightly more questionnaires were returned by mail from the nonmetropolitan group, but when we consider the greater number of questionnaires that were not delivered to the metropolitan group, the small difference in percentage has no significance, and we can conclude that response before the telephone follow-up was the same from metropolitan and nonmetropolitan groups.

193

Table 21. Number of Questionnaires Mailed to Metropolitan and Nonmetropolitan Groups and Number and Percentage Returned by Mail or Phone and Not Returned

Item	Metropolitan		Nonmetropolitan		Total	
	Number	Per Cent	Number	Per Cent	Number	Per Cent
Number of questionnaires mailed	1283		1452		2735	
Loss by bad address, etc......	37	3	2	.1	39	1.4
Returned by mail ..	804	63	1006	69	1810	66
Returned by phone .	311	24			311	11
Not returned......	131	10	444	31	575	21
Total returns......	1115	87	1006	69	2121	77

The total percentage of questionnaires returned by the metropolitan group, including those returned in response to the telephone follow-up, was 87 per cent, whereas the return by the nonmetropolitan group, who received no telephone follow-up, was 69 per cent. If we are willing to assume that the *rate* of return to a mailed questionnaire was the same for metropolitan and nonmetropolitan groups (and the day-by-day tally kept of questionnaires returned indicated this assumption was justified), then the telephone follow-up resulted in the return being increased from 69 to 87 per cent, or an increase of 26 per cent.

Since only the Minneapolis–St. Paul areas were followed up by telephone, and not the Duluth area, the total return from the Twin City area approximated 95 per cent, an increase in return resulting from telephone follow-up amounting to 38 per cent.

The four sub-samples to whom questionnaires were mailed (metropolitan boys, metropolitan girls, nonmetropolitan boys, and nonmetropolitan girls) were compared with the total samples from which they were drawn on the basis of their after-high-school plans. The chi square test provided probabilities indicating the two male groups and the metropolitan girls were representative of their total samples in this regard. A probability between .01 and .001 indicated, however, that the sub-sample of nonmetropolitan girls was not representative of the total group of nonmetropolitan girls in terms of their after-high-school plans. The sub-sample selected for the follow-up had in it significantly more girls who were planning on going to college than did the total sample. Inasmuch as the same procedures were used in selecting all four sub-samples, no explanation occurs to us as to why this difference appeared except that it is a chance difference of the order that would appear one time in every 500. The effect this difference has upon the results obtained is not known.

Of the 2121 students who returned the follow-up questionnaire, 887 (42 per cent) indicated on the original questionnaires that they planned on attending college. Of these 887 people, 657 (74 per cent) reported one year later on their follow-up questionnaires that they actually attended college. Table 22 shows no significant difference between the proportions of metropolitan boys and metropolitan girls planning on college who actually attended. The metropolitan boys were similar to the nonmetropolitan boys in this respect. Significantly fewer of the non-metropolitan girls planning on college actually arrived there, as compared with the other three groups. In the group of students planning on going to college but reporting they did not, the girls showed a greater tendency to get jobs, whereas the boys tended to join the armed forces. Apparently girls from nonmetropolitan areas are less able to follow their plans to attend college than are girls from metropolitan areas or boys from either metropolitan or nonmetropolitan areas.

Of the 2121 students reporting in the follow-up, 723 originally planned to go to work after graduating from high school, and 527 of these 723 (73 per cent) reported they did obtain jobs. Table 23 shows that of those planning on working, significantly more girls followed their plans than did boys. Even if those who actually worked for their parents are added to those who obtained jobs, relatively fewer nonmetropolitan boys than nonmetropolitan girls among those planning on working actually did work. Most of the male group planning on working, but failing to follow these plans, entered the armed forces. In none of the groups was there a marked tendency for those planning on working to attend college instead. Apparently, in the group of high school seniors planning on working after graduation, relatively few, under existing conditions, will change their plans and attend college.

The other side of the picture is obtained by looking at Tables 23 and 24. In Table 23, of the 743 students who reported they were actually attending college (35 per cent of the 2121 students reported they were attending college), 657 (88 per cent) were following the plans they had reported a year earlier. The proportion of nonmetropolitan boys in college who originally had so planned was significantly less than the pro-

Table 22. What the 887 High School Graduates Planning to Go to College
Reported They Actually Did

What College-Planning Graduates Did	Percentage of Metropolitan Group		Percentage of Nonmetropolitan Group	
	Boys (N = 305)	Girls (N = 216)	Boys (N = 162)	Girls (N = 204)
Got a job................	11	21	8	19
Worked for parents........	1	0	4	1
Went to college...........	78	74	77	66
Went to other school.......	5	4	3	8
Joined armed forces.......	5	0	8	1
Went into nurses' training...	0	1	0	4
Miscellaneous	1	1	0	2

Table 23. What the 723 High School Graduates Planning to Go to Work
Reported They Actually Did

What Job-Planning Graduates Did	Percentage of Metropolitan Group		Percentage of Nonmetropolitan Group	
	Boys (N = 161)	Girls (N = 222)	Boys (N = 140)	Girls (N = 200)
Got a job.................	73	86	42	80
Worked for parents........	2	1	14	4
Went to college...........	4	4	9	3
Went to other school.......	4	2	3	6
Joined armed forces.......	13	0	32	1
Went into nurses' training...	0	1	0	1
Miscellaneous	4	7	0	7

Table 24. Original Plans of the 743 High School Seniors Who Reported
They Actually Went to College

Original Plan	Percentage of Metropolitan Group		Percentage of Nonmetropolitan Group	
	Boys (N = 258)	Girls (N = 180*)	Boys (N = 155)	Girls (N = 150)
Get a job................	3	5	8	4
Work for parents..........	0	0	1	0
Go to college.............	93	89	80	89
Go to other school.........	3	6	5	6
Join armed forces.........	2	0	5	0
Go into nurses' training....	0	1	0	1
Miscellaneous	0	0	0	0

* Two of these expressed no original plans.

portion of other college students who were following their original plans.

Of the 858 boys and girls who reported they were actually working, 527 (61 per cent) had originally planned to work, and 130 (15 per cent) had originally planned to attend college. None of the differences between the four groups in Table 25 is statistically significant.

Thus, of those who during their senior year planned to attend college, 25 per cent failed to follow those plans. Of those who had jobs, 15 per cent had originally planned on college. Table 26 presents figures showing the number of students planning on and attending college, according to area and sex.

The major question approached in the follow-up study was this: How did those who followed their plans differ from those who did not? The

Table 25. Original Plans of the 858 High School Seniors Who Reported They Actually Went to Work

| Original Plan | Percentage of Metropolitan Group | | Percentage of Nonmetropolitan Group | |
	Boys (N = 203*)	Girls (N = 302†)	Boys (N = 106)	Girls (N = 247)
Get a job................	57	63	56	65
Work for parents..........	0	0	9	1
Go to college.............	17	15	12	15
Go to other school.........	16	16	8	15
Join armed forces..........	6	1	12	0
Go into nurses' training.....	0	2	0	2
Miscellaneous	2	3	2	1

* Three of these expressed no original plans.
† One of these expressed no original plans.

Table 26. Number and Percentage of Each of the Four Groups Reporting They Attended College

| | Metropolitan Group | | Nonmetropolitan Group | |
	Boys	Girls	Boys	Girls
Planned on college and went.....	239	160	124	134
Didn't plan on college but went...	19	20	31	15
Total in college................	258	180	155	149
Total not in college............	287	345	316	331
Total number.................	545	525	471	480
Percentage in college..........	47%	34%	33%	31%

rest of this chapter will attempt to answer this question. Of the 2059* individuals considered in the following sections, 1327 (64 per cent) followed their original plans. In one sense, this can be called the "realizability" of the plans of high school seniors. The respective "realizabilities" for metropolitan boys and girls are 68 and 68 per cent, for nonmetropolitan boys and girls, 65 and 55 per cent. The nonmetropolitan girls followed their original plans statistically significantly less often than did those in the other three groups.

METROPOLITAN BOYS

Inspection of Tables 27, 28, and 29 allows comparisons to be made between those metropolitan boys who reported they followed their original plans and those who reported they did not. In Table 27, those who followed their plans are divided according to those plans. Those who did not follow their plans are divided in Table 28 according to their original plans and in Table 29 according to what they actually did. The N's in Tables 28 and 29 are not the same because some individuals who provided information about plans did not provide information that could be coded about what they did.

There was a tendency for those boys planning on and attending college to have been younger than those planning on but not attending college, and a tendency for those planning on working and actually working to have been older than those planning on working but not working. These differences were not statistically significant,† but they do suggest that the stability of plans may be somewhat related to age — the *younger* boys who planned on college had more stable plans than the older boys who planned on college, and the *older* boys who planned on working had more stable plans than the younger boys who planned on working.

There was a slight, but statistically insignificant, tendency for those whose fathers were still alive to have followed their plans to a greater extent than did those whose fathers were dead.

A statistically significant tendency appeared for those who planned on college and actually attended to have come more frequently from

* Of the 2121 boys and girls who returned questionnaires, information regarding either plans or actual behavior was ambiguous for 62 cases, and these were eliminated from this analysis.

† In this, as in the other chapters, if the difference between two percentages is at the .05 per cent level of probability, it is labeled as statistically significant.

homes where the income was derived from professional fees, profits, or fixed salaries than did those who failed to follow their original college-going plans. This difference is related to the distribution of fathers' occupations. Of those who planned on attending college and did attend, 39 per cent had fathers in professional or managerial jobs, while of those who failed to follow their college-going plans, only 23 per cent had fathers in such jobs. Of the 44 sons of professional workers who planned on college, 89 per cent reported they attended college, whereas of the 48 sons of skilled tradesmen who planned on college, only 67 per cent actually attended. Of the 40 sons of factory workers who planned on college, 75 per cent actually attended. In general for this group, the higher the level of the father's occupation, the greater the probability that college plans would be realized, but this was far from a perfect relationship.

In terms of following original plans, regardless of what they were, 80 per cent of the sons of professional workers followed their plans as compared with 75 per cent of the sons of business owners and managers, 72 per cent of the sons of office workers, 66 per cent of the sons of skilled tradesmen, and 71 per cent of the sons of factory workers. Thus, with the exception of the last group, a direct relationship appears for metropolitan boys between the realizability of post-high-school plans and the level of fathers' occupations.

Of the 546 metropolitan boys, 56 reported that their mothers had been teachers prior to marriage. Of those who planned on going to college but did not attend, 5 per cent had mothers who had been teachers, while of those who planned on and actually attended college, 13 per cent had mothers who were teachers. Having a mother who had been a teacher apparently improved one's chances of carrying out plans to attend college.

Of those who planned on going to work and actually did go to work, 3 per cent had mothers who had been teachers, but of those so planning who did not go to work, 7 per cent had mothers who were teachers. The occupation of the mother before marriage bears a definite relationship to the extent to which plans for after high school are realized, perhaps regardless of what those plans are.

Closely related to parental occupation, particularly to paternal occupation, and to source of income, is the size of the family income as perceived by the pupil. Of the 34 metropolitan boys who indicated their

Table 27. Descriptive Data in Percentages According to Metropolitan-Nonmetropolitan Source, Sex, and After-High-School Plans of Those Who Followed Their Original Plans

| | Metropolitan Group | | | | | | | | Nonmetropolitan Group | | | | | | | | |
| | Boys | | | | Girls | | | | Boys | | | | | Girls | | | |
Item	Work	Col.	Other Schl.	Mil. Ser.	Work	Col.	Other Schl.	Nurs.	Work	Wk. for Work Parent	Col.	Other Schl.	Mil. Ser.	Work	Col.	Other Schl.	Nurs.
TOTAL NUMBER*	117	239	13	5	191	160	10	5	59	44	124	9	21	161	134	18	17
Age																	
16	7%	10%	23%	0%	9%	14%	0%	20%	5%	5%	10%	11%	10%	11%	5%	11%	0%
17	65	75	38	40	77	79	100	60	63	82	73	67	57	71	90	44	100
18	25	11	38	60	10	7	0	20	24	14	13	22	24	15	4	39	0
19	1	1	0	0	1	0	0	0	5	0	1	0	5	2	1	6	0
20	0	0	0	0	0	0	0	0	3	0	1	0	0	0	0	0	0
23	0	0	0	0	0	0	0	0	0	0	2	0	0	0	0	0	0
No information	3	3	0	0	3	1	0	0	0	0		0	5	1	0	0	0
Status of father																	
Father living	91	95	92	100	89	91	100	100	90	93	96	89	90	95	95	83	94
Father dead	9	5	8	0	10	9	0	0	10	7	4	11	10	5	5	17	6
No information	0	.4	0	0	.5	0	0	0	0	0	0	0	0	0	0	0	0
Source of income																	
Prof. fees, profits	4	25	15	0	13	24	10	20	25	93	39	44	19	37	58	50	53
Fixed salary	19	48	15	20	19	40	20	20	22	5	37	22	33	22	22	11	24
Wages	69	25	62	80	61	25	60	60	49	0	18	33	48	32	14	28	24
Investments	0	1	0	0	1	5	10	0	0	2	2	0	0	1	2	6	0
Pensions	7	.4	8	0	6	1	0	0	3	0	2	0	0	3	2	0	0
No information	1	1	0	0	.5	5	0	0	0	0	2	0	0	5	2	6	0
Occupation of father																	
Profession	4	16	8	0	2	14	0	0	3	0	20	0	0	1	13	6	0
Owns or manages business	4	23	0	20	12	29	0	20	7	9	24	33	5	11	27	6	29
Office work	9	12	8	20	7	8	20	20	2	0	10	0	10	1	1	6	0
Sales	5	16	15	0	5	15	10	0	5	0	2	0	5	2	6	11	6

200

Owns or manages farm......	1	0	0	2	1	0	20	82	15	22	5	32	31	22	41
Skilled trades...	13	8	0	33	16	40	14	0	10	11	33	17	12	6	12
Factory work..	12	38	40	19	2	10	31	2	6	22	24	25	4	28	6
Other occupation	2	15	0	9	6	20	7	0	6	0	5	2	2	0	6
Disabled	.4	0	0	0	0	0	0	0	0	0	0	1	0	0	0
Retired	0	0	0	1	1	0	0	0	2	0	0	1	1	6	0
Unemployed ...	0	0	0	0	0	0	0	0	0	0	0	0	0	0	0
No information .	4	8	20	10	8	0	10	7	4	11	14	6	3	11	0
Occupation of mother before marriage															
Don't know....	47	23	60	35	13	40	12	27	19	33	62	30	13	44	12
Teacher	3	23	0	3	17	0	46	20	27	11	0	8	33	11	24
Other	41	38	40	53	63	50	27	30	37	33	33	40	44	22	47
No information .	9	15	0	8	8	10	15	23	16	22	5	21	10	22	18
Size of income															
Frequently have difficulty..	3	0	0	2	1	0	10	0	2	0	5	2	3	0	0
Sometimes have difficulty	5	8	0	6	1	0	7	2	2	0	5	7	2	11	6
Have necessities, but not many luxuries	38	46	0	22	18	30	24	18	25	33	38	29	16	11	18
Comfortable ...	45	46	80	65	58	70	49	70	65	55	48	58	66	67	65
Well-to-do	3	0	20	3	17	0	3	9	4	11	5	0	0	0	0
Wealthy	0	0	0	0	1	0	0	0	1	0	0	2	13	0	6
No information .	5	2	0	3	6	0	7	0	2	0	0	2	1	11	6
High school curriculum															
Commercial ...	12	0	0	58	5	50	3	5	2	0	10	61	10	33	18
Agriculture	1	0	0	0	0	0	3	20	2	11	0	0	0	0	0
Shop or technical	15	8	40	0	0	0	29	16	2	11	29	1	1	6	0
College preparatory....	9	46	20	4	79	30	14	11	67	22	14	7	63	33	35
General	60	46	40	35	15	20	51	48	27	44	43	30	25	22	47
Other	3	0	0	2	0	0	0	0	0	11	0	1	0	6	0
No information .	1	.4	0	2	1	0	0	0	0	0	5	1	0	0	0

* The only category in which the total numbers are different is indicated in a note (‡) on p. 203.

Table 27 — Continued

Item	Metropolitan Group								Nonmetropolitan Group									
	Boys				Girls				Boys					Girls			
	Work	Col.	Other Schl.	Mil. Ser.	Work	Col.	Other Schl.	Nurs.	Work	Wk. for Parent	Col.	Other Schl.	Mil. Ser.	Work	Col.	Other Schl.	Nurs.
Reasons for making plans†																	
Prepare for a vocation	26	69	54	80	18	76	60	100	36	39	75	44	43	24	81	78	76
To be with old school friends..	0	1	0	0	0	0	0	0	3	0	2	0	0	0	1	0	0
To get liberal education	3	35	15	0	.5	43	10	0	2	2	35	11	19	2	32	6	6
To start making money quickly..	33	.4	8	0	20	1	0	0	29	30	1	11	5	28	1	6	0
To please parents or friends......	2	1	0	0	3	7	10	0	2	9	5	0	0	4	4	6	6
To be independent ...	20	5	8	20	38	9	0	0	19	22	13	0	10	24	14	28	12
To make friends and helpful connections	21	6	0	0	8	15	10	0	7	0	9	0	10	11	14	33	12
It's the thing to do........	7	7	0	0	4	4	0	0	10	9	10	0	5	4	6	0	0
Foregone conclusion, never questioned why	5	4	0	0	8	4	0	0	2	11	4	0	0	6	6	0	6
Will enable me to make more money	15	17	38	0	15	4	0	20	17	30	20	0	14	23	12	11	6
Everyone else does it	0	0	0	0	0	1	0	0	0	0	0	0	0	0	0	0	0

Table with questionnaire responses (percent). Figures are arranged by group, sex, and post‑school plan.

	Metropolitan Group						Nonmetropolitan Group						
	Boys			**Girls**			**Boys**				**Girls**		
	Work	Other Schl.	Mil. Ser.	Work	Other Schl.	Nurs.	Work	Wk. for Parent	Other Schl.	Mil. Ser.	Work	Other Schl.	Nurs.
Tired of studying, had enough education	3	.4	0	40	2	0	0	0	8	5	0	0	0
Only thing I could afford....	19	0	8	0	16	0	0	19	7	0	1	14	6
Like school....	1	8	15	0	.5	18	20	3	0	11	10	23	12
Family help on expense													
Pay all expenses	16			42			11				38		
Pay most expenses	33			30			40				36		
Pay some expenses	41			24			36				20		
Pay no expenses	9			2			10				6		
No information .	1			3			2				0		
If not going to college, would you change your plans if you had more money?													
Yes	36	38	20	26	10	20	39	30	11	29	36	11	6
No	53	38	60	63	30	20	51	57	33	57	54	22	29
No information .	11	23	20	11	60	60	10	14	55	14	10	67	65
If yes to above, how much money would you need?‡													
Enough to pay all expenses....	50	40	0	45	0	0	48	38	0	50	57	50	0

† More than one reason may be checked by any given individual.

‡ The total numbers in this category were as follows:

	Metropolitan Group						Nonmetropolitan Group						
	Boys			**Girls**			**Boys**				**Girls**		
	Work	Other Schl.	Mil. Ser.	Work	Other Schl.	Nurs.	Work	Wk. for Parent	Other Schl.	Mil. Ser.	Work	Other Schl.	Nurs.
	42	5	1	49	1	1	23	13	1	6	58	2	1

203

Table 27 — Continued

Item	Metropolitan Group								Nonmetropolitan Group								
	Boys				Girls				Boys					Girls			
	Work	Col.	Other Schl.	Mil. Ser.	Work	Col.	Other Schl.	Nurs.	Work	Wk. for Parent	Col.	Other Schl.	Mil. Ser.	Work	Col.	Other Schl.	Nurs.
Enough to pay half	36		40	100	49		100	100	48	62		100	50	38		50	100
Enough to pay less than half	10		0	0	6		0	0	0	0		0	0	3		0	0
No information	5		20	0	0		0	0	4	0		0	0	2		0	0
If not going to college, could you afford it if you wished?																	
Easily	7		8	0	14		10	0	8	27		11	10	8		0	12
Barely	21		38	40	17		10	0	19	16		33	29	23		6	0
Many sacrifices	34		15	0	31		10	60	22	41		11	19	22		6	18
No	31		8	40	30		20	0	42	11		11	33	36		12	12
No information	8		31	20	7		50	40	8	5		33	10	11		78	59
Attitude of family toward college																	
Insists I go	1	19	0	0	0	10	0	0	0	0	12	0	0	0	9	0	6
Wants me to go	44	74	54	20	24	82	40	60	34	32	74	89	38	28	81	56	71
Indifferent	42	3	31	40	59	6	50	20	46	57	10	11	38	54	9	28	18
Doesn't want me to go	3	0	0	0	5	0	10	0	2	9	0	0	5	8	0	6	0
Won't allow me to go	1	0	0	40	0	0	0	0	2	0	0	0	0	0	0	0	0
No information	9	4	15	0	12	3	0	20	17	2	3	0	19	10	1	11	6
Approximate number of books in home																	
0–9	10	1	8	20	3	2	40	60	8	14	5	0	5	18	7	11	18
10–24	18	6	15	0	19	6	10	0	36	27	13	44	29	24	13	17	12
25–49	26	18	0	40	29	11	30	40	29	25	19	22	29	24	25	33	35
50–99	23	26	8	20	28	28	20	0	15	16	27	11	14	21	18	22	18
100–up	18	49	69	0	18	51	0	0	8	14	37	22	19	12	37	17	18
No information	4	.4	0	20	3	3	0	0	3	5	0	0	5	1	0	0	0

Table 28. Descriptive Data in Percentages According to Metropolitan-Nonmetropolitan Source, Sex, and After-High-School Plans for Those Who Did Not Follow Their Original Plans

Item	Metropolitan Group Boys Work	Col.	Other Schl.	Mil. Ser.	Metropolitan Group Girls Work	Col.	Other Schl.	Nurs.	Nonmetropolitan Group Boys Work	Wk. for Parent	Col.	Other Schl.	Mil. Ser.	Nonmetropolitan Group Girls Work	Col.	Other Schl.	Nurs.
TOTAL NUMBER*	44	66	46	16	31	60	70	9	81	27	38	41	24	39	70	60	10
Age																	
15	0%	0%	0%	0%	0%	2%	0%	0%	0%	0%	0%	0%	0%	0%	0%	0%	0%
16	5	8	4	13	6	15	14	22	1	4	3	2	0	10	3	5	20
17	75	67	67	69	81	67	70	67	65	63	74	51	91	67	80	75	40
18	11	23	26	13	13	15	10	11	27	26	16	34	4	18	17	18	30
19	2	2	2	6	0	2	4	0	4	4	3	10	4	3	0	2	0
20	2	0	0	0	0	0	0	0	1	0	3	2	0	0	0	0	0
21	2	0	0	0	0	0	1	0	1	0	3	0	0	0	0	0	0
No information	2	2	0	0	0	0	0	0	0	4	0	0	0	3	0	0	10
Status of father																	
Father living	86	89	89	100	87	88	93	100	89	100	95	98	91	90	96	96	80
Father dead	11	11	11	0	10	12	7	0	11	0	5	2	8	10	4	3	20
No information	2	0	0	0	3	0	0	0	0	0	0	0	0	0	0	0	0
Source of income																	
Prof. fees, profits	11	18	15	13	6	10	11	0	44	89	45	51	25	69	49	57	60
Fixed salary	16	36	20	25	19	42	29	33	22	7	24	15	37	5	20	8	10
Wages	70	41	63	63	65	42	57	67	25	4	26	29	0	23	21	28	20
Investments	2	2	0	0	3	3	0	0	1	0	2	2	4	0	3	3	0
Pensions	0	0	2	0	3	0	1	0	4	0	2	2	0	3	6	2	10
Commissions	0	0	0	0	0	0	0	0	1	0	0	0	0	0	0	0	0
No information	0	2	0	0	3	3	1	0	2	0	0	0	33	0	1	2	0
Occupation of father																	
Profession	5	8	7	6	3	7	10	11	2	0	13	2	8	5	3	0	0
Owns or manages business	9	15	11	6	6	18	7	0	14	22	13	20	4	3	14	15	10

* The only category in which the total numbers are different is indicated in a note (‡) on p. 209.

Table 28 — Continued

Item	Metropolitan Group Boys Work	Col.	Other Schl.	Mil. Ser.	Metropolitan Group Girls Work	Col.	Other Schl.	Nurs.	Nonmetropolitan Group Boys Work	Wk. for Parent	Col.	Other Schl.	Mil. Ser.	Nonmetropolitan Group Girls Work	Col.	Other Schl.	Nurs.
Office work	5	9	11	19	3	8	6	22	0	0	5	2	0	0	7	0	0
Sales	7	15	2	0	6	8	9	11	0	0	0	5	4	3	7	3	0
Owns or manages farm	0	2	7	0	3	3	0	11	32	67	37	37	33	59	34	43	40
Skilled trades	39	24	28	50	26	20	31	44	19	4	8	15	21	15	10	15	10
Factory work	16	15	24	6	32	13	26	0	17	7	16	15	25	8	13	17	20
Other occupation	9	2	0	13	3	10	3	0	2	0	2	0	0	0	4	3	0
Disabled	0	0	0	0	0	0	1	0	0	0	0	0	0	0	1	0	0
Retired	0	0	0	0	3	0	0	0	0	0	2	0	0	0	1	2	0
Unemployed	0	0	0	0	0	0	0	0	0	0	0	0	0	0	0	0	0
No information	11	12	11	0	13	12	7	0	7	0	2	5	4	8	4	1	20
Occupation of mother before marriage																	
Don't know	36	27	43	18	48	17	20	22	43	41	32	54	33	33	31	37	20
Teacher	7	5	7	6	3	7	9	0	11	19	24	5	21	10	13	7	0
Other	43	53	33	63	45	60	56	78	26	22	26	29	17	38	39	33	60
No information	14	15	17	13	3	17	16	0	20	19	18	12	29	18	17	23	20
Size of income																	
Frequently have difficulty	5	6	2	0	3	2	6	0	7	0	0	10	0	5	9	0	10
Sometimes have difficulty	11	2	0	13	0	0	1	0	9	0	5	5	8	8	1	7	10
Have all necessities, not many luxuries	36	21	48	50	23	22	19	22	28	22	21	32	46	28	21	28	30

	1	2	3	4	5	6	7	8	9	10	11	12	13	14	15	16	17
Comfortable	43	59	39	31	68	67	73	67	47	67	61	41	42	56	64	58	40
Well-to-do	5	8	9	0	3	7	0	11	6	4	11	7	0	3	3	3	10
Wealthy	0	0	2	0	0	0	0	0	1	0	0	0	0	0	0	0	0
No information .	0	5	0	6	3	3	1	0	1	7	3	5	4	0	1	3	0
High school curriculum																	
Commercial ...	14	3	13	13	32	12	36	22	6	4	0	10	0	41	26	37	10
Agriculture	2	3	2	0	0	0	0	0	10	22	3	0	0	0	0	0	0
Shop or technical	11	5	15	19	0	0	0	0	14	11	0	29	12	0	0	0	0
College																	
preparatory	9	56	11	6	10	63	23	22	11	7	53	5	17	15	37	20	40
General	64	33	54	56	52	25	39	44	56	52	45	54	71	44	37	42	50
Other	0	0	4	0	6	0	3	11	1	0	0	2	0	0	0	2	0
No information .	0	0	0	6	0	0	0	0	2	4	0	0	0	0	0	0	0
Reasons for making original plans†																	
Prepare for vocation	30	64	70	38	0	72	67	88	25	30	79	80	50	0	80	80	70
To be with old school friends ..	2	2	0	6	16	2	0	0	1	4	0	0	4	0	1	2	0
To get liberal education	2	29	11	6	0	38	1	0	2	0	26	7	8	3	21	5	30
To make money quickly	27	5	4	13	0	0	9	11	52	19	8	7	8	36	0	7	0
To please parents and friends	5	3	4	0	23	2	3	0	5	15	3	0	4	3	6	3	0
To be independent ...	39	11	17	19	0	8	19	11	25	15	16	15	21	23	7	17	10
To make friends and helpful connections	9	12	2	6	35	7	7	22	6	7	11	5	12	13	9	10	10
It is the thing to do.........	11	5	9	0	13	0	1	0	6	15	11	10	21	8	4	3	10
Foregone conclusion, never questioned why.	5	3	0	0	10	2	1	0	2	7	0	2	12	5	0	3	0

† More than one reason may be checked by any given individual.

Table 28 – Continued

Item	Metropolitan Group								Nonmetropolitan Group								
	Boys				Girls				Boys					Girls			
	Work	Col.	Other Schl.	Mil. Ser.	Work	Col.	Other Schl.	Nurs.	Work	Wk. for Parent	Col.	Other Schl.	Mil. Ser.	Work	Col.	Other Schl.	Nurs.
Will enable me to make more money	20	24	13	0	3	5	20	0	27	15	24	37	8	18	17	25	10
Everyone else does it	0	0	0	0	23	0	0	0	1	0	0	0	0	0	0	0	0
Tired of studying, had enough school	5	0	0	0	0	0	0	0	2	11	0	2	0	8	0	0	0
Only thing I can afford	20	0	0	13	16	0	0	0	25	11	0	0	25	21	0	5	0
Like school	0	9	0	0	0	8	3	0	1	0	13	0	8	3	13	7	0
Family help with expenses																	
Pay all expenses		2				12					3				19		
Pay most expenses		8				38					32				39		
Pay some expenses		21				42					47				36		
Pay no expenses		53				7					16				4		
No information		17				2					3				3		
If not going to college, would you change your plans if you had more money?																	
Yes	48		22	44	32		21	22	47	22		24	37	28		28	20
No	45		37	31	55		47	33	42	48		29	54	56		27	40
No information	7		41	25	13		31	44	11	30		46	8	15		45	40

If "yes" to above, how much more money?‡

	Metropolitan Group						Nonmetropolitan Group						
	Boys			Girls			Boys				Girls		
	Work	Other Schl.	Mil Ser.	Work	Other Schl.	Nurs.	Work	Wk. for Parent	Other Schl.	Mil. Ser.	Work	Other Schl.	Nurs.
Enough to pay all expenses	43	20	14	30	53	0	53	17	30	44	36	53	0
Enough to pay half	52	80	71	60	47	100	47	67	70	56	55	47	100
Enough to pay less than half	5	0	14	0	0	0	0	0	0	0	9	0	0
No information	0	0	0	10	0	0	0	17	0	0	0	0	0

If not going to college, could you afford it if you wished?

	Metropolitan Group						Nonmetropolitan Group						
	Boys			Girls			Boys				Girls		
	Work	Other Schl.	Mil Ser.	Work	Other Schl.	Nurs.	Work	Wk. for Parent	Other Schl.	Mil. Ser.	Work	Other Schl.	Nurs.
Easily afford	11	7	13	19	17	22	15	14	17	0	10	7	10
Barely afford	7	13	31	16	20	33	41	14	24	17	26	18	10
Many sacrifices	27	22	25	39	16	0	22	31	20	29	31	25	10
Couldn't afford	41	22	31	16	17	22	7	32	5	46	28	12	20
No information	14	37	0	10	30	22	15	10	34	8	5	38	50

‡ The total numbers in this category were as follows:

Metropolitan Group					
Boys			Girls		
Work	Other Schl.	Mil Ser.	Work	Other Schl.	Nurs.
21	10	7	10	15	2

Nonmetropolitan Group						
Boys				Girls		
Work	Wk. for Parent	Other Schl.	Mil. Ser.	Work	Other Schl.	Nurs.
38	6	10	9	11	17	2

209

Table 28 – Continued

Item	Metropolitan Group								Nonmetropolitan Group								
	Boys				Girls				Boys					Girls			
	Work	Col.	Other Schl.	Mil. Ser.	Work	Col.	Other Schl.	Nurs.	Work	Wk. for Parent	Col.	Other Schl.	Mil. Ser.	Work	Col.	Other Schl.	Nurs.
How does your family feel about your going to college?																	
Insists I go	11	11	2	0	0	5	16	0	2	4	3	0	0	0	6	0	10
Wants me to go	7	68	65	44	42	77	49	33	42	26	66	54	29	26	73	45	40
Indifferent	27	12	28	50	45	12	31	44	44	41	24	41	62	59	14	47	30
Doesn't want me to go	41	0	0	0	6	3	4	11	2	7	0	2	0	8	1	2	0
Won't allow me to go	0	0	0	0	0	0	0	0	1	0	0	0	0	0	0	0	0
No information	11	9	4	6	6	3	0	11	7	22	8	2	8	8	4	7	20
Approximate number of books in home																	
0–9	5	5	0	0	3	5	6	12	12	11	8	15	8	10	7	8	0
10–24	7	15	17	13	13	10	16	23	23	22	13	32	25	36	9	40	20
25–49	27	23	37	25	35	8	21	31	31	19	16	22	25	26	33	22	10
50–99	30	26	24	31	26	35	31	16	16	26	26	15	17	10	23	13	40
100–up	30	30	17	31	19	42	23	12	12	19	37	0	17	8	29	15	30
No information	2	2	4	0	3	0	3	5	5	4	0	17	8	8	0	2	0

Table 29. Descriptive Data in Percentages According to Metropolitan-Nonmetropolitan Source, Sex, and What They Reported They Actually Did for Those Who Did Not Follow Their Original Plans

Item	Metropolitan Group								Nonmetropolitan Group									
	Boys				Girls				Boys					Girls			
	Work	Col.	Other Schl.	Mil. Ser.	Work	Col.	Other Schl.	Nurs.	Work	Wk. for Parent	Col.	Other Schl.	Mil. Ser.	Work	Col.	Other Schl.	Nurs.
TOTAL NUMBER*	86	19	24	42	111	20	20	8	47	38	31	16	82	87	15	33	15
Age																	
15	0%	0%	0%	0%	1%	0%	0%	0%	0%	0%	0%	0%	0%	0%	0%	0%	0%
16	9	11	4	5	16	10	15	13	0	5	0	13	0	5	13	9	7
17	62	74	92	55	67	85	70	50	70	58	87	69	63	75	67	73	73
18	26	11	4	31	13	5	10	38	26	37	13	6	24	20	13	12	20
19	2	5	0	5	3	0	5	0	2	0	0	6	9	1	0	3	0
20	0	0	0	0	0	0	0	0	2	0	0	6	1	0	7	0	0
21	0	0	0	2	1	0	0	0	0	0	0	0	3	0	0	0	0
No information	2	0	0	2	0	0	0	0	0	0	0	0	0	0	0	3	0
Status of father																	
Father living	93	89	87	83	90	100	90	88	97	97	97	94	88	94	87	97	87
Father dead	7	11	13	14	10	0	10	13	4	3	3	6	12	6	13	3	13
No information	0	0	0	3	0	0	0	0	0	0	0	0	0	0	0	0	0
Source of income																	
Prof. fees or profits	12	21	8	14	9	10	5	0	43	79	48	69	38	51	60	73	40
Fixed salary	26	16	33	26	32	35	35	25	15	5	32	19	23	13	13	12	20
Wages	59	63	58	52	54	50	55	63	38	5	19	13	31	26	27	12	27
Investments	1	0	0	2	1	0	5	0	0	5	0	0	1	2	0	0	7
Pensions	0	0	0	2	0	0	0	13	4	0	0	0	6	6	0	3	7
Commissions	1	0	0	0	0	0	0	0	0	0	0	0	1	0	0	0	0
No information	1	0	0	2	4	5	0	0	0	5	0	0	0	2	0	0	0

* The only category in which the total numbers are different is indicated in a note (‡) on p. 215.

211

Table 29 — Continued

Item	Metropolitan Group								Nonmetropolitan Group								
	Boys				Girls				Boys					Girls			
	Work	Col.	Other Schl.	Mil. Ser.	Work	Col.	Other Schl.	Nurs.	Work	Wk. for Parent	Col.	Other Schl.	Mil. Ser.	Work	Col.	Other Schl.	Nurs.
Occupation of father																	
Profession	5	16	8	5	7	20	10	0	4	0	10	19	4	0	0	6	7
Owns or manages business	8	16	4	14	12	10	10	0	9	18	13	6	18	7	7	15	27
Office work	13	11	4	5	6	0	10	25	2	0	6	0	4	6	0	0	0
Sales	8	0	4	9	6	10	10	0	0	3	6	0	4	6	7	9	0
Owns or manages farm	2	5	0	0	1	0	5	0	38	71	39	56	18	44	40	52	13
Skilled trades	29	26	46	31	29	20	20	38	19	0	3	13	23	9	20	3	27
Factory work	23	16	17	14	23	35	15	25	21	5	16	6	18	17	13	9	7
Other occupation	3	5	0	7	5	5	10	0	0	0	3	0	3	3	7	0	7
Disabled	0	0	0	0	1	0	0	0	0	0	0	0	0	1	0	0	0
Retired	0	0	0	0	0	0	0	0	2	0	0	0	0	1	0	0	0
No information	8	5	17	14	10	0	10	13	4	3	3	0	9	6	7	3	13
Occupation of mother before marriage																	
Don't know	34	32	29	36	21	25	20	25	36	53	45	38	44	39	40	27	27
Teacher	5	11	4	5	5	15	10	25	13	5	23	44	9	3	13	12	20
Other	44	58	42	45	56	60	65	38	32	24	19	13	27	34	33	52	40
No information	17	0	25	14	18	0	5	13	19	18	13	6	21	23	13	9	13
Size of income																	
Frequently have difficulty	2	0	8	5	3	10	5	0	0	5	0	0	10	8	0	3	13
Sometimes have difficulty	5	0	0	9	1	0	0	0	4	8	10	0	6	3	7	12	7

Have all necessities, not many luxuries	36	47	29	33	19	15	30	25	28	24	23	19	38	26	13	21	13
Comfortable ...	42	47	58	48	70	70	60	63	62	47	61	63	37	56	67	55	60
Well-to-do	9	5	4	2	3	5	5	13	0	10	6	13	6	1	13	9	7
Wealthy	1	0	0	0	0	0	0	0	0	0	0	0	0	0	0	0	0
No information .	5	0	0	2	5	0	0	0	6	3	0	6	4	5	0	0	0
High school curriculum																	
Commercial ...	8	21	4	7	29	20	15	0	2	8	6	6	5	33	13	52	0
Agriculture	2	5	0	2	0	0	0	0	4	16	3	13	5	0	0	0	0
Shop or technical	16	5	8	2	0	0	0	0	13	10	10	13	17	0	0	0	73
College preparatory	24	21	38	33	32	35	40	63	19	5	19	31	18	23	33	18	20
General	47	42	46	55	35	45	40	38	60	58	58	38	52	44	53	30	0
Other	0	5	4	0	5	0	5	0	0	3	3	0	0	0	0	0	0
No information .	2	0	0	0	0	0	0	0	2	0	0	0	3	0	0	0	7
Reasons for making original plans†																	
Prepare for vocation	59	47	62	43	63	35	50	100	53	39	48	50	45	11	33	33	13
To be with old school friends ..	2	5	0	0	1	0	0	0	4	0	0	0	1	76	47	55	87
To get liberal education	15	5	29	9	17	5	15	25	9	5	16	13	5	2	0	0	7
To make money quickly	7	16	0	24	7	10	5	0	6	34	26	19	33	15	0	15	13
To please parents and friends	5	0	4	5	3	5	5	0	6	3	6	13	3	5	27	12	0
To be independent ...	15	26	21	31	15	5	10	13	26	13	16	19	20	7	0	6	0
To make friends and helpful connections ...	9	11	4	12	9	10	10	13	9	10	10	13	5	10	13	18	13

† More than one reason may be checked by any given individual.

Table 29 – Continued

	Metropolitan Group								Nonmetropolitan Group								
	Boys				Girls				Boys					Girls			
Item	Work	Col.	Other Schl.	Mil. Ser.	Work	Col.	Other Schl.	Nurs.	Work	Wk. for Parent	Col.	Other Schl.	Mil. Ser.	Work	Col.	Other Schl.	Nurs.
It is the thing to do	3	11	8	9	2	10	0	0	15	8	6	31	5	9	0	12	13
Foregone conclusion, never questioned why	3	11	0	2	1	5	10	0	9	3	3	0	3	6	7	3	7
Will enable me to make more money	0	0	8	19	13	10	10	0	21	37	23	13	23	3	0	6	0
Everyone does it	0	0	0	0	0	0	0	0	0	0	0	0	1	0	7	0	0
Tired of studying, had enough of school	0	0	4	2	0	0	0	0	4	3	3	6	1	0	7	3	0
Only thing I can afford	2	5	4	12	1	15	10	0	9	8	16	19	17	1	27	6	0
Like school	3	0	4	5	5	5	5	0	0	3	3	19	1	6	13	18	7
Family help with expenses																	
Pay all expenses		0				20					6				7		
Pay most expenses		16				10					13				20		
Pay some expenses		16				20					23				13		
Pay no expenses		5				0					10				6		
No information		63				50					48				53		
If not going to college, would you change your plans if you had more money?																	
Yes	22		25	28	17		25	13	22	13		31	41	26		18	27
No	25		17	31	32		30	0	39	58		31	31	21		21	7
No information	52		58	40	51		45	88	39	30		38	28	53		61	67

214

	Metropolitan Group						Nonmetropolitan Group						
	Boys			Girls			Boys				Girls		
	Work	Other Schl.	Mil. Ser.	Work	Other Schl.	Nurs.	Work	Wk. for Parent	Other Schl.	Mil. Ser.	Work	Other Schl.	Nurs.
If "yes" to above, how much more money?‡													
Enough to pay all expenses....	37	33	42	42	100	0	60	60	100	29	57	50	50
Enough to pay half........	58	33	58	58	0	100	40	40	0	65	4	33	50
Enough to pay less than half...	5	17	0	0	0	0	0	0	0	3	0	17	0
No information.	0	17	0	0	0	0	0	0	0	3	39	0	0
If not going to college, could you afford it if you wished?													
Easily afford ...	8	4	9	15	0	0	13	13	19	10	3	12	0
Barely afford...	7	8	9	15	10	0	19	21	13	16	13	9	27
Many sacrifices .	19	17	14	5	20	13	15	32	31	23	18	9	7
Couldn't afford .	20	12	31	14	20	0	21	16	6	23	14	9	13
No information .	46	58	36	50	50	87	32	18	31	28	52	61	53

‡ The total numbers in this category were as follows:

	Metropolitan Group						Nonmetropolitan Group						
	Boys			Girls			Boys				Girls		
	Work	Other Schl.	Mil. Ser.	Work	Other Schl.	Nurs.	Work	Wk. for Parent	Other Schl.	Mil. Ser.	Work	Other Schl.	Nurs.
	19	6	12	19	5	1	10	5	5	34	23	6	4

Table 29 – Continued

| | Metropolitan Group | | | | | | | | Nonmetropolitan Group | | | | | | | | |
| | Boys | | | | Girls | | | | Boys | | | | | Girls | | | |
Item	Work	Col.	Other Schl.	Mil. Ser.	Work	Col.	Other Schl.	Nurs.	Work	Wk. for Parent	Col.	Other Schl.	Mil. Ser.	Work	Col.	Other Schl.	Nurs.
Attitude of family toward college																	
Insists I go	6	74	0	9	3	0	0	0	2	0	3	6	1	1	7	6	0
Wants me to go	59	21	79	45	56	65	60	63	30	21	61	38	59	54	40	49	67
Indifferent	27	0	17	28	27	25	20	13	51	68	29	50	28	34	40	33	27
Doesn't want me to go	0	0	0	0	3	0	20	0	2	5	0	0	3	3	0	3	0
Won't allow me to go	0	0	0	0	0	0	0	0	0	0	0	0	1	0	0	0	0
No information	8	5	4	17	12	10	0	25	15	5	6	6	9	7	13	9	7
Approximate number of books in home																	
0–9	1	0	4	5	5	5	5	0	13	18	6	6	11	10	7	3	0
10–24	15	11	17	14	16	5	10	0	19	26	23	6	20	29	40	27	13
25–49	28	32	29	21	20	30	5	0	17	24	29	44	26	25	13	27	27
50–99	24	16	25	28	24	25	50	50	30	8	13	19	23	16	20	18	13
100–up	27	42	21	31	32	35	25	50	17	13	29	25	18	17	13	21	47
No information	5	0	4	0	2	0	5	0	4	11	0	0	3	7	7	9	0

216

families frequently or sometimes had difficulty obtaining life's necessities, 56 per cent reported they followed their original plans, while of the 331 boys who reported their families were financially comfortable, well-to-do, or wealthy, 72 per cent had followed their plans. Again, this is evidence that the economic status of the family is related to the extent to which youths' plans are realized.

The student's curriculum in high school also bears a relationship to the outcomes of these plans. Of those metropolitan boys planning on and attending colleges, 79 per cent had taken the college preparatory course and only 17 per cent had taken the general course. Only 4 per cent had taken vocational curriculums. Of those planning on college but not attending, only 56 per cent had taken the college preparatory course, while 33 per cent had taken the general course and 11 per cent had taken vocational courses.

High school curriculums are usually selected prior to entering grade 10. The 44 boys who as seniors were in other than college preparatory courses and who nevertheless were planning on attending college, although they actually did not attend college, might to some extent have laid their resulting frustration to selecting the wrong high school curriculum. Since the majority of boys who planned on college and did not arrive there actually had taken the college preparatory course, however, this certainly is not the only explanatory factor. The available data do not indicate whether or not the 44 boys in other than college preparatory courses who planned on college but did not attend should have attended.

The stated reasons for making plans supply a possible index of a student's motivation, and yet there are but few significant differences between those who followed their plans and those who did not, as far as their reasons for making plans were concerned.

For those planning on college, the reason "to make more money" was checked more frequently by those who actually did not attend than by those who did attend, but this was not a statistically significant difference. Of those who followed their plans to work, 11 per cent checked "desire for independence" as a reason for their plans, while of those who did not follow their work plans, 20 per cent checked that reason, a statistically significant difference. Apparently not only was there a difference in family status between those who did and did not achieve their plans, but also there was some difference in motivational structure.

The extent to which a student perceived his family's willingness and ability to subsidize his college training provided an index to both family attitude and family financial resources. Of the metropolitan boys who planned on going to college, 16 per cent of those who attended said their families would pay all expenses and 2 per cent of those who did not attend said this (a statistically significant difference). Of those who did attend college, only 9 per cent said their family would pay none of their expenses, while of those who did not attend, 53 per cent said their family would not pay any of their expenses.

Of those who said they were going to work and actually did work, 36 per cent said they would go to college if they had more money, while of those who planned on working but did not work, 48 per cent said they would go to college if they had more money. Although this difference is not statistically significant, it does approach significance.

The extent of the influence of family attitude upon college attendance was suggested by the fact that of those who planned on college, 93 per cent who attended said their families either insisted they go or wanted them to go, whereas only 79 per cent of those who did not attend college reported their families favored college, a statistically significant difference. Of those students who planned on working, 45 per cent of those who followed their plans had parents who favored college and only 18 per cent of those who did not work had parents who favored college. One might expect that if a student who planned on working had parents who favored college, this would influence him so he would not follow those plans, but this was not the case.

Of the entire group here who followed their plans, 75 per cent had parents who insisted on or favored college, while of the group that did not follow their plans, only 57 per cent had parents favoring college. This difference was statistically significant.

The number of books reported in the home provided another index to home status. Of those students who planned on college, 49 per cent of those who actually attended college indicated they had 100 or more books in their homes, whereas of those who did not attend, only 30 per cent reported this many books, a statistically significant difference. Of those students who did not follow their plans, regardless of what their plans were, 27 per cent reported 100 or more books in their home, while of those who followed their plans, 39 per cent reported that many. Apparently, the greater the number of books reported in the home (and by inference, the higher the educational level of the home), the greater the probability that metropolitan boys will realize their after-high-school plans, particularly if these plans involve college.

Another aspect of this general problem is shown by the figures presented in Tables 27 and 29, which compare those boys who were pursuing the activities they had originally planned with those who were in the same activities although these were not the activities they had originally planned. The prior discussion compared those who followed their plans with those who did not, this latter group considered according to plan. Now we will discuss the former group and the latter group considered according to what they actually did. Thus, the boys in the first group who planned on working and who actually did work will be compared with those who originally did not plan on working but nevertheless did work. Because the number of cases was sufficiently large only in the "get a job" group, the other groups cannot be considered. It is interesting to note, however, that although only 5 of these metropolitan boys planned on entering the military service, 42 of them actually did so. Only 19 boys who originally had not planned on college were attending college. Any efforts that might have been made to influence boys not planning on college in order to encourage them to attend were relatively ineffectual.

Of the boys who went to work, those who originally planned on working did not differ statistically significantly from those who had not so planned in regard to age, whether the father was living, source of family income, occupation of father or mother, size of income, or number of books in the home.

Of those actually working, the boys who had not planned on working had statistically significantly more often taken college preparatory courses in high school. The group not originally planning on working had given more frequently as a reason for their original plans "to prepare for a vocation," whereas the group originally planning on working more often presented as reasons "to make more money" and "to make money quickly." The boys who originally planned on working and did work more often stated this was the only plan they could afford.

Of the boys who were working, 36 per cent of those who planned on working said they would go to college if they had more money while only 22 per cent of those not planning on working said they would go to college if they had more money. In the first group, 45 per cent said their parents wanted or insisted they go to college, whereas in the group originally not planning on working, 65 per cent had parents with these attitudes. Parental attitude, as much as parental status, appears to be related to whether or not youth follow their after-high-school plans.

The same comparisons made among the metropolitan boys were made among the metropolitan girls, as shown in Tables 27, 28, and 29. Of the 536 metropolitan girls, 366 (68 per cent) followed their original plans. The accompanying tabulation shows the breakdown by plan. Working

Plan	Number Who Originally Had Plan	Realized Plan	
		Number	Per Cent
Work	222	191	86
College	220	160	73
Other schools...........	80	10	13
Nursing	14	5	36

appeared to be the most realizable plan for these girls and going to "other schools" the least realizable.

There was a tendency for the girls planning on and attending college to be somewhat younger than those planning on but not attending college. There was a similar tendency for the girls planning on working and so doing to be younger than those planning on working but not working. Stability of plans, for this group, appeared to be inversely related to age.

No statistically significant difference appeared between the metropolitan girls who followed their plans and those who did not in terms of whether the father was living, occupation of the mother before marriage (although there was a tendency for more of those who went to college to have mothers who had been teachers than did those who did not go to college), size of income, family's attitude toward college, and the number of books in the home.

Statistically significantly more of the girls planning on and attending college had fathers in the professional and managerial occupations than did the girls planning on but not attending college. Of the former group, 43 per cent had fathers in these occupations and of the latter group, 25 per cent. Of the girls planning on college but not attending, 33 per cent had fathers in the skilled trades and in factory work, as compared with 18 per cent of the girls planning on and attending college. Similar statistically significant differences were found, as one would expect, in sources of family income. Of those who followed their college plans, 24 per cent of the families derived their income from professional fees and profits and 25 per cent from wages, whereas of those who did not follow their college plans, 10 per cent derived income from fees and profits and 42 per cent from wages.

Clear-cut and significant differences distinguished the two groups in regard to the type of curriculum followed in high school. Of those girls planning on working, 58 per cent of the girls who did work took a commercial course and 35 per cent took a general course, whereas 32 per cent of the girls who did not work took a commercial course and 52 per cent took a general course. Of the girls planning on and actually attending college, 79 per cent took a college preparatory course, while of those so planning but not attending college, 63 per cent took that course. Apparently students who follow their plans tend to be the ones who have selected high school curriculums most appropriate for those plans.

Although no statistically significant differences were found within the group planning on college in terms of reasons for making post-high-school plans, the girls who planned on working and did work differed from those who planned on working but did not work. Of the girls who followed their working plans, 18 per cent indicated they planned on working because this would give them vocational preparation, whereas none of the girls planning on working but not working reported this. On the other hand, 16 per cent of the latter group said their planning had been influenced by the desire to be with old friends, but none of the former group said this. Of those who followed their plans to work, 20 per cent said they wanted to make money quickly and 15 per cent said plans to work would enable them to make more money, whereas of the group who planned on working but did not work, none gave as a reason the desire to make money quickly and only 3 per cent thought plans to work would enable them to make more money. In the group not following their plans to work, 23 per cent said, "Everyone else does this," whereas in the other group, none made that comment.

Apparently, for these metropolitan girls, the stability of plans to work was directly related to the extent to which a girl was financially motivated and inversely related to the extent to which she was influenced by her friendships.

The girls anticipating more financial help from their families were more likely to follow their college-going plans than the girls not anticipating such help. Of those who followed their college plans, 42 per cent expected their families to provide full financial support, whereas of those planning on but not attending college, only 12 per cent had expected such support. Of the girls who did not attend college, 51 per cent expected less than "most of their support" to come from their family, while of the girls who did attend college, only 29 per cent expected so little support. Only 6 of the 220 girls planning on college expected no financial help from their families.

Although not statistically significant, a difference in family attitude was suggested when those girls planning on working and actually doing so were compared with those who did not carry out their plans to work. Of the former group, 24 per cent said their families wanted them to go to college, whereas of the latter group, 42 per cent said this. Perhaps family wishes do influence girls to change their plans from working to continued schooling.

When the metropolitan girls who did not follow their original plans were divided according to what they reported they actually did do, the only group with enough cases for comparison was the group of girls who went to work. Thus, we were only able to compare the girls who were working in accordance with their original plans with the girls who were working although their original plans were different.

No statistically significant differences appeared between the two groups in regard to age, whether the father was living, parental occupation, or size of income.

Of the working girls who followed their original plans, 19 per cent had families whose incomes were derived from fixed salaries, while of the working girls who were not following their plans (which had been other than working), 32 per cent were in families with incomes derived from fixed salaries. Perhaps this demonstrates a tendency for girls from middle-class families, in terms of income source, who are not planning on working to be forced eventually to the realization that work is what they will have to do.

Again, the high school curriculum differentiated the two groups. Significantly more of the working girls who originally planned on working took the commercial course and significantly fewer took the college preparatory course than was true for those working girls who originally did not plan on working. Only 4 per cent of the former group took the college preparatory course as compared with 32 per cent of the latter group. What was the extent of the frustration experienced by the 36 girls in this group when their college-going plans failed to materialize after three or four years of preparation?

The two groups also differed statistically significantly on the basis of reported reasons for making their post-high-school plans. Of those originally planning on working, only 18 per cent gave as a reason "to prepare for a vocation," whereas of the group with plans other than working, 63 per cent gave this as a reason for those plans. Of the working group who planned on working, 20 per cent said they wanted to make money quickly and 38 per cent said they wanted to be independent; in the working group originally not planning on working, the respective percentages were only 7 and 15 per cent. Of the former group, only .5 per cent indicated a need for a liberal education, whereas 17 per cent of the latter group reported this as a reason. In the group following plans to work, 16 per cent had said this was all they could afford. Of the group working in spite of other plans, 1 per cent had given this as a reason. These differences, all statistically significant, are suggestive of some of the dynamics that influence a student in carrying out his plans.

Of the group originally planning on working, 63 per cent said they would not go to college even if they had more money, whereas of the group originally not planning on working only 32 per cent, statistically significantly fewer, said this. Of the former group, 61 per cent said they could not afford college or it would involve many sacrifices, whereas in the other group, only 19 per cent reported this. Those girls who planned on working and actually did work apparently at the time they were high school seniors perceived themselves as having less money than those who did not plan on working but eventually did work.

Family attitude also differentiated the two working groups. In the group planning on working, 24 per cent of the families wanted the girls to attend college, as compared with 56 per cent in the group not planning on working; 59 per cent of the families in the former group were indifferent to college, as compared with 27 per cent in the latter group. Those working girls who originally had other plans were perhaps influenced in the making of these original plans by their perceptions of their families' wishes, but their actual behavior may have been more influenced by other factors in their situations.

The number of books reported in the home also differentiated between the working girls who had planned on working and the working girls who had not planned on working. Of the working girls who had not planned on working, 32 per cent reported 100 or more books in their homes whereas only 18 per cent of the work-planning group reported this.

In general, those working girls who originally had other plans tended to come from middle-class families having more favorable attitudes toward college and having more books in their homes, and tended less often to take vocational curriculums in high school than did those working girls who originally had planned on working.

NONMETROPOLITAN BOYS

Of the 468 nonmetropolitan boys, 55 per cent followed their original plans. A breakdown by plan is shown in the tabulation. Going to other

Plan	Number Who Originally Had Plan	Realized Plan	
		Number	Per Cent
Work	140	59	42
Work for parents........	71	44	62
College	162	124	77
Other schools	50	9	18
Military service.........	45	21	47

schools was the least realizable plan and going to college the most realizable plan.

No statistically significant differences appeared between the nonmetropolitan boys who followed their plans and those who did not in terms of whether the father was living, size of income, amount of financial help for college expected from family, attitude toward change of plans if they had more money, and amount of money needed to change plans.

The boys planning on entering military service and actually doing so were significantly older than the boys who had so planned but had not entered the service. Changes then pending in selective service legislation might have been related to this difference.

Among those boys planning on working and so doing, statistically significantly fewer came from homes where income was derived from professional fees and profits and more came from the homes of wage earners. Of the boys planning on military service and following these plans, 48 per cent came from the homes of wage earners, while of the group planning on military service but not following these plans, none came from families of wage earners. In this group planning on but not entering service, one third of the boys gave no information regarding source of family income.

For those boys planning on working, on college, or on military service, a significantly higher proportion of those who failed to follow their plans had fathers who owned and/or managed farms than did those who followed these plans. Thus a relationship appeared between stability of post-high-school plans and occupation of father, with sons of farmers having less stable plans. Relatively more of the boys who followed their plans to work had fathers who were factory workers than did the boys who failed to follow plans to work. This was a statistically significant difference.

Of the boys who followed plans to work and actually did work, 46 per cent had mothers who before marriage were teachers, as compared with 11 per cent of those who did not follow work plans, a statistically significant difference. Of those failing to follow their plans, significantly more did not know or failed to report the occupation of the mother.

Of the boys who planned on working and followed their plans, 29 per cent took a technical course in high school while 14 per cent of those who planned on working but did not took such a course. Of the boys who planned on college, 27 per cent of those who attended college took a general course in high school, while 45 per cent of those who did not attend college took such a course. Of the boys who planned on going into the military service, 43 per cent of those who entered the service took a general high school course, while 71 per cent of those not entering the service took such a course. A general relationship appears here — boys taking the general course in high school had less stable post-high-school plans.

In regard to reasons for making post-high-school plans, only one significant difference appeared. Of the boys planning on working, 29 per cent of those who did work gave the reason "to start making money quickly" while 52 per cent of those who did not work checked this reason.

Of the boys planning on working for their parents, 16 per cent of those who did so work said they could barely afford college, as compared with 41 per cent of the boys with plans to work for parents who did not follow them; 41 per cent of the boys who followed plans to work for

parents said they could afford college, but it would require many sacrifices, as compared with 22 per cent of those who did not follow their
plan to work for their parents.

In making comparisons involving the number of books in the home,
only one difference approached statistical significance. Of the boys
planning on working, 36 per cent of those who did work reported
between 10 and 24 books in the home, while 23 per cent of those who
did not work reported this number. No consistent pattern appeared here.

A comparison of figures in Tables 27 and 29 shows differences between
the boys following given courses of action in accordance with original
plans and the boys following the same courses of action despite other
plans. The two groups did not differ statistically significantly on the
basis of whether or not the father was alive, source of income, or number
of books in the home.

Of the boys working for parents who previously planned on so doing,
82 per cent were 17 years old and only 14 per cent were 18 years old,
while of those working for parents despite other plans, 58 per cent were
17 years old and 37 per cent 18 years old. These statistically significant
differences suggest that older students were likely to be the more frustrated, if frustration results from failing to follow original plans.

Only one comparison between these groups on the basis of paternal
occupation was statistically significant. Of the boys in college who originally planned on college, 15 per cent had fathers who were farmers,
while of the boys in college who originally had other plans, 39 per cent
had farmer fathers. Those boys who were in college as a result of
changed plans tended to come from farm homes.

Of the boys who were not following their original plans, significantly
more were unable to report what the occupation of the mother was
before marriage. Of the boys working, 46 per cent of those who had
originally planned on working had mothers who had been teachers,
whereas 13 per cent of those who originally had other plans had teacher
mothers.

Of the boys working for parents, 70 per cent of those originally
planning on working for parents indicated their economic status was
"comfortable, but not well-to-do," whereas only 47 per cent of the boys
with other plans indicated this.

Pre-college training was related to stability of plans. Of the boys in
college who originally had planned on college, 67 per cent had taken

the college preparatory course in high school and only 27 per cent the general course. The respective figures for those in college who originally had other plans were 19 and 58 per cent.

Significant differences were found among these groups in terms of reasons for making post-high-school plans. Of the boys in college originally planning on college, 75 per cent gave as a reason "to prepare for a vocation" and only 1 per cent gave "to make money quickly." Of the boys in college who originally had other plans, 48 per cent gave as a reason for their original plans "to prepare for a vocation," and 26 per cent, "to make money quickly."

Of the working boys who had originally planned on working, 29 per cent gave as a reason "to make money quickly," but only 6 per cent of the boys working despite other plans gave this as a reason.

Of the boys in college, 51 per cent of those who planned on college reported their parents would pay all or most of their expenses, while only 19 per cent of the boys who originally had other plans had reported this. Of the boys who went to college, the more financially secure were able to anticipate college and perhaps to plan accordingly.

Of the working boys who had originally planned to work, 42 per cent said they could not afford college, while of the boys working despite other plans, only 21 per cent said they could not afford college. In the group of boys working despite other plans was a significantly greater proportion who failed to answer this question.

Reported family attitudes differed significantly only for the boys in military service. Of the boys originally planning on entering the service, 38 per cent had families who insisted they go to college, or who wanted them to go, while of the boys in the service despite other plans, 60 per cent had families with these attitudes. The first group perhaps contained a greater proportion of volunteers than the second, and family agreement is perhaps important in determining whether or not a student volunteers.

NONMETROPOLITAN GIRLS

Comparisons between various groups of nonmetropolitan girls are also presented in Tables 27, 28, and 29. Of these 509 girls, 330 (65 per cent) followed their original plans. The accompanying tabulation indicates the breakdown by plan. As with the metropolitan girls, working was the most realizable plan and going to other schools the least realizable plan.

Plan	Number Who Originally Had Plan	Realized Plan	
		Number	Per Cent
Work	200	161	81
College	204	134	66
Other schools..........	78	18	23
Nursing	27	17	63

No statistically significant differences appeared between the non-metropolitan girls who followed their plans and those who did not when the groups were compared on the basis of whether the father was living, size of income, family attitude toward college, or number of books in the home.

Of the girls who planned on college, the girls who actually attended college tended to be younger, on the average, than the girls who did not attend. Of the girls who planned on attending other schools, those who actually attended other schools tended to be older than the girls who did not. Of the few girls who planned on nursing, all 17 of the girls who actually entered nurses' training were 17 years old, while only 4 of the 10 girls who did not enter were 17. Thus the girls who followed their plans to enter nursing tended to be younger than the girls who had those plans but failed to follow them.

Of the girls planning on working, 37 per cent of those who did work came from homes where the source of income was fees or profits, while 69 per cent of the girls who did not work came from similar homes. Perhaps pressures in "professional or business" homes influenced girls who planned on working to seek further education instead. Of the girls planning on college, 27 per cent of the girls who attended college had fathers who owned or managed businesses, whereas 14 per cent of the girls who did not attend college had fathers in this category. Of the girls planning on working, 32 per cent of those working had farmer fathers while 59 per cent of the girls who did not work had farmer fathers. These differences were statistically significant and again demonstrated a positive relationship between family background factors and realizability of after-high-school plans.

The influence of the occupation of the mother before marriage was shown by the difference between the two groups of girls planning on college. Of the girls actually attending, 33 per cent had mothers who had been teachers, while of the girls planning on college but not attending, only 13 per cent had teacher mothers.

Differences were apparent also regarding the high school curriculums of the groups. Of the girls planning on working, 61 per cent of those who did work took a commercial course in high school while only 41 per cent of the girls who did not work took such a course. Of the girls planning on college, 63 per cent of those attending college took a college preparatory course and only 10 per cent a commercial course, while 37 per cent of the girls not attending college took a college preparatory course and 26 per cent took a commercial course. These differences were statistically significant. If a student was in a high school course appropriate for her after-high-school plans she was more likely to realize those plans than if she was in an inappropriate course, but nevertheless, a surprising number of students did not appear to be unduly restricted by what might have been considered inappropriate high school curriculums. High school courses and post-high-school opportunities, including opportunities for college, are far from being perfectly rigid.

Only one difference was significant among the reasons checked for making after-high-school plans. Of the girls planning on working, 24 per cent of those who did work checked the reason "to prepare for a vocation," while none of those who did not work checked that reason. Did this indicate a stronger vocational drive in the girls who followed their working plans?

Of the girls planning on college, 74 per cent of those attending college indicated all or most of the money needed for college would come from their families, while 58 per cent of the girls not attending college said this. Twice as many in the former group as in the latter group reported their families would pay all expenses. These girls' perceptions of their families' ability and willingness to pay have a direct relationship to whether or not they were able to achieve their plans for going to college.

When the nonmetropolitan girls who did not follow their original plans were divided according to what they reported they actually did, as in Table 28, the only group with enough cases to justify comparison was that group of girls who went to work. Thus, again, the girls who were working in agreement with their original plans were compared with those who were working although their original plans were different.

No statistically significant differences appeared between these two groups in regard to age, whether the father was living, occupation of father, occupation of mother before marriage, size of income, or approximate number of books in the home.

Of the girls who planned to work and did, 37 per cent came from families where the principal source of income was fees or profits, while of the girls who had other original plans but who actually worked, 51 per cent had family incomes from these sources. As with many of these differences, this one is difficult to explain.

The greatest difference between these two groups appeared when comparisons were made on the basis of high school curriculum. Of the girls following their original plans to work, 61 per cent had taken a commercial course, 7 per cent a college preparatory course, and 30 per cent a general course, whereas of the girls working despite differing plans, 33 per cent had taken a commercial course, 23 per cent a college preparatory course, and 44 per cent a general course.

Statistically significant differences appeared regarding the reasons the two groups checked for making their original after-high-school plans. Of the working group who planned on working, 24 per cent saw these plans as preparation for a vocation, whereas of the working group who had not planned on working, only 11 per cent saw their original plans as vocational preparation. Of the group who worked although they originally had other plans, 76 per cent gave as one reason for making their original plans "to be with old friends," while none of the other group checked that as a reason.

Of the group planning on working and actually working, 28 per cent gave as a reason for these plans "to make money quickly," and 23 per cent "to make more money," whereas the respective percentages for the other group were 15 and 3 per cent. Of the group planning on working and actually working, 24 per cent gave as a reason "to be independent"; only 7 per cent of the other group gave this as a reason for their original plans. These differences perhaps provide some clues to differences in motivation between the groups.

Of the group following their plans to work, 54 per cent had said that even if they had more money they would not change their plans and attend college, while of those girls working in spite of other plans, only 21 per cent had expressed this fixity of plans. A peculiar difference showed that significantly more of the latter group than of the former group did not answer this question. For the girls who did say they would change their plans if they had more money only 61 per cent of the group planning on working and working said they would need enough to pay one half or more of their expenses, whereas 95 per cent of the working group originally having other plans said they would need this much. Of the working group who planned on working, 14 per cent said they could not afford college even if they so wished, whereas in the working group who had not planned on working, 36 per cent said they could not afford college.

Differences in family attitude as well as in the student's perception of her ability to afford college were also statistically significant. Of the group working in accordance with plans, 28 per cent said their families wanted them to attend college, and 54 per cent said their families were indifferent toward college, whereas of the group working despite other plans, 54 per cent said their families wanted them to attend college and only 34 per cent said their families were indifferent. The girls who were working despite other plans perhaps reflected not only their own personal frustrations resulting from their failure to follow these plans but also their families' frustrations.

The results of this follow-up study throw light upon the validity of the generalizations based on the analysis of students' plans. A close relationship exists between the plans made by students during their senior year in high school and their subsequent behavior during the following year. Just as important is the information suggesting why students succeed or fail in following the plans they make.

It appears that a succession of psychological and situational barriers must be overcome before an adolescent can attain his educational and vocational goals. One group of these barriers must be overcome before appropriate plans can be defined. Another group of barriers must be overcome before these plans are placed in operation. The same factors, however, appear to be effective in overcoming both sets of barriers. That is, those conditions which result in a student's formulating a given plan tend also to be the conditions which determine the extent to which he is able to follow those plans.

Index

⚐ Index

Ability: previous findings on, 13–15, 21; and after-high-school plans, 64–66, 98–111; measures of, 98; sex and geographical differences in A.C.E. scores, 99–106; sex and geographical differences in high school ranks, 107–11

Access to colleges, 75

Activities, extracurricular, 21, 84. *See also* Organizations

"After High School — What?" questionnaire, 49, 51–54

Age: effect on plans, 11, 68–69; previous findings on relation to college attendance, 16; of parents, 19; and stability of plans, 71, 198, 219, 220, 224, 226, 228, 229; of college-planning students, 113; of job-planning students, 126; of high-ability students, 135–36, 152; of girls planning to enter nursing, 160; of girls planning to attend business school, 167

American Council on Education, study of factors related to college attendance: high school achievement, 15; sex, 16; parental occupation, 18; family background, 19; geographical area, 21

American Council on Education Psychological Examination, 56, 83: scores of high-ability students, 57–58, 149; relation of paternal occupation to scores, 59–61; relation of plans to scores, 98–111, 135

Anderson, G. L., study of Minnesota high school graduates: activity after graduation, 9, 57; high-ability students, 14, 58; high school achievement, 15; paternal occupation, 18, 60; geographical factor, 21; comparison with later study, 95

Anderson, John, 89, 91

Anderson-Goodenough Occupational Classification Scale, 18

Aptitude, college, *see* College aptitude

Arkansas high school students, *1949* study of, 10, 14

Attitudes of parents: differ according to child's sex, 16; in case histories, 28, 30, 31, 33, 36, 39, 42, 44, 45, 46; effect on students' plans 68, 71; of work-planning students, 131–32; of girls planning to enter nursing, 165; differences in, 173–77

Attitudes of students, 22, 82

Baker, F. E., 17

Barber, L. E., 17, 22

Beauty culture, schools of, 95

Benson, V. E., 14

Berning, T. J., study of Minnesota high school graduates: activity after graduation, 9, 57; high-ability students, 14, 58; high school achievement, 15; paternal occupation, 18, 60; geographical factor, 21; comparison with later study, 95

Books in homes: influence on plans, 8, 70; and realizability of plans, 71, 218–19, 220, 224, 226, 228; of college-planners, 123; of job-planners, 133–134; of high-ability students, 147–48, 158–59; of girls planning to enter nursing, 166; of girls planning to enter business school, 172

Bulletins, college, inadequacy of, 29, 84

Business school plans: characteristics of group with, 70–71; sex differences in, 95; frequency of, 97, 167; and age, 167; and family status, 167; and parental occupation, 167–68; and language background, 168–69; and family income, 169; and high school curriculum, 169–70; and family attitudes, 170–71; and occupational goals, 171; and material possessions, 171–72; and parents' membership in organizations, 172; and books and magazines in home, 172

California, college attendance in, 21

Choice points, and plans, 8–9

Church-affiliated colleges, 176

Class structure, and desire to attend college, 86

College aptitude, 69: previous studies of, 13–15; sex differences in, 59; of students